THE BANDOR CHILD

THE BANDOR-MAGE WAR
MIKE MCKINNON

Copyright © 2023 The Bandor Child by Mike McKinnon

All rights reserved. This book or any portion thereof may not be reproduced or used in any manner whatsoever without the express written permission of the author except for the use of brief quotations in a book review.

This is a work of fiction. Unless otherwise indicated, all the names, characters, businesses, places, events, and incidents in this book are either the product of the author's imagination or used in a fictitious manner. Any resemblance to actual persons, living or dead, or actual events is purely coincidental.

Mike McKinnon Publishing
www.MikeMcKinnonAuthor.com
Developmental editing by Jo Thompson
Copy edit and proofread by Hana Kennedy

Printed in Canada.
First Printing, 2023
ISBN: 979-8-89109-335-5 - paperback
ISBN: 979-8-89109-336-2 - ebook

GET YOUR FREE BONUS CONTENT

The world of Tal'am is vast, and this book only scratches the surface of it. This is why I have written bonus chapters and a companion short story that will never be sold and are only for fans of the series.

Please visit the link below to grab these exclusive freebies:
https://www.mikemckinnonauthor.com/Newsletter-Sign-Up

This one is for you, Shanna.

CONTENTS

1. Birth — 1
2. Stampede — 9
3. Creet — 19
4. The Fires of Creet — 35
5. Tales from the Drunken Owl — 51
6. Waking in a New World — 55
7. Burn it Away — 71
8. The Journey — 79
9. Tales from the Drunken Owl — 89
10. Dronoch — 93
11. The Gathering — 103
12. Fire Light — 111
13. The Bath — 121
14. The Strike Team — 133
15. That Which We Cannot Control — 147
16. Machinations in the Magisterium — 153
17. Mistakes — 161
18. The New Assignment — 173
19. Council of Archons — 183
20. Preparation — 193
21. The Trials — 209
22. Empty Bunk — 217
23. The Assault — 225
24. Tales from the Drunken Owl — 239
25. Flashes in the Dark — 245
26. The Carriage — 255
27. The Decision — 265
28. Over the Wall — 277
29. Distraction — 287
30. Alarm Bells — 293
31. A Dark Place — 299
32. Eye of the Storm — 305

33. Titus Arrives	317
34. Blood and Chains	323
35. Fire	337
36. Escape	349
37. Reunion	367
38. Repercussions	379
39. Tales from the Drunken Owl	385
From the Author	389
Acknowledgments	391
About the Author	393

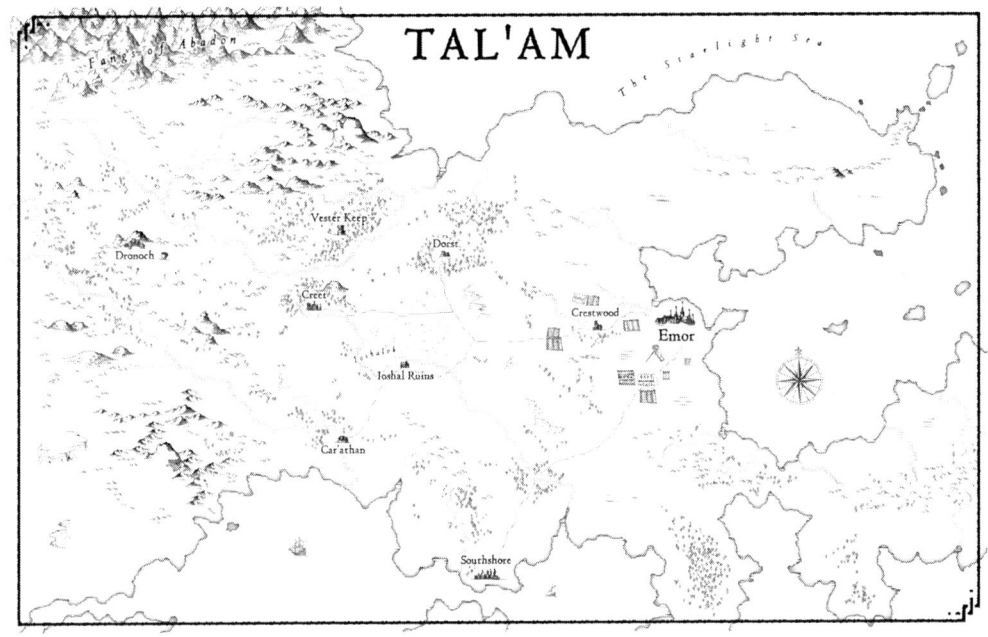

CHAPTER 1
BIRTH

Beginning

710: Year of the Second Era

Cairn tightened his cloak, shielding himself from the cool night air. He rested on the bench outside his friends' tent, listening to the fading cries of their newborn son he had helped deliver. He gave his friends time to relish the blissful moment, however fleeting. The nearby fire crackled, and he silently counted his heartbeats. He hated this part; as the shaman, he had helped them bring the baby into their world, but now he would have to take it away.

Bao and Brakan had looked elated when he had last left them inside. Bao, exhausted, had melted into the soft furs that made up the bed while the father, Brakan, half-sat on the bed beside her, had held Bao close while he extended his other hand out to their baby boy. His fingers had poked the babe's palm, smiling at every movement.

The two warriors had looked almost childish as they giggled at their baby's subtle interactions; Brakan, always the muscle-bound warrior, was like a little boy, his eyes lit up under a mop of auburn hair. Bao, always so composed, was vulnerable and joyful. She had named the boy Jaxon in a whisper and brushed her lips over his soft fuzzy patch of hair, then kissed the top of his head, breathing in his gentle, newborn scent. Their excitement did not make his duty any easier.

In front of Cairn, an ember now flickered out. The time had come; he had given them long enough. Cairn slapped his hands on his knees and pushed off to stand up from the bench. He stepped to the tent's entrance and paused, took a stressed breath in, let it go, and entered the circular tent.

A small fire burned in the centre of the dwelling, lighting the inside. Criss-crossed slats covered by tightly pulled animal hide and felt kept the home warm and sturdy. The couple still sat on the bed where he had left them. Bao's sweat-soaked brown hair stuck to her face as she lay, half propped up by folded furs. Her expression was relaxed as she leaned into Brakan's embrace.

Bao saw Cairn, and her eyes darkened as a shadow passed over her beautiful face. Although Cairn was good friends with both, at that moment he felt like an enemy. Brakan's face also darkened, but held a hint of uncertainty as he looked back and forth between Cairn and Bao, ready to protect his new family if Bao asked.

Sweat beaded on Cairn's forehead. He looked at Bao, taking note of the fear and worry in her eyes, and felt a pang empathy.

"It is time, Bao. May I see the child?"

Bao did not respond. She glanced at her son, then back at Cairn who moved towards her cautiously, as if approaching a wild animal.

"I know you are afraid, Bao. Afraid he may not pass The Inspection." Her eyes looked fierce once again. Cairn had to tread carefully. "But that is beyond your control, my dear. It will be as the tests decide. You have done your part and done it well either way. Look at the little guy. He is bright and healthy looking."

Bao's eyes softened as she looked down at the child and the

anger melted from her face. Brakan's look softened as well, and he gazed comfortingly at Bao.

"It will be alright, love," Brakan said.

Cairn reached a grey-skinned hand out to take the child, but he did not grab it. Instead, he opened his arms to allow her to place the babe within them.

Bao hesitated for a moment, eyes flicking between her baby, and Cairn's outstretched arms, concern pressed her eyebrows together; maternal instincts battled with a rational mind. They all knew what was next.

She sighed and lifted the child to the shaman. Cairn tenderly held the child to his chest to keep him warm and prevent him from crying at being separated from his mother.

He gave Bao a small nod of understanding and drifted to the tent flap that Brakan held open for him.

Cairn looked back as he reached the exit, quickly glancing at the mother who did everything in her power to contain her fear. Yet, a single tear ran down Bao's cheek and she blinked, attempting to clear her eyes, and her chest heaved with a silent sob. Cairn knew she was strong. She would be. For Brakan. For herself.

Brakan cast a final look at the baby. He said nothing, but nodded at Cairn before he turned away and approached his wife. He sat down next to her on the bed and his hand caressed her cheek. She nuzzled into him, seeking solace as he pulled her into a tight, comforting embrace.

With babe in hand, the shaman lowered the tent flap and left the new parents. This part was hard for all mothers, but they all knew it was necessary. And in the end, it was a mercy.

Cairn carried the baby into the chill night air. The child had cried as Cairn removed him from the warmth of his parents and home but, as the clan's healer, he had long since tuned out the effect of crying children.

He had seen the fear flicker in Bao's eyes, but she had less cause for concern than most. Years of carrying out Inspections on children had given him a knack for knowing when a child was unlikely to fail. He had a promising read on this boy. His parents were strong, and the birth had gone well. Then again, they wouldn't have The Inspection if intuition alone was sufficient.

Cairn appreciated the quiet at this time of night. He walked briskly through the camp to his medical tent; the moon was bright enough in the sky that he needed no other light to guide his way as he passed through the throng of tents and firepits still smoking with hot coals.

The baby settled as it became used to the cool night air, and by the time that he had reached his tent, the child had calmed to a gentle whimper. He raised the tent flap and stepped into the warmth of his home. The clan chieftain, Gaer, was already there, waiting for him. No words were exchanged between the men as Cairn placed the child down on the examination table, unwrapped him, and began his examination.

He had many tools, as well as concoctions for use during the process. Cairn began by measuring the baby: length, arm span, head size. Every defect that he could consider was inspected. The boy was not small or disfigured; he had no visible weakness and was not pale of skin. Still, he looked for any abnormality that was possible. If one was found, the child would be disposed of, but he could see none. *Not yet.*

Cairn took a sharp needle, one often used to sew a wound shut, and pricked the baby's right arm. The child turned his head as if to see what had happened, but he did not cry as some children would. *Interesting.*

With delicate fingers, Cairn lifted the blood that had enveloped the point of the needle, and carefully held it above a flask of semi-transparent yellow liquid. He tapped the needle once to let a drop of blood fall into the flask. The blood slid into the mixture, feathering as it sank deeper into the liquid. It turned a gentle shade of orange as it diffused further, but nothing abnormal seemed to happen, even as Cairn swished the liquid around. He placed it carefully back down onto the table. Gaer, who had been watching the process closely, let out a low grunt of approval at the sight before him.

Lastly, Cairn took both feet of the child in his hands and lifted the baby upside down to inspect him in the dim candlelight of his tent. He expected the baby to cry or let out a noise, as babies so often did at this point in the examination, but the child remained quiet. He slowly turned the child to analyze it from all angles. It was at that moment that Gaer also leaned in close to observe the child; he, too, was curious to see the child's reactions. When Cairn finished his inspection, he looked into the boy's eyes, anticipating to see tears or hear whimpering. But the child made no such noise. He just looked back at Cairn, unmoving, almost glaring, as if the child purposely refused to satisfy their expectations and challenged Cairn to find something wrong with him.

Very Interesting.

However, imperfections could not be tolerated; only the strong and healthy survived to become Bandorians. More tests were needed before he could say if they would keep the child, or it would be tossed out to return to the earth from whence it came.

After another half hour of poking, prodding, weighing, measuring and all manner of inspecting the baby boy, Cairn looked over at the chief with satisfaction.

"It is done," He stated, "The child is strong and healthy. I can find no cause to dispose of this one. He will be acceptable and can join the others when he is ready." Cairn laid the child back down on the table, this time on the blankets the babe had come in, and began wrapping the child again.

The chief gave a nod of approval. "Good. Bao and Brakan are powerful warriors. This one will bolster our ranks and, if he is as smart as his parents, he will make a good leader. We will need children like him in the days to come. Congratulate both of them for me when you see them."

Before Gaer could turn to leave, noises arose from outside; the sound of people rushing about and the raised voices of other Bandorians.

Gaer and Cairn shared a look of concern. Then, with the baby still in his arms, Cairn followed the chieftain out of the tent.

As soon as they exited the shaman's tent, the smell of smoke assaulted Cairn's nostrils. A breeze coming from the east carried the smell of burning wood into the camp. Bandorians ran to-and-fro, waking others, and investigating the east end of camp.

Cairn jumped when a panicked deer ran past him. He now noticed other small animals skittering past in a panic. Farther down the valley, less than a league away, he saw a faint light.

Forest fire.

"Stampede!" Gaer yelled. "Protect the camp!"

The fire looked too far off to be an imminent threat, but larger wild animals tearing through the camp in a panic would be a problem.

"We need to get a handle on the situation," Gaer called out. "Where is Axton?"

It was natural for him to want his unofficial second-in-command. Axton was young, but well respected.

"Cairn, get the baby back to Bao and Brakan, then head to the front for aid."

"Of course," Cairn responded.

Gaer ran off into the night to help the others. Cairn clutched the babe close to his chest, still wrapped in the warm bundle.

Bao and Brakan's tent was no farther from the danger than his own and, as he rounded a corner, he paused to let a small wild boar dart past him. Its panicked squeals blended with the thunderous rumble of hooves and the piercing cries of terrified animals. The stampede tore through the camp with unrestrained force, toppling tents, scattering supplies, and sending warriors scrambling. Cairn cradled the newborn, shielding the fragile life in his arms as he pushed forward through the chaos, leaping over fallen debris and dodging charging animals. Sweat poured down his face as he tried to push closer to Bao and Brakan's tent amidst the tumultuous frenzy.

A lull in the chaos let him push forward to his destination when he heard a loud crashing sound coming from a thicket of trees. The full moon was still the best light he had, and it was just enough for him to make out a massive shadow coming out of the forest at a full run. It was twice the height of a man and headed right towards him.

CHAPTER 2
STAMPEDE

Axton woke to the sounds of yelling and commotion outside his tent. He opened one eyelid, considered ignoring the noise, but once he heard commands being called, he knew it was imperative that he rise immediately. He brought his large hand to his face and wiped the sleep from his eyes.

His previous night's companion still lay beside him; naked save for a vestige of a blanket covering one of her legs. Her blonde hair spread over most of her face, hiding her beauty.

He pushed himself off his bed of soft furs, his movements slow and weary; groggy as his energy tried to awaken. Axton grunted, stood up and shook his body to toss off any remaining exhaustion. He pulled on his leggings and looked around the room; his large battle axe lay against the wall of his tent, and he was quick to grab it and throw off the cover that protected its edge. The metal blade's edge gleamed razor-sharp, and the pick was spiked to puncture steel.

"What is it?" his companion asked, fatigue clear in her soft voice.

"I'm not sure," he said. "Get up and get ready."

He rushed out of his tent, hoping his axe would be enough for whatever the disturbance was.

"Where is Axton?" a voice called out from somewhere in the distance. It sounded like Gaer.

Small critters ran by him, and he could smell burning timber. *Not good.* He ran towards the voice, past a smouldering campfire, and a bucket of tools knocked over in the commotion. He saw his clan quickly gathering equipment and moving towards the action.

Before he reached the source of the call, a sight made him pause. It was Cairn, holding a strange bundle in his arms. *Was it a baby?* The sound of soft thunder rumbled from the distance, interrupting his thoughts, but it was too close to be from the clouds.

Cairn was unarmed, but he spread his legs in a ready stance, preparing for a threat that Axton couldn't see.

Suddenly, a large creature with murder in its eyes charged at Cairn. Twice the height of a man, it had the body of a horse, but where its head should be, there was a man's upper torso, wielding a large two-handed sword.

Centaurs.

In an instant, Axton's feet were propelling him forward into a full sprint, his axe ready at his side, hoping to intercept the creature before it could reach Cairn.

His legs protested the quick exertion, but despite his efforts, he would not reach Cairn before the horselord. *Time for another tactic.*

As he continued to sprint, he wound back his great axe, and, with all his strength, he swung it forward, letting the axe fly.

The horselord, blinded by madness, brought up his sword to cleave Cairn in two. As the sword fell, Axton's axe bore into his abdomen. He staggered sideways, crashing down at Cairn's feet, axe still embedded into his side, blood streaming out.

The other animals bounded off into the darkness, continuing with their stampede through the camp.

"Axton?" Cairn asked, noticing him as he approached.

"Cairn," Axton said. "Baby?" He eyed the bundle in Cairn's arms. "Wait, is that Bao and Brakan's baby?"

"That's right, just born this hour. Thanks, by the way."

"Of course," he said, his eyes scanning the area, "it is unlike them to attack us; likely this one was in a panic. You should get the baby back to them and then help me clean this up. Oh, and congratulate the two of them for me."

"Good suggestion. I'll be back as soon as I can," Cairn said. He bounded off, babe still in arms.

Axton noted the baby had not cried through any of the action. Cairn disappeared into a distant tent, and Axton turned back.

He looked down at the injured creature that lay before him; a male centaur, fully grown, still breathing. Blood flowed, but Axton knew better than to remove the axe for fear of doing more damage. The horselord's chest rose and fell, and his eyes blinked open before closing again. His arms moved, alternating between trying to push himself up to a sitting position and carefully touching the axe, considering pulling it free to remove the pain.

"I... I..." The horselord struggled to get words out.

"Easy friend, easy. Our healer will be back here in just a moment. Try not to move," Axton said, placing a gentle hand on the horselord's flank. He was wary of the creature lashing out, but its rage seemed to have disappeared.

"There, there. We will see what we can do to patch you up. I make no promises, but we will try."

Axton found a nearby piece of cloth from a collapsed tent. He ripped two pieces off it and wrapped them around the embedded blade. Axton pushed down with both arms to keep blood from pouring from the wound.

"I will talk, if you don't kill me..." The centaur spoke once more, slowly, with deep breaths, ensuring it did not strain itself in the effort.

"We'll not hurt you."

Another Bandorian approached with a folded bundle to place below the creature's head and a small group formed around them, eager to help if they could. Soon enough, Axton saw Gaer approach with Cairn.

"What the hell happened here?" Gaer demanded as he approached Axton and the group gathered around the injured horselord.

Axton knelt beside the horselord and watched the others clear a space for the chieftain and shaman to get close as well.

"He will talk, Chief," Axton said. They had to find out what had caused this.

"You," Gaer said, speaking to the horselord, "why did you attack us?"

Axton put a gentle hand on the creature's slowly rising chest.

Cairn knelt closer to the horselord and inspected the wound. Axton stared at Cairn with an unsaid question, but the shaman frowned and shook his head.

"You didn't attack us?" The centaur asked.

Gaer shook his head and parted his lips to answer, but the horselord cut him off.

"No, I suppose not," he continued, "It becomes clear now."

"What is clear? What are you saying?" Gaer asked.

The creature shifted his weight and gave out a low grunt of pain. "You are Bandorians. I see it now. Not the Imperials that killed us."

Of course. The Venesterium Empire, the conquers of Glenmore and scourge of the Barbarian tribes before Bandor. But what were they doing so far west? Had they expanded to the Craeg already? It's too soon.

"The humans, they came to us almost one week ago. Wanting us out of the forest they claimed was on their land. We told them they could not lay claim to the forest we've lived in for generations. Others would stand against them if they marched on us. We warned them of this, and they listened. They *pretended* to listen." Water collected in his eye, and a tear crept down his face. "They said *so be it*, and that they would leave us be. They would find other forests."

Axton doubted they would.

"Why would they not leave well enough alone? Their words are lies. Oath breakers... murderers."

Cairn unstoppered a flask and held the creature's head up. He poured a small amount of the liquid down the centaur's throat. "For the pain," he said. It would ease the passing. The centaur swallowed, then continued.

"They did not march on us. In that way, they held true. But it was a corrupt truth."

"Tonight, as I slept, I was woken by screams of flames and smoke. A fire came from the east, growing quickly. Beyond the fire, through the flames, just barely, we could see shapes. Humans."

"Ashes," Axton cursed under his breath. *That did sound like the Empire. Gaer had been warning them for years.*

"The fire flew on a fell wind, one that had changed direction in less than an hour and unnaturally carried the fire. Never have I seen fire spread that fast before."

"Magi," Gaer said. "Must be."

"We don't know that," Axton replied.

Gaer just grunted and the horselord continued, "The fire surrounded us. We tried to save as many as we could, but trees burned and fell upon us. Smoke made sight impossible. When I escaped, only a handful of others were behind me, and the fire chased after us."

Axton had already lost someone to the Empire. This creature had now lost his entire species.

He would not admit it out loud to Gaer, but it was sounding like the work of the Magisterium, the wizards of the Venesterium Empire. Axton often worried Gaer focused too much on the Empire and the conflict to come. *It would come in time and there was no need to rush it.*

"We saw you as humans; no distinction did we warrant. Rage filled me, wanting revenge for the murder of my people. All you humans look the same. Only now, as I lie dying, seeing this orc spawn tend my wound, do I realize you are not just humans. Not of the Grand Venesterium Empire. Before I die, it must be known. You must carry this last memory for me. For I can carry it no longer; what has happened here. They have killed us all, for I am the last. I feel it…

The truth of their Empire is laid bare." The horselord looked down. "Now I will rest..."

He closed his eyes and rested against the dirt. His chest rose and fell, still living, but not for long.

After this, it would be hard for Axton to convince Gaer not to proposition the other Bandorian clans to prepare for war. Though the Bandorians had grown in numbers over the century, they remained in hiding, and to reveal themselves to the enemy would require a unanimous agreement among all the clans. War with the Empire would be inevitable, especially when the Empire discovered their existence, but that should have been many decades away, maybe even beyond his lifetime. Now, perhaps not. If his life had to end eventually, it would be better to die in battle than in a bed.

Gaer stayed there, kneeling beside the dying creature, deep in contemplation, so Axton took charge. "Everyone, disperse. We have all we will get from the horselord for now, and we all have damage to tend to. Get to it."

The other Bandorians raised no objections, and left to clean up overturned baskets, knocked over campfires that ran a risk of igniting nearby items, and collapsed huts. Cairn left with them to tend to the wounded. Thankfully, the damage had been minimal.

Axton laid his hand upon the centaur's flank once more, feeling the breaths in and out become slower and less pronounced. He felt the final rise and fall of the lungs, then no further movement came from the creature. Axton sighed.

"They are getting closer, Axton," Gaer said as he stood. "War is coming." Gaer spoke to his friend without taking his eyes off the dead horselord. "Every year their world grows closer to ours. They claim the land for themselves, and they clear it to make way for their industry. They don't care who or what they destroy."

Gaer spoke of the Venesterium Empire. Axton had heard these remarks from him before.

"It is not just them, Gaer," Axton said in a lighter tone than his friend, trying to ease the tension. "We have grown bigger every year as well. Expanding from the north, we cover most of the Craeg now."

"That's different. We don't claim the lands, and we don't spread like locusts. They do."

Axton looked to Gaer but Still he did not move.

"And to what end? To continue the cycle until they cover all Tal'am? And after that?" Gaer took a deep sigh, "Mark my words, Axton: there will come the day when our worlds collide. We will need to be prepared. And on that day, we will need to deal with them."

Axton said nothing, but his brow furrowed. He knew his old friend had spoken true, but he did not see what could be done beyond what they were already doing. He saw no reason to worry about something that he could not control at that moment, but he recognized they were heading straight for a large-scale confrontation. The Venesterium would not just stand down and keep within their borders. They had already spread too far, and the clans would not allow the lands to be overrun; not by the Empire.

The war would not end swiftly. He knew it would be a costly and bloody war, but he did not know which of the two cultures would come out the victor. All he could do now was to spend his time from this day to that preparing for the war that would inevitably come.

Beyond the trees and across the open space of the Bandorian camp, a figure watched the flames light Gaer's expression. A crooked grin came to Damitus's lips as he watched from the shadows of the forest. A stern look was visible on the chieftain's face. Excellent. He would see the Empire as an unavoidable opponent.

Damitus spied on them from too far away to hear the conversation between the horselord and Gaer, but he could tell by the expressions that the beast had mentioned the Empire.

His plan was early in its phases, but he beamed to see it go as intended. He always had backup plans, of course, but it was reassuring to see his scheme come to pass.

After all, this had been a mere test, to see if he could manipulate events as he saw fit; to confirm that he could plant seeds that may take years to grow. It would take time for it to spread to the other clans of Bandor, but Damitus could wait. He had the patience.

He clung to the tome that he had taken when the horselords had fled. It had no name, but he had seen references to it in old forgotten scrolls in the basement archives of Emor. Mentions of the ancient knowledge it contained; knowledge from before the Empire, older than anything in the Magisterium's libraries. Perhaps even from the time of Ancients.

Damitus turned to go. He had seen enough, and there was still so much to do. So much he still needed to learn. He moved quietly between the trees. Unlike the other mages in the Imperial Academy, he did not wear the long flowing robes that would catch in a forest; instead, he had opted for pants and short robes, slit in the front and back, bound to his waist and body with belts and buckles. It allowed him to show off his opulence while serving more practical purposes. Purposes such as sneaking off into the forest as he needed to at that very moment.

With his vision heightened to the darkness, he stepped lightly, moving away from the night's events, brushing a twig to the side with his foot. He had the skills of the forest that no other Imperial mage would have understood. *Fools, the lot of them.*

The Magisterium and even the Empire had no clue of the Bandorian threat that existed just off their borders. But Damitus knew. He knew much that others did not. Including how to spread the fire that the lumbermen and farmers started, and have it blaze past the barriers that centaurs set up to protect themselves from such things.

If it had not been for him, the ignorant border men would have been murdered in their attempt to take the land. But he bore them no more care than one bears for a tool; they had served their purpose.

He pulled up his cowl to further conceal his head, then turned back to get one last look at the Bandorian camp before disappearing once more.

CHAPTER 3
CREET

Eleven Years Later
721: Year of the Second Era

Trisstiphina carefully balanced the last dirty bowl on top of the precariously high pile of dishes that sat on the edge of the wooden table so she could wipe the rest of the surface. She liked the look of a tidied table, in contrast to the mess that had been there just a moment before. With a quick flick of her wrist, she sent a stray blonde strand of hair behind her ear before grabbing the semi-damp rag and brushing the crumbs and food off the table. The dog would get those that fell upon the ground; anything that was left, she would get when she swept later.

Trisstiphina enjoyed cleaning the tables at the Cask and Barrel, the quaint local taphouse in Creet. She was grateful that the owner had allowed her to work there even though she was only eleven years old. He had told her she was mature for her age, so he didn't mind.

She was proud to bring money home for the family, even though her father had said it was nothing and that she was wasting time.

But he didn't stop her, so she ignored his comments. She worked there for the chance to overhear rumours from around town and, if she was really lucky, she would hear stories from throughout the Empire. Those were what excited her.

Travellers often stayed in the attached inn and regaled them with stories of the wider world. Usually, it would only be a simple farmer, merchant, or drifter. But if she was incredibly lucky, there might be a travelling bard.

Bards told the best stories. Tales of love and adventure; tales of pirates on the eastern seas, raiders from the north, or the wizards of the royal court in the capital. Even tales of gnomes, dwarves, and all other manner of creatures from the far southwest.

Though her favourite stories were the tales of the mysterious and magical elves; stories of their wondrous cities deep in the forests, their amazing magical powers, supernatural beauty and mischievousness. She would imagine running away and falling in love with a handsome elven lord.

She had been told that most of these tales were often exaggerated and rarely affected the people of Creet, but it did not diminish her wonder.

Compared to the bard's tales, her town was dull, small, and hardly of any importance. Apart from the Government House, where adults dealt with taxes and debts, and the barracks, where the town garrison trained, it had nothing of importance.

A crooked old wizard ran the barracks; he had some magic, but Triss had never heard of him using it. She did not know the wizard's name, but she knew he was a spiteful man who never smiled and only cared for the money he could drag out of this town. At least that was the rumour she had heard. He was old and withered, and he had unnerving eyes that made the hair on Triss's arms stand on end.

Unlike the old wizard though, the regional governor beamed friendliness from the steps of the Government House that he ran. He was a plump old businessman with some part ownership of every business in the town. Most loved the governor, for he was the one that secured trade with the capital and the production of goods from the west. He brought in all the elegant clothes, fancy jewels, household wares, but most valued of all were the magical devices.

Shiny and vibrant trinkets and elixirs were infused with magic by wizards to do many wondrous things to ease and excite people's lives. Trinkets that could purify water, heat food, change hair colour, hide pockmarks, make babies sleep better, play music, or tell stories.

These goods from the capital were highly desired and people would pay much to own such things. The governor was the one that ensured that these goods continued to be supplied, so he was often idolized in the town. And because he partially owned most businesses, he was seen as the one that hired and kept the populace employed. Triss could not verbalize it, but something about it all felt off to her.

As she scrubbed the table, she strained to catch the conversation a few tables over where two men from out of town were enjoying drinks and had attracted a few of the locals with their talk of the events from the north. They had spoken of some conflict with Bandits or raiders, Triss, had not caught exactly who the attackers were.

When four men from the table next to them began shuffling and gathering their things, Triss watched them. The table cleared, and she took advantage of the opening. She abandoned the dishes where she had stacked them and moved to the newly emptied table. A length of her hair fell in front of her face again, and she used the excuse to untie her long hair, grab it in a bunch and begin tying it back again. Anything to drag out the time she could spend listening.

From the table next to her, she could hear a rough middle-aged stranger speak, with a slight slur from the drink, "That's right, Vester Keep. A bunch of savages. Since Vester, they have been raiding and attacking the northern garrisons for the last month."

Another man quickly jumped to his feet to add details to the reports, "They are monsters. Some of them look like men, but demons run among their ranks and those that do look like men, attack with ferocity only demons would possess. They are not humans. Some of them breathe fire. Some can fly, some can rip you into pieces with their claws, others will appear out of thin air."

The man's hands flew about in wild gestures, emphasizing the details of his story, his movements slightly unsteady from the effects of alcohol.

"Sure, sure, next you'll tell me they shoot lightning out their rears," laughed Gabe, a local man that Triss had seen before selling goods from his farm. The other local men around the table snickered.

Trisstiphina again stacked the dishes in one corner of the table and began washing the wooden planks with her rag as she eavesdropped.

"You laugh, but you will not be laughing in the night when your home erupts in flames, and you face the demons in the dark."

"Hah, being a little dramatic there, aren't you Blyth?" Master Shaw asked.

Master Shaw was town's blacksmith; usually a somewhat rational man, even if he did charge quite a premium for his goods. He knew he was the only one in town to craft those goods, at least until spring when the traders would return and undercut his prices, forcing him to return to a fair deal.

"We get your point. They're fearsome. But demons? Really? More likely some feral barbarians."

"Well, demons or not, you all need to be wary," responded the man that Master Shaw had referred to as Blyth.

Triss would usually have pegged this man as an attention seeker, but he was not the first man this month to make such claims. It worried her. She had heard this tale a few times already, and she had also heard it from men that were much more believable than Blyth.

"Girl, stop your dawdling." A nagging hiss came from the hall to the kitchen, not quite loud enough to distract the patrons. The alewife stood with hands on her aproned hips, glaring at Triss, before turning and marching back to the kitchen. She was a miserable woman. An older boy had called her an "old bag" once, and it suited her.

Regardless, Triss snapped her head back to the work she was supposed to be doing. A puddle had formed under the rag she held. Her eyes furrowed. She had paused longer than she had thought, distracted by the conversation at the next table. The story intrigued her, but she shivered, thinking about what they had said.

Triss drew the rag back and forth over the oak surface, scrubbing away some spilled beer. The wood darkened with the moisture and shone, once again clean.

Who were these raiders? Why would they just attack the Imperial Army? No one did that. What did they want? She decided that these were not questions for one as young as her and she should forget issues she could do nothing about. Besides, they had a large force in the barracks, and they even had a wizard stationed there. Certainly, the governor would make the wizard defend them with his magic if it came to that.

Yes, that's it. The wizard will protect us.

Trisstiphina collected up all the dishes from the table and brought them back to the kitchen. She imagined enormous monsters attacking people in the dark but tried to clear her mind and focus on her work. She was on her way back when her father's name grabbed her attention.

"Bill?" Master Shaw asked. Triss had missed the beginning of the conversation.

"Yeah, that worthless shit, Bill. He hasn't paid the last two months interest on his loans. I told Gus we should just make an example of him; he's a deadbeat."

Triss returned to the empty table beside them, her fists clenched. *How could this man say such things about her father?* She was fairly certain that the man's name was Samuel. He was one of the debt collectors for Gus, the lender that her father dealt with. The lenders seemed to run the town, or at least everyone seemed to do what they said. Her father had told her they were part of a guild, but that did not mean much to her.

Triss looked down to see her hand trembling as she tightly gripped a knife and involuntarily dragged the blade along the table, etching a mark in the wood.

"It might not actually be bad if those Barbarians did come around," Samuel said. "They could clear out some of the trash like Bill that has been clogging the drains of this town. Put the man out of his misery."

"Shut up!" Triss yelled at the man. "My father is not a deadbeat."

The men all turned to her, only now noticing that she had been there.

"Deus's shit, Samuel," Master Shaw cursed. "Look around to see who is here the next time you open your trap like that."

Samuel ignored Shaw, though, and just gave Triss an intense, dark glare.

"Your father is a deadbeat girl. And even if your mother was once pretty, she is withered now. It would be better if you all just disappeared."

It was not his comment that pushed Triss over the edge; words only cut so deep. It was that none of the other men disagreed with him or told him he was wrong.

Rage reached a boiling point in Triss, and her vision turned red. Hardly registering what she was doing, she saw her arm throw a wooden bowl as hard as she could. Samuel just barely moved his head out of the way in time; the bowl thumped as it bounced off a table and clattered to the ground.

"Bill's little bitch pup is a crazy witch. She tried to take my head off. You all saw what she did."

Triss heard more curses trail off, but she did not hear anyone argue with Samuel as she stormed out of the tavern. Dust kicked up around her feet as she stomped down the street. She had no plan, no destination in mind, just fury.

How could no one stand up for her father? She knew Samuel had been called an asshole before, but no one said anything. They all knew her father; they had acted like his friends when she saw them together. *How could they not tell Samuel that he was wrong?*

Tears blurred her vision as she replayed the scene over in her head. She felt a strain in her clenched fists and the heat in her ears, like she could explode at any moment.

After she calmed down, she found herself sitting on the grassy western ridge just beyond the town limits, staring down at her home. With the forest to her back, she held her knees to her chest and looked down to the chimney smokes catching the rays of the setting sun.

Why were people like this? How could she trust people if they could so easily talk this way behind your back? Why would someone say something like that about her father?

She gazed out over her town and a memory surfaced. She recalled an evening, possibly half a year before. Her parents had been arguing, her dad sitting at the table yelling about something. Money maybe. They had been in the kitchen half of their main room, and she had been lying among the pillows on their wooden couch, trying to pretend that she was not there. There had been a knock at the door, which halted the argument.

Trisstiphina's father raised his considerable bulk to walk to the door. He rested against the door frame and opened the door. He only opened it about halfway. In the door frame stood a tall and heavily built man that Triss had seen a few times around town. She knew he worked with the bank men, but was not sure what his actual job was.

"Hey Thorpe," her father said. "I know. I missed the payment today, but listen, the crops are still coming in. They will... Wait a moment, why are we even talking about this now? Can't this wait until the morning? This is my house, Thorpe. Why can't we discuss this in town tomorrow?"

Her father had started apologetic, but now seemed to push back at the man in the doorway, apparently named Thorpe.

"Bill..." the man took a deep sigh, "You missed the payment last month. Today was just us doing you an extra favour. They sent me to see if I can extract the payment from you in some other way."

"Like hell you will," her father said. "Well, I ought to—oof."

Her father keeled over, clutching his stomach, and then dropped to the ground like a sack of potatoes. Thorpe had delivered a quick, powerful blow to her father's abdomen that knocked the wind out of him and his response.

"Don't worry, Bill, I'll look around the house for anything of value before I consider taking either of the women."

He sounded sincere in his distaste for what he now had to do. He stepped over her father and began looking through the cupboard for valuables. Her mother just sat there crying. Triss lay frozen. The entire event confused her too much to know what to make of it.

Thorpe finished looking through the main room, not finding anything of interest, and headed for the bedroom. *What would happen if he could find nothing to take? What did he mean by "taking either of the women"?*

"Thorpe," her father said, gasping for breath. "What about that?"

Her father had caught Thorpe attention and pointed directly at Triss. Shock and terror filled Triss; her hands became sweaty as she kneeled on the couch. Her father then coughed to clear his throat, "The amulet. The girl has an amulet. Surely it must be worth something. Take that."

Shock tore through Triss, followed by rage, "No!" Triss said.

The amulet was the only thing that Triss had that she cared about. Her nana, whom she loved dearly and missed terribly, had given it to her.

Thorpe looked at Triss for a moment, glimpsing the amulet before Triss could clutch it in her hand for protection.

"Nah. That looks like a cheap piece of shit. There is no way it is real."

Thorpe looked around once more before focusing on her father again.

"It is a promising idea, though. Now *that* I know I could get something for." Thorpe gestured to the wedding ring resting on her father's finger. "Give me the ring and I'll be gone. At least until next month."

"Yeah, of course," her father said. He slipped the ring off his finger and held it out. "Take it."

Triss sat on the couch clutching her amulet, unable to speak or move. Her father had tossed away the ring that represented his love for her mother like it was nothing. Triss turned her head to her mother to see her reaction. There was none; neither of her parents did a thing.

Thorpe snatched the ring, and then he was gone. Just like that.

Her parents had gone back to tasks around the house after that, as if nothing had happened. Triss had sat there for a while longer, trying not to make any noise before she snuck away to feed her pet lamb; any excuse to not be there anymore. As strange as it had been, the one thought she had dwelt on was that at least her parents had stopped arguing that night.

Her father had done some questionable things over the years. She had always been told by him that none of the things had been his fault. She didn't believe him, but there may have been a sliver of truth to the claim. Her father wasn't perfect, but he also had little control; he could not escape his debts. Nor could he control how little people paid for the apples they sold. People had so little money these days.

Everyone was in debt to someone else and was forced to work for terrible wages just to pay off the debts they had. No one even thought it was strange; she had seen it time and time again happen to others besides her father.

She sat on the hill that afternoon until the sun finished setting, then went straight home.

That night, as she lay in bed, she could not help repeating the encounter over and over in her head. But as she continued to hover on the edge of sleep, her mind mingled and moved to other things.

Samuel's cruelty mixed with her imagination, showing monsters from the tales told by the tavern merchants.

Giant men with animal heads. Demonic faces shrieked and red tails whipped. Sharp talons tore at her. Monsters of every sort that her young mind could imagine plagued her dreams. She tossed and turned in the night and every time she got close to sleep, she woke to sweat-soaked sheets. Her mind raced, thinking about the threat she really knew nothing about.

She found no rest that night.

Triss made her way through the orchard, picking any ripe apples she could find. It had been two days since the incident at the Cask and Barrel and she had not returned, choosing to hide in her work in their orchard instead.

The orchard did not look great. It may not have been the best place to start an orchard in the first place. Her father had been too greedy and planted the trees too close together, hoping to get more trees and fruit out of the space that they had. She remembered the words her nana had once said. "I'm sorry, love, but your father is not the wisest." She had since learned the truth in those words.

She had struggled with her opinion of her father in the last few days. Some part of her still loved him. He was her father, but she felt embarrassed by him and frustrated with how he treated her.

She remembered a younger version of herself, excited by the beautiful dresses that her father would bring home. She would rush to put them on and twirl around in them as she imagined the dancers of old would. That was until she realized that her father only got them for her before parading her to a boorish party, mostly filled with creepy old men, their wives, and some spoiled brat of a child that would just torture and taunt her because of her family's lower status.

Her father was constantly trying to cozy up to the higher-class people in town. All of his actions were just an attempt to appear wealthier than they were.

She was sad to admit it, but she had to agree with her nana; her father had a habit of making life more difficult for the whole family. Once they had owned a lovely farm, but it was far from town and her father had dragged them to this orchard. "You don't want to be a farmer your whole life, do you? Of course not!" her father had said. "We need to become city folk. People respect city folk."

But what good is respect? Respect didn't make a person's debts go away.

Trisstiphina had to laugh at herself for a moment; these were her nana's words in her mind. She had developed this dislike of how the world worked from her nana. "Sweetheart, just because this is the way it 'is done' does not mean it is still the right way."

Triss gently touched her amulet, smiling at the memory of her nana; she was a wise and kind woman, even if she tended to point out Triss's mistakes. She liked that her nana was the only person who never talked down to her or acted like being a child kept you from being smart. Her nana was the only one to call her little lady, instead of her silly childhood name, Trissy.

Unlike the other adults that would respond to her questions with a dismissive answer of "that's just how it is" or "that is no question for a little girl", her nana had always answered every question she had about the world. Though she had always avoided questions about her past.

She reached up as she found another ripe apple and pulled it away from the branch. There was a subtle noise as the branch released its grip and swung back to its position. She softly placed the apple in her basket as she continued walking.

She missed her nana deeply; her nana did not visit anymore, and it had been over two years since Trisstiphina had seen her nana. An ache of grief made Triss close her eyes. She didn't know what had happened to make her nana stop visiting every summer; her parents would not talk about it though she remembered the last time she had seen her nana.

It had been a lovely, warm afternoon in the summer of Trisstiphina's eighth year. Her nana had come to visit her, and the two of them had spent much of their time gathering berries from the bush on their farm, close to the house. The air was not too hot, and the sun's rays through the leaves had warmed her skin in a blanketing embrace. Birds had chirped a song high above in the treetops, and a gentle breeze had kissed her skin and let the branches dance in the air.

"These ones look good, little Fae," her nana said.

Her nana was kind and wise, and she had a funny habit of never using Trisstiphina's real name; she was fairly certain her grandmother was the only one that knew that she did not really like her name and wished she had been given another.

Her nana would always use nicknames such as "Love", "Dear", "Little Lady-bug", "Little fairy", or "My little Fae". She found her nana pleasantly odd.

"The berries are growing excellently this year, my dear. Have people at the market been enjoying them?" her nana asked without looking away from her picking.

"Oh yes, old lady Agatha said they are the best berries she has ever tasted, and she is old, so she has probably had lots of berries," Trisstiphina responded with enthusiasm, barely taking a breath.

Her nana giggled at the commentary on Agatha's age but gave a nod.

"But... But Papa said we might get rid of them next year. He said we need to make more room for the apple trees. He said they make us more proof... profa—"

Trisstiphina stumbled on the word, trying to remember what word her father had used.

"Profit?" her nana asked.

"Yes. That's it. He said they make us more profit, and we need to focus more on that. But I told him that even if people buy our apples, they only come to us because they like the berries. I told him what Agatha said, and she buys more fruit and vegetables from us than anyone."

Her nana paused from her berry picking, and one eyebrow raised slightly.

"But Papa said I'm just a girl and I don't know anything about it. He doesn't listen to me."

"Yes, well, your father does not always make the wisest decisions or see wisdom when it is handed right to him."

"What do you mean, Nana?"

"Well, you must understand, my dear girl, your father has lived in the Empire his entire life. He has a good enough heart, but his mind is clouded by what that life has taught him, and just as importantly, the things that life has not taught him. Your father always yearns for more: more wealth, more goods, more status, and he is quick to forget that which he already has. He has impressions of the world that have been instilled in him-" her nana cut herself off realizing that Trisstiphina may not understand all her words, "-or ideas that have been taught to him, that may not be correct, but he sees them as correct, anyway because he does not know any better."

Triss sat there thinking as her nana returned to picking berries.

"Nana, where are you and mommy from then?"

"Pardon?" her nana asked, caught off guard by the question.

"You said Papa has always lived in the Empire, but where else is there to live then? Where else could someone live? Where did you and mommy live?"

Her nana put on an expression of innocence.

"Did I say that?"

Triss never got an answer to her question as her father returned home at that moment, barging across the yard and bragging about the new orchard they were going to move to. Triss did not catch all of what he said as he exclaimed to her mother, who was working on some potatoes around the corner of the house.

Triss could only hear a few things, the two most important ones being "Move to a small apple orchard just on the edge of town," and "Jake is not even living there right now, so we can move in as soon as we are ready."

At the last comment, Trisstiphina bristled and spoke up, "I don't want to move. I want to live here. The city is loud and busy, and people are not always nice there, and the men always stink of ale." She did not mention that her father also smelt of ale.

Her father looked over at her, and his look of condescension made Triss squirm.

"What? What do you know? You're just a young girl. You'll be chasing the town boys around in no time and making more friends than you ever had here? Besides, it doesn't matter what you want. I am the man of the house, and we do what I say."

He waved his hand to dismiss her, accenting the fact that her opinion was meaningless in case his words were not evidence enough.

Before he could say more, though, Trisstiphina's mother walked over to her father and grasped his arm to turn him away. She could hear them speaking in hushed voices and it sounded like her mother was upset.

Trisstiphina looked up at her nana, "Nana, I don't want to leave here. I like our farm and I like all the things we have planted here. Please tell me I don't have to move. Do I?"

Her eyes were a little sore as tears formed. Her nana did not look down at her but gave a serious stare at the back of her father's head.

"I do not know, child, but I will find out. Get back to picking those berries."

With that, her nana gestured her back to the berries and marched towards her father. Triss heard the three of them talking in hushed but serious tones. They seemed upset with one another, but Trisstiphina decided she should leave her mother and nana to deal with the problem and do as her nana instructed.

Even then, she had known she did not want to move to the town. She did not want to leave her quiet little farm and she had not understood why they had to move; they had everything they needed there.

She put her hope in her mother and nana's abilities to change her father's mind. But they had failed. She and her family moved within the month, and she had not seen her nana since that day.

Her mind returned to the present, and she reached for another apple. She missed her nana terribly and she let out a hopeless sigh.

Why did she have to be stuck in this town? If only she could find her grandmother again. Triss frowned as she searched another tree, noting that it was bare of any sellable apples. She imagined living with her nana, picking delicious berries or planting flowers in the sunshine and drinking warm tea in a cabin when it was chilly. No bothersome people to worry them.

Why couldn't she do it? The world couldn't be that big. Other people in other towns must have seen her grandmother before. She stuck out a bit from other elderly women.

Triss was not sure how old her nana was; she seemed youthful, unlike the old and withered husks the other children called grandmothers. Most grandmothers she had seen before looked elderly while they sat around and nattered about other people. They rarely said pleasant things and were overall unpleasant people, but her nana was not like that at all. She had been full of energy and loved to play in the fields with her. The fine wrinkles on her nana's face told Trisstiphina that she was older than her parents, but sometimes she felt that the sparkle in her nana's eyes was that of one who should have been much younger. She had been lean and nimble and would have stood out to those that passed her by.

Triss could pack a bag and run away and find her nana. She could even take Lammy with her; she couldn't leave her pet lamb.

Lammy was the single sheep they kept for milk and wool; Triss had given it the nickname of Lammy, despite her father's annoyance at the sheep having a name at all. "Farm animals are for food and resources; they are not friends," he had said.

She could sell Lammy's wool and milk; maybe hire a guide. She was eleven; she was almost an adult after all and if she didn't run away, her father would just sell her off to one of his creepy friends.

She would do that. She would spend the next week planning, then she would take Lammy and go find and live with her nana.

She shook her head as she reached the end of the orchard row; for now, she had to act normal and do her chores. She had as many apples as she could get that day, so made her way to their cart. It was time to head to the market and while she did, she would plan her journey.

CHAPTER 4
THE FIRES OF CREET

Trisstiphina made her way back from the clothesline with her bundle of dried laundry. The sun was nearly setting, and she knew she was late—or at least late in her mother's eyes. *Why had she let the other boys talk her into following them over the ridge? Just to throw rocks at gophers.*

She wasn't allowed to go over the ridge though she had been there twice in one week and the younger boys knew she was the oldest child around who was still willing to break the rules. Now she was late getting home, and her mother would want to know where she had been. Hopefully, her mom would be out in the yard and she could walk to the front door without being seen from the orchard.

She approached her front door and heard nothing. The house was silent. Triss pressed on the wooden door carefully and she grimaced as the hinge creaked softly. She had a clear view of the kitchen now and her mother was not there. Triss sighed.

Then she heard someone clear their throat. The sound was familiar, and she imagined the stern look of her mother before even turning to see her.

As she expected, her mother was in a chair beside the window, glaring at her, "Dammit, Trissy, were you with those younger boys again?" Her mother pressed her fingers to her forehead. "No, you know what? I don't even want to know. Just go put those clothes away. I'll think of what we will do with you."

Triss grated at that name. Others around town would call her that, but her mother rarely did. Despite her annoyance, Triss tried to put on the most sheepish look she could as she walked to her parents' room. She hoped that by looking remorseful, her mother may not give her a punishment.

"And I better not find any of the clothes bunched up in the drawer," Trisstiphina's mother called from the main room.

Triss opened the drawer and began putting clothes away. It was odd that her mother was sitting by the window. She had not seen her mother do that for a long time, though she had once done it regularly.

Triss recalled a time when her mother would tell her stories from the chair by the window. A time when her mother still had a sense of wonder and excitement. Though she had once had such spirit and energy, the years had worn her down and had slowly changed her to become more like the women of the town, condemned to a simple life.

Her mother used to tell her stories of her time as a dancer in the capital, with an uncharacteristic enthusiasm; they were Trisstiphina's favourite memories of her mother. She remembered a specific story her mother had told her about a love affair in the capital.

In their old farmhouse, her mother had been sitting in the chair once more by the window. Triss, only six or maybe seven, had been playing on the floor below her mother, asking questions, and attentively listening to the stories.

"The auditorium was aglow," her mother said. "Aristocrats from every house arrived in golden carriages to see the performance. The chandeliers shone like brilliant spirits on high, brightening the hall with magic just for us. Dancers all around us ran to and from the stage as we quickly changed between scenes. It was all very exciting."

Trisstiphina looked up at her mother expectantly, eager to hear another tale.

"The dresses were beautiful. Reds, greens, blues, and even purples. The stage was infused with magic to create colours you could not even imagine. Oh, how they swayed that day as we spun across the stage. I felt like a magical flower petal dancing in the wind. I was the lead dancer that night." Her mother's face held a hint of pride, and she smiled down at Trisstiphina. "The elven prince threw me into the air and would catch me in his graceful arms."

"You danced with a prince?" Trisstiphina cut her mother off with excitement. Her mother gave a gentle smile.

"No sweetie, he was just dressed as a prince. His name was Thaddeus. He was playing the role of the prince. Like an actor in a play. Do you understand?"

"Oh, I see. Who watched your performance this time? Was there an elven prince in the audience?" Trisstiphina asked.

"No love. There are no elves in the Empire, only humans."

"Oh. Right."

"But there were royals there, like the daughter of the Veneshal. She was called the Marchioness, and she was beautiful. Gorgeous, and decorated with diamonds. I still remember how her tiara glittered in the soft light of the mezzanine. Her dress, it was a soft gold that streamed along the ground. And her neckline... it was scandalous. It dipped down low enough that you could almost make out the edges of her chest." Trisstiphina let out an innocent gasp. Her mother leaned forward, as if to share something conspiratorial. "Do you want to know a secret?"

Trisstiphina eagerly shook her head in excitement.

"The Marchioness was there to watch her lover. She pined over Thaddeus. He was the lead dancer and was very handsome. This was unheard of. The Veneshal would never allow it. His daughter, and a commoner? It was reprehensible." Trisstiphina's mother gave her a mischievous smile. "They kept the affair secret; no one could know. But us dancers knew. Performers always know."

Trisstiphina leaned forward, excited to learn more.

"To make things worse, Thaddeus was not even in love with the Marchioness. She was cruel and vain, and Thaddeus had a good heart. He wanted to end the relationship, but he feared the wrath of the Marchioness. She could end his career if she wanted or do even worse to the dance company."

Trisstiphina's mother leaned back in her chair now, staring out the window. "She didn't deserve him. She didn't know him, didn't really love him. Not the way he was meant to be loved." Her speech slowed, and she stared out the window.

"He was so handsome, brown hair that flowed; you could run your hands through it. That was just the outer layer, though. He was gentle and kind. And passionate. I remember his hands, the way he held me, his arm pressed across my chest, clutching me in his embrace. I still remember..." Her voice trailed off as her eyes seemed to stare into the distance.

"Mommy, can we go see the dancers in the capital sometime?"

"They do not dance in the capital any longer. They are not allowed... not anymore." Her voice sounded sad. Though she was sitting right in front of Trisstiphina, she seemed to be far away.

Triss waited for her mother to continue, but not for very long. She had become used to her mother ending a story this way. Usually trailing off, deep in nostalgic thought with a forlorn look in her eyes. Trisstiphina became bored, and wandered off, while her mother continued to sit on the chair, and stare out the old dusty window.

That had been years ago. Trisstiphina loved her mother, but she felt she was always sad, and usually seemed far away. Since they had left the farm, it seemed to not change for the better. Triss missed her mother's old stories, but they had not been told since her nana had stopped coming around. *Maybe that was what was missing; perhaps her mother's spirit would return if they saw her nana again.*

Triss decided then; she would take her mother with her when

she left. Her mother was certain to see how great their lives could be, but her dad would never come; he was more concerned with his position in the town.

Triss had been thinking about leaving much in the last week. She had everything she needed ready to go, in a bag under her cot in the loft. She had asked an older boy, who had run away before, what to pack. All she would have to do was pack some clothes and she could leave. She just had not yet committed to leaving. Nothing had pushed her drastically since her encounter in the tavern the previous week.

Triss took the remaining clothes up to her sleeping area in the loft but did not put them away. Instead, she left them there and climbed down the ladder, excited to discuss going to find her nana with her mother.

When she reached the floor, her mother was in the kitchen putting some cups up on the board. She approached hesitantly, still wary of her mother's anger at her tardiness earlier.

"Mommy…" Triss said.

Her mother paused what she was doing, then turned to look at her daughter.

"I was thinking. We haven't seen Nana since we moved here."

Triss spoke hesitantly, nervously grasping her hands together in front of her. Her mother's emotionless stare turned into a frown at the mention of her nana, but Triss was determined to push forward.

"I thought that, maybe, you and I could go see her. We could go find her… and maybe live with her for a bit. Do you know where she is?"

"Trissy, I have told you before and so has your father. We do not speak of your nana in this household." her mother's tone was stern. It made Triss flinch, but anger also flickered in her. Her mother continued. "That woman is just a crazy old witch, with unsavoury ideas about life and no sense of how the world works."

Vile words. Triss had heard them before; they were echoes of her father. *Why would her mother say such things?*

"She's not crazy."

"She is crazy. She was my mother, but she is not anymore. She has gone away for good, and it is better for everyone."

Her mother's voice grew; she was angry. Tears were in her eyes, but Triss was not sure why. *How could she say such things?*

"We will not go see her and we never will. I don't want to hear you ever mention her again. Do you understand?"

Triss was too angry to answer. She had hoped her mother would run away with her. But her mother was gone. Triss stomped her feet and ran to her ladder. She scurried up to her loft, while her mother continued yelling at her.

"Trisstiphina, you get down here right this instant."

Triss ignored her mother and reached under her cot, grabbing her travel bag. She stuffed a small blanket in it and pulled the not-yet-emptied basket of laundry over to herself.

She heard her mother approaching the stairs and something warned her she could not get past her mother with a travel bag, but she was too angry to care right now.

Before her mother began climbing the ladder, Triss heard the front door open.

"What is all this racket?" Trisstiphina's father asked. "I am coming home from my afternoon business and all I hear is yelling?"

Triss could not hear her mother's response, but she heard stern voices from below. Her pack was slung over her shoulder, but she paused. She changed her plan; she would stow the bag and run away, then come back for it at night when no one was awake in the main room.

Before she had the chance to unsling her pack, though, she heard a shocked voice from behind her.

"What in the Abyss are you doing?"

Triss spun around to see her father's head sticking up over the loft edge.

"Are you packing a bag to run away?" her father asked.

Triss did not say a word, instead she pressed her lips together and glared furiously back at her father. *Wrong move.*

"You stupid girl," he said. He grabbed Triss's ankle and pulled her to the lip of the loft. "You get your hide down here right now or I swear to Deus, I will take off this belt and beat you bloody with it."

Triss scrambled down the ladder but continued to glare at her father. She was so angry and scared that her ears began to tingle and flush with heat.

"I just found out today from Samuel what you did to him last week. You tried to take his head off with a bowl. And in the middle of a crowd? And now I come home and find you disobeying your mother and trying to run away?" Her father looked furious; he waved his hands in the air and paced back and forth as he yelled at her, "Do you have any idea how this looks for our family? For me?" He asked.

His pacing slowed and he towered over her, looking even more menacing, "Now, you are going to go over to the Cask and Barrel, where I hope you will find Samuel, and apologize to him as well as anyone else present. Then you will ask him what you can do for him to earn his forgiveness."

"What?" Triss yelled. "Do you even know why I got angry at him? He was making fun of you behind your back. He called you a deadbeat and said he hoped Barbarians would kill you and the other riffraff of Creet."

"I don't give two shits what Samuel said. You will not embarrass me in front of the people of this town. And you will apologize and do what I say, young lady."

Triss couldn't believe it. Her father did not care about her, her mother, or even his own dignity. He only cared about his station.

"I will not!"

Triss ran past her father before he could grab her again and pushed the front door open. It was dark out and her eyes did not immediately adjust to the dusk, but she heard the noises of the town which were slightly more active than usual. She slammed the door behind her, hard enough to make a bit of noise.

Bang!

A loud explosive noise rocked the porch and rattled the door; she almost lost her balance. *That wasn't the door slamming.* No, the noise had not come from behind her; it came from somewhere else in the town. Suddenly, she realized the raised racket of the town was not just the usual hustle and bustle. There were shouts and screams coming from all directions.

She took several steps out into the street, looked down the lane, and halted. She saw a scene that was unlike anything she had seen before, and her mind took a moment to register it. Part of the Imperial Barracks was on fire, and the fire was spreading. Small fires here and there scorched wooden buildings. She could hear metal clank against metal from the direction of the barracks. Smoke trailed across the streets from sources she could not see, and when a tendril of it cleared, she saw a body lying there, in a military uniform. Then she noticed another.

Curiosity, confusion, and shock placed her in a trance. She shambled down the road; feet shuffling of their own accord. She should have been terrified, but it was as if she were in a dream, as if sleepwalking toward the noises.

After only a few moments of walking, she could now make out the forms of Imperial soldiers behind the smoke. *Fighting against.... what? another army? No, she saw no matching banners or standards. Bandits? No, they appeared to be men but seemed too organized or at least disciplined for bandits. To Triss's surprise, they were beating the soldiers back. No Bandits would stand up against professionally trained soldiers.* She had learned these things from the men in the tavern; Bandits were usually untrained and only fearsome because they preyed on those who could not defend themselves. *Then what was going on?*

She could make out the smell of charred wood as she made her way closer. Her body froze as wind cleared the smoke further, and light illuminated an enemy. The attacker was much larger than most men, covered in fur, and... and it had the head of a bull! *These must be the savages from the north the men had spoken of... what had the men at the tavern called them? Barbarians? Demons?*

The bull man swung an axe and felled the soldier in front of him. After the first soldier collapsed, two crossbowmen fired at him, but both bolts ricocheted off his metal chest armour. He tilted his head down, horns pointing at them like a threat, and charged at the two crossbowmen before they could even reload. His head contacted their bodies with a clear crunching noise and launched them into the air. They landed a few meters back in a heap. They did not get back up and the bull man disappeared from Triss's view as he charged through a cloud of smoke.

A flash of light caught her attention, and she noticed that the fire had spread beyond the barracks as more buildings were in flames. As she searched for the source of the flash, she saw the wizard from the barracks standing at the intersection of two roads, and he ignited two orbs of fire in the palms of his hands.

The wizard threw fire at the intruders, seemingly not caring if he hit the enemy or the houses of innocents around him. He flailed and tossed the orbs of fire in desperation at anything he could make out through the smoke. The first flame hit one raider square in the chest and threw him back, killing him instantly. But the second fireball flew clear of the raider and hit the general store on the other side. It quickly went up in flames.

An arrow whipped past her vision, just in front of her head, snapping her back to her senses, suddenly aware of the current danger of her situation.

She looked right to follow the trajectory of the arrow when another raider advanced up the street behind her. He did not look at her. His focus was beyond her up the street.

There stood three crossbowmen, one reloading, having been the one that nearly hit her. The other two raised their crossbows for shots, but before they could fire, the raider shoved her aside, moving in front of her. He shielded her with his body so the two bolts that would likely have also hit her only hit the raider. The first one bounced off his armour, but the second one found a gap. He staggered and fell to his hands and knees. *Why had this raider done that?*

The crossbowmen approached the downed raider who raised his right hand, and on his wrist was a small, attached crossbow. It looked strange to Triss. The raider pointed it at the three crossbowmen, and she heard a mechanism click. He fired it. Instead of launching a single bolt at the unsuspecting crossbowmen, it fired multiple bolts, like a porcupine shooting quills. They peppered the three crossbowmen with tiny needles, and the men dropped to the ground, dead.

Captain Titus could see the town of Creet in the distance. So far, there were only small fires coming from a few of the buildings. His men would certainly be capable of putting out that fire and fixing up the town… but he knew that was not what would happen. He made his way on foot past the rows of archers, all waiting on his command. He approached his commander, an acolyte, perched on his large war horse.

"Report, Captain," the acolyte, Pious, said as Titus approached his horse.

No older than Titus, he was a junior amongst mages, but superior to Titus. The cloak of his acolyte robes was lowered, showing his raven black hair pulled back into a bun.

"Our scouts report that the main Barbarian force has engaged the battalion at the Creet barracks, but the fighting has spread throughout the town," Titus said. "The scouts have confirmed that there are no Barbarian reserves in hold outside of the town. Their entire army is inside, and within range of our archers, as you requested."

He paused for a moment, considering if he should say what he felt he must.

"Sir, there are also many civilians in the town. The entire population is still in there. No one has made it out yet. Not to mention the entirety of our barracks."

"I know it's not ideal, Captain. But these are just peasants out here. They are not out on the frontier because they are great people. Even soldiers only end up here when they do something wrong. The increased casualties will strengthen the Empires' resolve. We need this victory. We'll be heroes for defeating such a deadly threat."

"Pious, let me just take my men in and engage them. We can draw them out. Then we can ambush them. Save the town. Save our people and the townsfolk. The demons will be trapped between us and the garrison." His voice would have sounded like a plea, if not for the strength and conviction in his tone.

The acolyte leaned forward in his saddle towards the captain, to address him, and him alone.

"Captain, do you have any idea how much shit we are already in? You lost Vester Keep, and I risk losing the entire western border. If we return in defeat, with our existing troops lost, we'll lose everything. Our title. Our lands. Think of your family. Do you want to see them out on the street? Have to sell yourself, your wife, or your son into servitude just to survive? Do you know what this sort of mark can do to either of our careers?" he paused, "Dammit, Titus. We are hanging by a thread. We can't afford a risky engagement." The acolyte let his words hang for a moment, then he sat up tall and put on a cool face once more. "You have your orders. Carry them out."

"Yes, sir." The captain's eyes sunk, and his head lowered, but he knew his duty. The acolyte was right.

He took a few steps away from Acolyte Pious and towards his archers. He lifted his hand in the air and yelled, "Light!"

A squire with a torch ran along the line of archers, igniting the tar on the ends of each arrow that were already nocked on their bows.

Once the squire had passed each archer, the captain called his next command, "Ready!" He waited a moment to ensure each archer was prepared to draw. "Fire at will!"

Arrows let loose and soared like blades of fire and light through the air. They arched and came down on the town.

For a moment, the light dissipated as the arrows hit their marks, then, in response, the town erupted into a blaze of luminosity, with flames engulfing many houses and any other combustible objects within its reach.

Captain Titus' forces would spend the night there while the flames burned down what remained of Creet. They would take out any survivors fleeing the town while they waited and, in the morning, they would sweep through the town, cleaning up any remaining enemy forces. Then they would report the victory over the invading barbarians that had been plaguing the border for the last few months.

The captain's face darkened, sullen. He looked down at the ground, reservations about his role in this action weighing on his mind. *What had they just done? What was he still going to do? The civilians and the town of Creet, they would not see the morning. He had just been following orders. There was no choice; he must follow orders.*

Fire reflected off nearby windowpanes. The blaze grew as it engulfed building after building. Triss had to get away. Tears streaked across her face as the wind whipped her cheeks. Her eyes were red and sore from crying in terror.

She ran and ran without looking back at all. She ran right past her house, in such shock that her mind did not register it half burnt down. Flames burst from buildings all around her.

She ran straight for the shed and her pet lamb, surprised it was not burned down. As she approached, though, she found the door broken and thrown wide open. A man stood in the doorway, facing away from her. He was going to steal something.

She recognized the man. It was Master Shaw who she had last seen in the Cask and Barrel. *She had not considered him a terrible person, possibly even kind. Perhaps he only seemed that way because it was what he thought people expected of him. What was he doing?*

"You're gonna make a fine meal for me," he said.

Her body froze. He was looking straight at Lammy.

The blacksmith reached towards Lammy, as Triss realized he was going to steal and eat her best friend.

Without thinking, she rammed Shaw as hard as she could colliding her shoulder into the square of his back. The man grunted in surprise and lost his balance, crashing into the small wall of the pen.

Triss fell back, mostly bouncing from the impact, but she was quicker to get back up. She pounced on him, tearing at hair and skin. She banged her small hands on the back of his head and bit his finger when he tried to bat at her.

Lammy jumped, terrified, and bolted over the destroyed pen wall. She only had a moment to watch Lammy run into the woods before Shaw pushed her off, got back to his feet, and slapped her across the face.

"You bitch!"

She landed hard on the ground, but rage numbed the pain. Shaw launched himself at her, but she rolled out of the way. He grabbed her left leg, but she kicked and flailed with her free leg, finally landing a blow on the back of his neck.

He growled at the barrage of kicks, and his grip on her leg slipped.

She scrambled to her feet and turned to run, but Shaw lunged forward and grabbed her ankle again. She tripped, and he dragged her to the ground.

She slammed against the dirt and banged her head hard. Sharp pain shot through her skull, and she felt dizzy.

Before she had time to think, the man delivered a hard kick to her ribs. She had never felt pain like it before. Shaw dove on top of her, pinning her to the ground.

"I'm going to beat you for that girl. Teach you some manners."

She was having a hard time focusing her eyes, but she stull caught sight of his cruel sneer. His eyes slowly lowered to the locket around her neck.

"What is this? This looks shiny." He leaned his head forward to get a better look at the locket. Renewed anger flared in her and sharpened her mind.

Triss head-butted the man in the face. *Crunch*. Blood flowed out of his nose.

"You wretch!"

He slapped her across the face. She was terrified, but the pain in her head made it too difficult to think clearly. Her body felt limp, and her neck could no longer support her head.

Shaw seemed to gain his composure again. "Or maybe I'll just bloody you up a bit and then sell you to the slavers. Yeah, I'm going to enjoy—hrmph" Shaw let out a strange gurgle then slumped down lifeless on top of her. Confused, she looked up over him, but all she could see was a dagger sticking out of his back, near his neck. His weight crushed her, but then his body was thrown off her.

Above her stood a large, menacing man covered in armour and weapons. Blue, black, and red paint gave him a savage appearance. *Or was it blood?* She saw no eyes behind his helmet; hidden in the shadows.

He was strange. Unlike the soldiers of the barracks, whose armour would usually cover as much as possible, his armour only covered a few key areas. It would have looked patchy if it did not look so intentional, with feathers and beads braided into parts of it, and with many gaps, it would not be of much use against arrow fire. But she could make out a long shield on his back through her blurry vision.

He stood there unmoving, looking down at her. Light flickered off metal, and she noticed the throwing knives lining a leather belt wrapped diagonally across his chest; knives that matched the one in Shaw's back. A drop of blood dripped from the edge of a massive battle axe held in his left hand.

He must have stood six feet, which was quite tall for a man in her village. But it was not the armour, weapons, or the height that made him seem menacing. It was his presence; the way he held himself, and the confidence of a person tried in battle and found worthy.

Terror struck Triss, but she was too injured to make a run for it, and the pain in her head continued to throb. Her eyes felt so heavy, she tried to fight it, but she could feel the black consuming her. The man reached down to pick her up, and the last thing she saw was her home and town burning as he carried her away.

CHAPTER 5
TALES FROM THE DRUNKEN OWL

In the average sized town of Crestwood, stood a comfortable little tavern called the Drunken Owl. Above the door a wooden sign swung, with a large circle and what looked to be an owl half standing, half leaning against the inside of the circle. A drunken stance resembled the namesake of the tavern.

Along the bar within, three men sat on stools, conversing familiarly while Lucius stood close by, half listening while he tended to his bar, cleaning a glass with his damp rag.

He glanced at his long-time friends. They had been coming here since he opened the Drunken Owl. The right-most of the three men, Ox, was much larger than the rest, a symptom of a physical life on the farms. Dirt caked to his clothes and his hands still had soil between his nails, despite attempts at cleaning them.

Marcus leaned against the bar on the left of the group and was by far the cleanest looking of the bunch, with a tidy vest and a clean-shaven, sharp look to himself. He worked in administration within the town hall and was always the best dressed because of it.

But at that moment, the bartender, the farmer, and the administrator were all focused on the man between them, Beacher.

He was shorter than the others and skinny; a trader, but not successful enough to grow the pot belly common among the profession.

"That's right," Beacher said. "I heard it when I travelled through Dorst, then the same stories when I was in Creet. The Guards and military did not want to talk much about it, but I can be convincing."

The trader gave a sly smile, looking quite proud of himself for the information he knew though Lucius was used to Beacher's boasting at his bar and just rolled his eyes.

"The bartenders will usually help me buy the guards a drink to get them to open up and loosen their tongues."

Beacher seemed to enjoy the attention he was receiving from Ox and Marcus. Lucius didn't think Beacher even cared if they believed him, so long as they listened. He would take Beacher's information with an appropriate grain of salt.

"Beacher, you're full of it," Marcus said. "The Barbarian tribes were wiped out hundreds of years ago. They probably had just seen some wild men. A few are known to live in the dead hills."

"Ha! That was what I thought. But woodsmen in both towns have had sightings of people that look like barbarians and are not just dirty wildlings. There have been too many sightings to be a coincidence."

"Friend, I think—"

Before Marcus could continue, Ox cut him off, "Hold on, I want to hear him. What if that is just what the Empire has told us and wants us to think? What if the Barbarians were not completely wiped out?"

Lucius continued washing glasses with his hand rag. He liked to listen more than talk.

"Maybe that is exactly what they are doing," Beacher said. "But even if not, it seems like too many similar sightings to be a coincidence. The Barbarian Hordes have returned." Beacher emphasized this last point like a bard singing a song in proclamation.

Ox's eyes lit up with interest, but Marcus just glowered. Finally,

Lucius commented, "Beacher, isn't the word Horde a bit dramatic? At most, you said a few barbarians were sighted."

Beacher hunched a bit, deflated, "Fine, but the news is at least interesting. What's new around here for you guys? Marcus? What's your most interesting story?"

Marcus sighed and began, "Yeah Fine. Not too much new in administration—"

"Is there ever?" Ox cut in with a quip. He was clearly more interested in stories of the borders, but Lucius flicked the side of his head with a towel to tell him to shut up, so that Marcus could continue.

Marcus smiled in appreciation, "The Autumn Court has passed legislation restricting the use of indentured servants in the Empire. Now only certain people can be indentured. I heard it was a move to calm the plebeians, but the senate quietly increased the power of the banks and guilds, with a new law allowing them to venture into the ownership of mass property and reclamation of unpaid debts. They also removed some of the pre-existing monopoly laws."

Lucius saw the look of boredom and confusion come over Ox's face.

"Why does that matter? Fewer Indentures means less slavery, right?"

Marcus sighed, as if frustrated at having to answer a child, but he let out the breath and composed himself, explaining with exceptional patience.

"Because it means the banks and guilds can control the resources, property, and the money. Meaning that they control everything that a person needs, so that if a person does not do the work that the guild or bank want them to, they can just starve the person to death. It is just slavery hidden under a different name to not seem like it. If you don't want to starve, you will take whatever job they give you, no matter how shitty or life threatening it is. And with the banks so willing to give out money, they can track and drag you back to your job if you try to leave it without paying back your debt."

"Oh, so it is the same thing?" Ox asked, his face scrunched up, attempting to follow the logic.

"Yes, the same thing, though laws previously existed to protect the indentured and ensure the owners treat them to a certain standard, which may not exist with actual employees."

"Well, in that case, I am just happy that the big guilds do not have a large presence outside of the capital," Lucius said. "I can just run my tavern and mind my business."

"For now..." Marcus put in.

Lucius hoped he would not have to concern himself with the guilds for some time. He picked up the closest dirty mug and returned to cleaning. For a moment it was silent, as the tone of the conversation had taken a glum turn.

"Well, at least it is a lot better than having your innards eaten by ravaging barbarians!" Ox said. He gave a laugh that came from his belly. Glum faces turned up and smiled back at Ox.

"Here, here!" the rest of the friends gave a small cheer and clinked their drinks together.

"Ox, my friend, I am sure you do not need to worry. No one will ever eat you," Beacher said.

Ox raised an eyebrow as if to ask why, and Beacher continued first by slapping Ox on the shoulder.

"You, my friend, smell much too foul. Like a pig that rolled in mud, got into some spoiled hay, and let it fester."

Ox glared at Beacher and Lucius paused cleaning. He hoped Ox would not punch Beacher out again. Ox tried to look angry, but his sour expression burst, and he erupted into laughter. The other three quickly joined him as they chuckled together, slammed back their drinks and ordered another round.

CHAPTER 6
WAKING IN A NEW WORLD

Trisstiphina awoke slowly. The bed beneath her was firm but comfortable with soft blankets, warm and cozy. Yet, a gnawing sense of unease tugged at her senses. This was not her bed; something was not right.

Triss blinked her eyes open; everything was a blur, but shapes slowly formed. She did not recognize where she was, only able to make out pale brownish colours, perhaps a light coming from somewhere. She tried blinking further, but everything was still a fog, and a throbbing pain in her head swelled, forcing her to bring her hand to her forehead. It ached worse than it ever had before.

There was a flicker of movement out of the corner of her eye. She tried to turn her head to focus on it, but the pain intensified. She closed her eyes and felt like she would fall asleep at any moment.

This time, when she opened her eyes, she could make out a bit more. She could make out a roof and walls of cloth. It felt both strange and fascinating to be enclosed within these soft walls, held together by wooden poles, creating a circular room. The poles were spaced evenly, creating a rhythm that her curious eyes followed along the walls.

She was in a tent, and a fairly big one, it seemed.

Again, there was a subtle movement, and she focused her eyes on it as best she could. There was a man sitting in a chair near her bed. Her mind was still groggy, and she had a hard time focussing, but she made out some of his key features. He seemed wiry yet extraordinarily strong, with long, messy black hair and a scraggly beard. His chest was exposed, but he wore an animal skin skirt or kilt, and boots. Something seemed off about his skin. *Was it the colour? Was it grey?* She could not quite tell.

"Good. You're up," the man said, "At least partially."

She tried to recall where she was or what her last memory was, but her mind was too foggy. She remembered her home, but not much else. *This wasn't home. How had she gotten here?*

The memories came back in a wave, and she winced as they assaulted her mind. Her memories were still missing details, but the flashes told enough; there had been a battle in town and fire everywhere; it had trapped her in its midst.

She almost screamed when she remembered the sight of her house burning. She had been in shock when it happened and had not registered it, but the feelings kicked her in the gut now; an ache in her stomach that felt like stone. She knew her parents were most likely dead and so was everyone she had ever known.

Her eyes blurred with welling tears as she remembered the mage hurling fire at attackers and felt hatred. Remembered the monsters and felt fear. Remembered the fires and felt sorrow.

The initial onslaught of emotions passed, her mind cleared, and she remembered more. *Someone had assaulted her, but how had she escaped? Had she escaped?*

The image flashed into her mind; the memory bore into her brain. A fear tied to the memory. *A large man, her rescuer perhaps?* Or more likely her captor; she was uncertain.

She squirmed, panic settling in.

"Woah there now. Don't worry, child, you are safe now." The man put his hand on her shoulder, and she relaxed. His voice was deep, but comforting, like a man that had been through much but kept an empathy for others.

It was not her captor. She was certain of that.

Was she actually safe? What happened to the demons? The fire? The military?

"Where.... where am I?" she stammered as she tried to speak.

The man smiled at her, at least it seemed he did; he was still hazy, "You, my dear, are in the camp of Clan Kaltor, of the Bandorian clans, or more specifically, you are in my tent. The medical tent. And I am Cairn," he spoke in a comforting tone. "Do not worry, you are safe," he repeated.

He turned something over in his hand. Triss couldn't tell what it was, but his tone turned serious.

"Where did you get this locket? I have seen one like this before, but it does not come from your world."

"Mmm... my... my locket? It was from my nana. It belonged to her."

"Interesting. Was your nana a Fae? This is a Fae necklace, and the Fae do not often lose things that belong to them."

"A Fae? The Fair Folk?"

The man nodded.

"What? No, I have never met one of them."

Triss had heard tales of the Fae, Fair Folk that come from the otherworld. They were people and spirits that would come out of the forest to steal your babies and punish wicked children. But they were just tales, things that mothers would tell their children to keep them in line and away from the forest. Even her nana had used the term as a silly name for Triss, "my little Fae."

The man seemed to take a bedtime story surprisingly seriously.

"Hmm, perhaps you have met one, but did not know it." He let out a brief chuckle. "No matter. You should get more sleep; you need more rest."

"Yeah, you are probably right..." she said, but her response trailed off as she lowered her head back to the pillow. She sorted through everything she had known about her nana and wondered if she had overlooked some subtle detail.

A Fae? Were they real? What would her nana have to do with the fair folk? Why would she have a necklace of theirs? Her nana had always been mischievous and secretive about her life away from Triss.

She tried to think more about it, but her thoughts jumbled with memories of the night before. The waking world fell away as she drifted back towards dreams; she wanted to think more, find out where she was now. *How had she gotten here?* But the more she tried, the heavier her eyelids felt, until she could battle it no longer, and fell asleep.

"Get up."

A gruff voice barked at Trisstiphina, but it was the booted foot kicking her thigh that woke her. It did not hurt, but it was jarring enough to give her system a shock.

Her eyes snapped open and this time there was none of the haze that had filled her head when she had woken before. She felt rested and alert. Her hair was in her face, and she brushed a hand over her face to move the long blond lock. She looked up to see a large man towering over her, not the man named Cairn from before.

This man was bulkier and tall. No shirt obstructed her view of his powerful frame. Muscles on the man looked taut, like layers of whipcord stretched over his body. He stared down at her with a hard look in his eyes. Something about him seemed familiar and, with a shock, she realized he must be the man that had taken her. Her Captor.

"Get up," he repeated before he stepped back out of her vision.

She quickly noted that she was in a tent once more, though this one seemed smaller than the medical tent, only large enough for a nearby wooden frame bed, and the cot that she lay on along the floor of the opposite wall, but still large enough to stand in.

Triss lifted her head quickly, fearful of being kicked again and harder, before she pushed herself into a sitting position. Fear washed over her at the thought of being unconscious for a long time in the presence of dangerous people. She patted her hands down her body to make sure she was not injured and was relieved to notice that she was still wearing her simple village clothes. She brought her hand to her chest and gave a sigh of relief when it landed on her nana's locket. She clutched it, tucked it under her shirt, then looked back up at the man.

Wearing only short trousers and animal skin boots, he stood back a few feet from her and stroked his short red beard as he stared at her. He had a deadly look to him; even with his considerable bulk, he seemed like he could lunge at her at any moment, like a snake. She quickly hurried to get to her feet.

"Good," he said. "Now grab that bucket and get outside."

He did not wait for her to respond, instead, he turned on his heel, lifted the tent flap, and walked outside.

Triss saw a wooden bucket beside where she had laid on the cot. She quickly grabbed it by the handle and rushed to the door. *Making this man wait did not seem like a wise thing to do.*

Her dress rustled around her feet as she lifted the tent flap and made her way outside. Her vision filled with white as she passed through the door; it had clearly been some time since she had been outside.

Triss lifted her hand to cover her eyes, but at that moment her dress caught on her foot, and she tripped. The bucket flew from her hand as she threw her palms out to catch herself, but she could not see the ground coming. She skidded on the hard packed dirt and scraped her palms.

Dust kicked up around her, and she squinted to clear her eyes. She glanced up to see the large man standing there and fear filled her heart. She scrambled to her knees and grabbed the nearby bucket.

Her eyes had adjusted enough to see her surroundings. She was in a forest of thick oaks. There was only one other tent in the space between the trees, but she could make out the tops of other tents beyond the shrub and a small brook trickled close by.

"Sorry." She blurted the words out. "Master, I beg your pardon. Please forgive my clumsiness."

Triss hoped that her respect would earn his pity though the man said nothing, just stared at her as he stood beside an extinguished fire pit. The largest axe Triss had ever seen leaned against a log bench beside the man. It had subtle etchings along the length of it and flecks of red, likely blood, on the blade and handle.

Both tents in her small clearing were rounded and faced in towards the now cool firepit and wood log benches. The smell of other active campfires wafted through the air, and from all directions, sounds of a military camp echoed through the trees. *There was no hope of escape.*

Between the trees in a few places, she could make out the other tents, weapon racks, and savage looking people in animal skins wielding and sparing with deadly looking weapons.

Barbarians.

Everywhere she looked, she saw signs of battle hungry raiders through the trees; painted, half naked and dirty.

And she was their prisoner.

As a slave, or the spoils of war, intended to be sold off into slavery. She had heard tales of such before; raiders and barbarians had stolen people and traded them for gold. Even the Empire would take in new slaves, bought from other civilizations, though they called them servants instead.

Triss quickly got to her feet, keeping her head bowed to the man.

Her captor had just been staring at her. Finally, he gave a slight chuckle and spoke, "Master? Why do you call me master?"

He eyed her for a moment, as if trying to decide something. It made her nervous.

"I am no one's master. There are no slaves to be found here; we do not have time for those that cannot think for themselves."

He looked down at her dress as if trying to decide something.

Then he reached for his boot and drew his large knife out of its scabbard. He took one step towards her, and she flinched, hoping that her punishment would not be too permanent. He grabbed her roughly by the dress, and she tried hard not to let out a cry as she squeezed her eyes shut even harder than she had before.

She felt a gentle tug at the bottom of her dress and heard a quick ripping noise. She did not feel any pain, his grip released, and she opened her eyes, confused to see that he had taken a step back and was looking at her with a satisfied smile.

Wondering what he had done, she looked down at herself to see if there was any blood; there was none. He had not cut her at all but had cut away the bottom half of her dress, so that it now only came down to her knees instead of her heels. She imagined she looked ridiculous, but had to admit this would be much easier to perform chores in.

"Now pick up that bucket and clean those plates."

He pointed to two plates that were sitting on a bench and then at the small brook just behind the tent. Obediently, she walked towards the water to fill the bucket, wondering what he meant by 'no slaves here.' She doubted he meant they kept them somewhere else. *If they did not keep slaves, then why was she here?* She was not sure, but she suspected there was something important in his words that she was missing.

She was aware of nearby warriors that stared at her between the trees as she walked over to the brook. She first thought they must not be used to seeing a girl in a military camp. But as she filled the bucket with water, she noticed there was a woman among them. Two women, actually. Dressed in leather and hide armour like the men, not a dress as she expected. They were dressed for battle, not for doing dishes or any other womanly chore. Did they fight with the men? This was unheard of.

She finished filling the pale and returned to her captor. He was sitting on a log, focussed on dragging his knife across a leather strop.

Triss quickly washed the two wooden plates and looked around to see what she was supposed to do next. Without looking up from what the man was doing, he spoke.

"Good, now let's get some food. I am hungry, and you must be as well."

He hopped up, slid the blade into his boot sheath, grabbed the two plates, and began walking. Triss, not wanting to see that blade again, quickly fell into stride behind him.

While Triss had hoped for a chance to see more of the camp to get her bearings, they did not go far; only a few paces down the path to the next clump of tents over from theirs. In the distance, she saw a man, strong looking like Axton, but with sharp ears and a strange, grey colour to his skin. Another warrior caught her attention, and she initially mistook him for a child, but his proportions seemed off, and she decided it must be some other race. She had heard whispers of other races beyond the Empire from the travellers at the Cask and Barrel, but she had never laid eyes upon one.

She tried to strain herself to get a better view, but her captor handed her the plate, which she held, confused.

The clump of tents was made up of four tents—one of which was much bigger than the rest—arranged around a bonfire, with a large beast roasting on a spit. Felled tree logs lay arranged around the fire for sitting.

Her captor grabbed a knife that had been stabbed into a stump and cut a slab of meat off the roast and put it onto his plate, then cut another piece off and placed it on Trisstiphina's plate. He then grabbed a ladle that sat in a pot beside the fire and scooped cooked root vegetables onto both plates. Triss found this all terribly peculiar; *what kind of slave was fed with the masters?* She was starting to realize that things were not as she first assumed.

"Sir?" she asked, confused by how she was being treated. Perhaps she was being kept for ransom as she had heard of bandits doing that. But she was not worth anything, and no one would ever pay for her return. Before she could voice the actual question, though, he interrupted her.

"Sit down." They both had a seat, and the man picked up his piece of meat and began eating. Triss hesitated, not sure if she should eat or not, and she still wanted to ask her question.

"Sorry Sir, but I have to ask-"

"Why do you keep calling me 'Sir'?" he interrupted, giving her a quizzical look. "At least you stopped calling me master, I guess." He took another big bite of meat.

"You are in charge; you are the authority. I assumed I should show you respect." She was wary of some sort of trick, so she chose her words carefully. "You are in charge, are you not? Is it not expected for me to show respect?"

"Respect? Ha! Is that so? Have I shown you some sort of amazing wisdom and knowledge already? Wow, I must try to remember what I've done." Sarcasm dripped from his voice. "Have I earned your respect so quickly?"

"I... uh... um." Fear and confusion muddled her mind.

"Ha! Of course not. You don't even know me; how can you speak of respect so soon? Respect is for those who earn it. Authority is not exempt from the title of fool. Any ruler can be a fool; and you would respect a fool? That shows nothing except that you are a fool yourself."

He seemed amused by her confusion, then his eyes turned serious and contemplative. He spoke, almost under his breath and to himself, "No... but you are no fool... hmm," he trailed off, stroking his beard. "You do what I tell you to do right now, because if you do not or if you choose to run, I will wallop you. Not for disrespecting me, but for taking such rash action. Only a fool would act impulsively before understanding their surroundings.

"Do not call me sir. Titles are for the vain; my name is Axton, and you may call me that."

Trisstiphina noticed he did not ask for her name. She made note of his name and nodded in understanding.

Axton took another large bite of meat, then rested his wooden plate on the ground out of the way. He leaned forward, bringing his face closer to hers, "Child, you are not a slave."

Somehow, she knew the words to be true as Axton spoke them; but she still did not know how that could be. She was still afraid, even if Axton seemed to treat her well enough. *Who were these people that butchered towns but politely fed their captives? They had captured her during the raid on her town; was she not at least a prisoner?*

"I took you with me. After that brigand had injured you, just outside of what I can only assume was your home, I took you to save you."

His expression looked serious, but with a hint of something else; perhaps empathy, or at least what passed for empathy in his culture.

She stared blankly at him in confusion. It made little sense. *If she was not a prisoner or a slave, then what?* A hint of tension and fear peeled off her.

"Your home is destroyed," Axton said. "Your hometown has burned to the ground, and every person you have ever known is likely dead or gone." His tone carried no emotion; just facts.

She winced at the pain of the memory and as some of the fear left her, sorrow filled the gap. His words hit her like a wall, her stomach ached from the knot within, and the world blurred from the water welling up on her eyelids.

She had known these things, but she had been too afraid before to acknowledge them. When she had awoken somewhere strange and her memories returned to her, somewhere deep down, she had known she would not see her home again. This information had just confirmed what she already knew; but it still hurt.

Axton did not move. He just sat, waiting for her to process her situation.

The pain changed then; she felt it flare into a fiery anger in her chest towards Axton and his people. They had done this to her. She had to hold in her rage to ensure she did not lash out. After all, Axton still made her afraid.

She brought her arm to her eyes to wipe away the tears, then looked at him. As she stared up into his eyes, her rage became muted and subsided; still there, but pushed aside by something else. His actions confused her, and curiosity overshadowed that anger, forcing it to wait.

"We are Bandorians," he said, "and like the Barbarian hordes we descended from, battle is our way of life. But do not make the mistake of thinking we are the same as them. As you will learn, our ways differ from theirs. We have chosen a different path.

"Months ago, we began our campaign to battle the Empire. We attacked a few of the outposts that the Empire had established along the western border. Our aim was to destroy their seats of power and draw out their armies. Discover their military strength; to understand our enemy."

Trisstiphina's anger made her chest ache, but her fear and curiosity kept her from doing anything foolish.

Axton sighed deeply. "We succeeded. We came for Creet, not for the people or buildings, but for the Barracks and the wizard within. Despite what others believe, we are not demons; we do not butcher helpless people. When we attacked the barracks in your hometown, we incurred the wrath of your wizard. He unleashed an inferno, pinning us down within the centre of the town."

A flash of anger made her face hot as she remembered the strange cruelness of the local wizard. Her town burned and part of her buried anger redirected towards him. The wizard had brought these monsters down on her family and town.

"We underestimated the Empire's competence. Our previous actions attacking the Imperial outposts had gained the attention of the Empire and had brought out the western regional garrison. They knew we were approaching the town, and they laid in ambush, waiting for us to commit our troops. They surrounded the town with men and trapped us within, killing our people as quickly as they could. The town was burning, and it was time for us to leave."

He narrowed his eyes on Triss and leaned forward in his seat, so his eyes were level with hers.

"Your story begins when that man attacked you."

Her eyes locked with his.

"As I was surveying the outskirts of the town for enemy soldiers and any of my surviving kin, I saw you charge that man. I was curious how it would play out, so I watched as you fought a man four times your size and made him pay for every inch. You fought bravely and with heart, and I decided you did not deserve to die with the rest of your people. So, I brought you here to live on. To keep your story from ending and to see how the rest of your story plays out."

He saved her because she fought a man?

Axton waited, giving her time to think. Confusion and conflict came to her mind. His soft tone and eased demeanour contradicted the demons she had watched destroy the only home she had. Her mind struggled to understand the events that she had experienced. She had been sure these Barbarians were monsters, but what she had experienced was anything but. Axton was kind and practical; he painted a different picture than the one that had been in her memory, and yet, it filled in the gaps she could not explain herself.

Then an image flashed back into her mind. She had seen it with her own eyes; a monstrous demon through the fire and smoke.

"You say you are not monsters, but I saw demons with you," Triss said. "A massive one, twice the height of a man, with the face of a beast... a bull, and huge horns for goring people. He was covered in fur and blood. It was terrible..."

Her hands shook at the memory of the creature.

Axton slapped his knee and gave a good laugh.

"You mean Horst?" he asked. "Ha. I suppose he is a terror to behold."

Axton turned his head towards one of the nearby tents, the larger of the four, and called out a name.

"Horst! Get out here. I need you for a moment."

Triss froze. Her hands trembled. Was she about to see an actual demon, a monster from the Abyss? A fur covered hand pulled back the flap of the kitchen tent and, as Axton had stated, out came the demon from her nightmares.

She broke. Panicked, she kicked off quickly from her seat and tripped, falling backwards over the log she had sat upon. She scrambled, half running, half-trying to stand up. But she did not make it far. Thick hands grabbed her, and she felt herself falling. The next thing she knew, she was pinned and could not move. Axton had her wrapped and gripped tight in a hold, like a bear hugging a child. The more she struggled, the tighter his grip got.

"Whoa there, girl," Axton said. "Calm down. Calm down. Relax." His voice was slow and calming. But Triss continued to struggle. Only after she tired of squirming and her muscles relaxed did Axton relieve the tension. He did not let go or allow her to move, but he held her in more of an embrace than a crushing grip.

"It's ok," Axton said. "He won't hurt you."

Axton turned them both around on the ground to face the demon. She reluctantly looked at the creature she had feared so much.

Something was not right. Her mind fumbled, trying to comprehend what she was looking at. As she had said, it had the dark fur covered legs of a thick bull, a rippling torso of a giant, sharp horns that could spear a man, and a terrifying snout. But nothing else about it looked terrifying. It was wearing a stained white kitchen apron, like the one her mother used to wear, holding a large carrot in one hand, and a tiny peeling knife in the other. It stood there with a dumb look of confusion on its face and slouched, waiting impatiently to find out why it had been called.

The creature looked comical. Still terrifying, but like a drawing crafted by a child of a ridiculous monster. Axton was laughing at the sight, but finally calmed enough to speak. "The girl thinks you're a demon." Then Axton continued to chuckle.

Horst looked at the girl, then back at Axton. "Oh. Uh, I could give her a growl if she would like. I mean, I've been cutting onions though, so I can't promise anything impressive. I suppose I could swing this peeler around, but the carrot might actually do more damage."

Axton was reeling at the idea; he let go of Fae and slapped his knee. "No, no, my friend, I think it is fine. I just wanted to give the girl a look. You go back to those onions. Thank you." Horst shrugged, then walked back into the tent.

Axton stopped laughing and helped Triss back onto the bench. Her hands had only now stopped shaking.

"You will find in life that many things are not as they first appear. Horst is not a demon; he is a minotaur. A creature you have likely never been exposed to in your quiet life in Creet. We welcome people of any species or race, as long as they accept and adopt our culture. You will find humans, minotaurs, dwarves, gnomes, even the occasional half-elf or half-orc amongst the Bandorians. I don't think you will find a demon, though. Although, I suppose if they were not evil and accepted our way of life, it is possible. Though, to be fair, if you have ever seen a raging gnome, you would be forgiven for thinking it a demon. It's the small ones, the ones that have always had it tough, that you really must fear."

Triss could not imagine a small gnome being terrifying, but Axton seemed to be convinced.

A minotaur in a kitchen apron? Raging gnomes? Barbarians with a moral code and kindness?

"It is easy to fear that which you do not understand," she recalled her Nana telling her, "That which is a mystery to you."

She reached her hand up to touch the small amulet at her neck. Though she was afraid, her mind was beginning to accept the fact that perhaps things were not always as they seemed when the veil was lifted.

Axton leaned back and took another bite of meat before beginning again, "Now then, you have some options. You can leave, if you wish, and you can try to survive in the world by yourself. You may make it back to the Empire, but your town is not there, and your Empire will just put you in a refugee house for orphaned children, if you are lucky, or make you a slave if you are not. If you do end up in an orphanage, they will keep you there and give you nothing until you come of age. Then they will throw you out to starve to death on the streets."

Triss had heard of the orphanages before and knew this to be true; families sometimes took the babies in, but no one wanted an older child. She continued to nibble on her food, her bites becoming bigger as she realized it was not some form of trap. She had not noticed how famished she had become.

"Or... you can take what you are given," Axton continued. "You can join our clan, be fed, trained, and educated. We will forge you into a self-sufficient person of strength, however, we require that you follow our creed, our culture. No person who does not believe in our culture may stay within our clan. At any point you can leave, but when with us, you will be a part of our culture and follow our ways."

As they ate the rest of their meal in silence, Triss could hear cooking and cleaning noises from the tent Horst was in. When they were almost done, Horst came back out of the tent toward Axton.

"Axton, they are just wrapping up in there," Horst said.

Triss still tensed around the enormous creature.

"Good, we have tarried here long enough. Move throughout the camp and ask everyone to be ready to move out before the sun reaches its peak. I'll tell Farth to get the boys ready."

Horst poked his head into the cooking tent he had come from and said something Triss could not hear, before disappearing through the bushes to other parts of the camp.

"Come girl. Leave your plate, we will return for them."

Axton placed his plate down on the bench, and Triss did the same. Then she followed him down a small path past a few other tents with grizzled looking warriors packing equipment. She noticed bandages on some of them, a reminder that they too had lost many of their people.

"Axton, did a lot of your people die back in Creet?" Triss asked. "You said you lost the battle."

Triss worried that the question might upset Axton, and she looked up at him timidly. But the small smile on his face did not seem to fade as he kept his eyes forward on the path.

"Yes, many died," Axton said. "We did not bring many shields or counter-archer measures; we saw little need for them in a city. The regional garrison used arrows, and we were not prepared. Before this battle, we had been one of the largest clans in all of Bandor, but now we will be lucky if we are not the smallest."

It surprised her that he said it so matter-of-factly, with little emotion.

"Aren't you sad you lost?"

"You win, or you learn. Losing only happens to those that never learn."

CHAPTER 7
BURN IT AWAY

Trisstiphina and Axton did not go far before they approached a tent with a scraggly older man, who still had considerable lean muscle on him. Though balding, he had a large moustache, and a beard that seemed like he had cut it as short as he could with a simple boot knife. The man was short for a Bandorian, but he still looked strong and had been sharpening a long dagger on a wet stone when they approached.

He stopped sharpening the blade but kept it in his hand.

"Farth," Axton said. "Are the boys going to be ready to head out?"

"Aye, I've already got them packing up," the man, Farth, said. "What's with the kid?"

He waved his knife, pointing at Triss with it.

"She's the one I found in Creet. She'll be coming with us and joining the clan. Should be a good addition. I assumed you had heard."

Triss pulled back her shoulders in an attempt to look strong as coming off fierce seemed to be the best way to succeed with these people. It had been what convinced Axton to save her life.

"Yeah, I heard you picked up a tag along. But her?"

He rose to his feet, walking over to her. He pointed at her with the tip of his blade, then gestured to her arms with it.

"She's barely got any muscle on her. And what is that? A dress she's wearing?" He looked skeptically at her outfit. "You sure Ax? My boy Bullock would crush her bones in a scrap, and I ain't bragging. I'm just worried for her, is all." To Farth's credit, he had a concerned look on his face.

"Yeah, I'll crush it." A voice came from beyond the flap of the nearby tent. "Wait, what am I crushing?"

At the mention of his name, a boy came from within the tent. He could not have been much older than Triss, maybe twelve at most. He was a beast of a boy, large, stocky, and full of brawn and his light blond hair covered a square face that made the boy look more strong than intelligent. But Triss avoided any snap judgements; Axton had also seemed like a cruel barbarian at first sight.

Bullock caught sight of Triss and simply said, "Huh," as if he was not sure what she was doing here. He looked her up and down and appeared dumbfounded then he shrugged and waited for the adults to continue talking. Axton gave a short laugh and continued the conversation by replying to Farth's last comment.

"Farth, you're not that big of a man yourself," Axton said. "Besides, she is young. She will grow. And you didn't see her bloody the nose of a brigand back in town. I tell you she will be a feisty one."

Axton looked over at Triss, and she felt an odd sense of approval. Farth gave a shrug like the boy had.

"Fair enough," Farth said. "She will need something else if she is going to keep up." He pointed at her attire.

"Sara is already working on that," Axton said.

"Good," Farth said.

Axton placed a gentle hand on Triss's shoulder. Farth's words had cut her down, but Axton's confidence pulled her back up. She tried to look confident again.

The entrance flap of the tent pulled back once more and out stepped a strapping young boy, a thick mane of auburn hair and a handsome face. He was smaller than Bullock but seemed about Triss's age.

The boy gave Triss a quizzical look.

"That is the recruit you took on?" The boy said, "Axton, did the fire leave you blind?"

Trisstiphina's mouth dropped open at the insolence this boy showed to a clearly well-respected member of their war-band.

"I mean, look at her," the boy continued. "Those arms are like wet twigs."

"She will do just fine, Jaxon," Axton said to the boy.

The boy did not look convinced. He approached Triss and continued his critique. He grabbed one of her arms and swung it to show it flop but stopped just as she tried to tense up.

"Don't touch me," Triss said. She hissed it under her breath, but loud enough that the others could hear.

The boy, Jaxon, continued to act as if she was not even there. He poked at her chest, pushing her enough that she almost lost balance. Triss was very uncomfortable with this boy; she knew that she was not a slave, but this boy still made her feel like nothing.

"I don't see any potential here. Besides, I thought those people were just weak rats, spreading everywhere but not doing anything constructive."

Triss felt a hot anger rise in her as her ears became warm, and she gritted her teeth together. Axton and Farth did not seem to care about how the boy's words would affect her, they just watched.

"Didn't they just roll over and let their town go up in flames? I don't get it."

The boy seemed like he was about to say something else, but Triss lunged at him, catching him off guard. She brought her fist into his head and felt a satisfying impact. They both tumbled over. She tried to kick and hit, and felt limbs mix as they rolled on the ground.

She tasted dirt and could only see the ground pressed up against her face. She found she could not move, and a steady pain grew in her arm to become extreme enough for her to let out tears. Jaxon now sat on top of her back, holding her arm painfully behind her, and pinning her face to the ground.

She had taken him by surprise, but he was clearly an incredible combatant. She didn't belong here.

"Dammit Jaxon, get off the girl, and let her up," Farth said.

"Huh? Oh yeah, sure thing."

Jaxon jumped up off Triss, releasing her arm from its painful position. She rolled over and pushed herself to a sitting position.

"And what have I told you about opening your mouth?" Farth asked.

"Not to open my mouth until I think about how it might affect the other people around me," Jaxon said. He hung his head in slight embarrassment.

"The girl, though untrained, landed a hit on your face, Jaxon," Axton said. "I hope you see now why I think she has some potential."

Jaxon just gave a shrug, as if to suggest Axton's words made enough sense.

Triss got to her feet and rubbed her sore arm. Axton put a soft hand on Triss as if to lead her away, but the voice of the larger blonde boy, Bullock, made him pause.

"Axton. Will she be coming with us back to the gathering?"

Axton turned only his head back to address the boy, "Aye, that she will, lad. There, she will probably join you and the rest of your pack. She will have some catching up to do, but I am sure the rest of you will help her along."

"Uh, yeah, you bet Axton. You can count on us. We'll give her a proper challenge and show her the ropes." Bullock's tone shifted upwards with excitement at the further prospect of being able to prove himself.

"Good, get packed," Axton said. "We leave before the sun reaches its peak."

Axton led Triss away, and as she peaked back over her shoulder, Jaxon's face did not seem to show disapproval or excitement. He just stared at Triss with curiosity. He did not seem to be upset that she had attacked him, or that Farth had scolded him.

They picked up their plates from the campfire; another soldier was cutting up the pieces of the remaining beast. They returned to where Triss had woken up, and Axton packed the plates away.

Axton began packing and Triss, having nothing to do, awkwardly stood behind him waiting. Boredom and curiosity overcame nervousness, and she asked another question.

"Why do you hate us so much?"

Axton continued packing and did not look back at her, "Pardon?"

"Why did you want a war? Why do you hate my people?"

"The Empire. Not you. Not its people."

Triss did not understand the distinction.

"Fine the Empire then. Why not just leave them be?"

"Another time." Axton dismissed the question.

"My town is gone, my house burned to the ground, and my family dead; don't I deserve to know?"

The words burst from her mouth, and she feared a reprimand. Her flickering anger had produced the question before she had time to filter herself. Axton finally stopped what he was doing and turned to face her. Triss feared the worst.

"I've seen them throw people off the land that fed them, starve them because they no longer served a purpose. They strip the land until it is barren and divert water for only themselves, creating deserts. They have burned down forests, wiping out entire species. I've seen them transform a nation into a monster fed by the souls they have damned—a harvester of people's hopes, dreams, and every meager coin they possess. Contentment eludes them; they seek to expand like a relentless plague, tearing every living thing from the earth not realizing that it will leave the world a desolate husk. And even then, they won't be satisfied. It may not happen in my lifetime, or even your lifetime. But it will happen unless someone does something about it.

"So, you ask me why I hate them? I don't hate them. Hate does not help me. But I know what I must do—what we all must do. We must destroy them, their authority, their way of oppression. Crush it and burn their culture away."

Triss stood, her face numb, shock paralyzing her. *This man was unlike any she had met before. How could he be all emotion and all calm in the same moment?* Axton turned back to his packing, leaving her standing speechless. With nothing else to say, Triss found a tree stump to sit on until she was given some other tasks.

Not too long afterwards, a woman walked the path that passed by their tent. She wore strange clothing for a woman, form fitting, matching that of the men, but with support around her chest. Triss then noticed the bundle the woman was carrying before she called out to Axton, tossing it to him.

Axton caught it and thanked her before she disappeared down the path. He threw the bundle down at Trisstiphina's feet.

"Put these on," he said.

Triss said nothing, only stared down at the bundle. Whatever it was, it was wrapped in animal fur and wool and bound with a hempen rope. She bent down to unwrap it as Axton continued to pack things away. He took his time ensuring he tightly wrapped every item before putting it in his rucksack.

She unwrapped the bundle to find an outfit, one that seemed like it would fit her well. She was surprised by the craftsmanship, and that they would give her something of obvious quality. It contained a top, bottoms, and boots, all made from a combination of leather and wool. Also, inside she found a shawl of knit wool, but to her distress she realized that the small, form fitting top and short bottoms resembled the undergarments she tended to wear, but there was no dress or outfit to go over the whole thing.

Fool. Of course, they would not give her an outfit different from their own.

"Axton, sir?"

Axton looked up at her, and she thanked the fact that he did not comment on the accidental 'sir' she had let slip.

"Is there anything for me to put on top of this?"

"No. Just get changed," he said. "It is a long journey, and you will be hot enough in that outfit there."

She had figured that would be his response.

"Where can I go to change into this?" Triss asked.

"Just change right there," he said. He returned to packing things away.

"May I change inside the tent?"

Axton just waved a hand at her as if he didn't care. She crept towards the tent, watching for him to tell her not to, then slipped inside and changed.

Once she was done, she looked down at herself. She wore a fitted sleeveless leather and cloth top which did not cover all of her stomach. The pants were of a similar style and material, very short leather leggings, with an only slightly longer skirt-wrap to go over it. But even the wrap had slits in it; it would make it easier to run in, but was hardly appropriate. The outfit also included fitted leather boots that came to mid-shin and had a tougher leather sole just thick enough to ensure that the sharp rocks would not cut or harm her feet. More practical than the shoes she had been wearing.

She was thankful that they had given her the knit-wool shawl that she could use to at least cover her shoulders.

Uncomfortable and exposed; she had worn nothing so form fitting before. Her bottoms hugged her so tightly that people would be able to see her legs and rear almost as if she were wearing nothing at all. She wanted to cry at the outfit. *How humiliating. How many things would she have to change about who she was just to survive with these people?*

She tried to wear the shawl as loose as she could so that it would hang over her torso and at least cover her exposed shoulders and the tight top they had given her, but it did little good. She picked up her old dress and decided to try her luck. She pulled the dress back over her to hide her exposed skin. She had done what he asked. Maybe Axton would not care.

She left the tent with hope and optimism. But it was quickly dashed.

"Hrmph," Axton grunted. "Take off the dress. Don't be ridiculous."

Her heart sank, but she did as he ordered.

"Pass it here."

She passed him her dress. He took it from her hands and threw it on the still hot coals in the firepit.

She stared at the dress, scrunched up into a ball, black marks forming on the edges that touched the coals. A flame flickered to life. Then another. The fire grew, and the dress curled on itself as it turned to char.

Triss continued watching, not willing to take her eyes off the flame. The last of the dress burned away. The flame slowly sputtered back down, having consumed all the fuel available. All that remained was ash.

CHAPTER 8
THE JOURNEY

Just as Axton had said, the Bandorian army had the camp packed before midday, quiet and methodical as they strapped their hiking packs to themselves. Several times throughout the morning, Axton had to grab Triss and hold her tight to keep her from panicking at the sight of a Bandorian from one of the many strange or monstrous other races. The most terrifying sight of all, though, were the massive beasts of burden the Bandorians used. The gigantic wolves that Axton had called vargrs were the size of horses, with thick coats of fur that stuck out from beneath the pack straps.

The Bandorians had formed a long marching line. No one barked out orders, instead they'd simply left once each person was ready. With the lightly weighted scouts taking the front of the column and the sweepers taking up the rear, the remains of the army had travelled westward.

The trail they followed seemed like a game trail; it wound through the rocky hills and across streams. Triss struggled with the roots and sharp boulders, trying not to cut her hands on the sharp rocks but she had to admit that her new boots made it easier.

She was intent on keeping up with Axton and the column. While others carried large packs, they had not burdened her with one. This kept her light and losing her dress made the experience manageable.

It had been several days since she had woken in the camp, and the march began. The terrain had been rocky with hills and sparse trees, but now they came upon the south side of a densely treed hill. The trail travelled perpendicular to the slope. As they approached the woods, Triss could make out little of what lay beneath the forest canopy and her hair stood on end as she looked at the un-inviting entrance that lay before her. Not wanting to fall behind Axton, she pushed forward anyway.

The forest was dark, and as her eyes adjusted it took on a grey tone, as if something had drained all colour from beneath the canopy. The trees were old and gnarled and packed so close together that she found it hard to see far in either direction. As she looked around herself, to watch for what monsters may lie within, she noticed that the Bandorians behind her were doing the same, eyes darting from side to side. Their eyebrows furrowed in concentration, though, not fear. It did not make her more comfortable.

She crept as quietly as she could behind Axton, trying to keep his hulking form in front of her; she felt it could shield her from the fears.

They continued like this with no event for some time, possibly half an hour. She had fallen into a monotonous step behind Axton, wondering how long the forest journey would take. Axton talked little, so, to pass the time, she retreated into her own thoughts. It helped to distract her.

They were travelling further into the dead hills, or Craeg as Axton had called it. Away from everything she knew, and it would become harder the further she got for her to return to the Empire. The place was dangerous. She had heard tales of the monsters that lived here, making it inhospitable for any human to live in. Axton had claimed that half of those monsters had been the Bandorians, spreading fear and keeping imperials out, but that did not explain the other half.

Her head jolted up as a loud howl echoed through the forest. A chill whipped through her like a dive into an icy lake. *What was that noise?*

Perhaps it was the wailing stones they had passed earlier—large boulders at the tops of hills with holes ground into them to catch the wind and create a haunting cry. Another unsettling feature of the Dead Hills. No, this noise was sudden, not a slowly growing wail.

Before she could react, though, she heard another howl. This time it sounded as if the creature producing it was right on top of them.

A scream of pain pierced the air in response to the howl, followed by a yell from someone else about twenty people in front of them.

"Thistlebacks. Arm yourselves!"

All around Triss, Bandorians readied for a fight. Axton brought his hand to his chest and unfastened the chest strap for his pack, then shrugged it off his shoulders and tossed it to the ground with a thud. She could hear similar sounds all around her as other Bandorians did the same. Axton removed the latch that attached his sizable two-handed axe to his back and lifted it in front of himself.

Out of the bush, a massive beast leapt at them. Shaped like a fat mutated wolf, but much bigger and with sharp quills interspersed along its long back. Its eyes glowed red like burning embers, and a green mist trailed from drops of what looked like poison on its snapping jaws.

It soared at Axton, but he did not flinch. In a large cleave, he brought his axe up from the ground and through the face of the wolf. There was an awful crunch as flesh was hewn and bone crushed. Axton could not redirect the force of the creature's pounce, so instead he let go of his axe to sidestep the fall of the massive beast.

"Girl, get behind me," Axton said.

The beast was still moving.

Axton was not unarmed for long. He drew a dagger from each boot, flipped them to face down in his fists, and leapt at the creature. As the monster heaved on the ground, Axton dug his right dagger into its flank and used it as an anchor to swing his momentum onto the back of the creature and dig his left dagger into its left flank.

The beast howled. The noise was horrible. Fear and terror slammed into Triss. All around her, monsters attempted to pounce on Bandorians. Blades swung and blood sprayed. The fear and energy in her body hit a boiling point, about to burst.

She ran.

Despite the organized column the Bandorians had been marching in, they had spread out as the battle raged on. She fled away from the fighting. Ahead and to her right, a Bandorian she did not recognize felled one of the terrifying beasts and jabbed a large glaive down into it to encourage it to stay dead.

Triss glanced back, her panic surged again as she saw a menacing shadow racing towards her. The sight of giant fangs glistening with saliva sent a shiver down her spine, and her heart pounded in her chest. In a state of sheer terror, she let out a piercing scream and abruptly changed direction, running as fast as her young legs could take her, towards the Bandorian she had just seen.

He noticed her, and a confused expression crossed his face before it turned to determination as he saw the beast chasing her. Triss didn't look back as she ran past the man.

She bolted through the brush, crashing hard into something she had not seen. A thistleback picked at the remains of one of its dead companions. The creature did not budge when she hit it, but she bounced back to land prone beside it. Triss let out another scream of terror.

The creature turned its head towards her, its burning eyes focused purely on her. She scrambled backwards, trying to put space between them. The creature circled her, intending to play with its food first. It snapped and growled at her.

She pushed off the ground and got back to a half-standing position that would allow her to run. The creature leaped forward and swung out a paw, knocking her back onto her bottom. She screamed once more.

She tried to scramble backwards again until she ran against a slope. Terror gripped her, but she closed her hands around the dirt. The creature prowled closer to her. It lunged at her, and she threw up her hands, spraying it with gravel and dirt.

The beast collided with Triss, but it hurriedly pulled back to wipe at its eyes. Feeling a sliver of triumph, she tried to stand up and get away. But it was no use.

Even though the creature had recoiled, its paw had her leg pinned, and it seemed to almost have enough of the dirt out of its eyes. Triss looked from side to side, desperate for something to help her defend herself.

She heard a low whistling noise.

A large spear impaled the beast's neck. It collapsed to the ground beside Triss, blood draining from its.

Triss looked up the slope to the source of the thrown weapon and saw a young Bandorian, about fifteen paces up, raise his hand in triumph before running off for another opponent.

With her leg free, Trisstiphina got to her feet. It was chaos all around her. *These people were mad to live here. Keeping a constant eye out for monsters. What was she doing here?*

Again, she ran.

"I have to get away. Have to get away," she repeated over and over as she ran.

Trees, bushes, and large stones whipped by her. The thought that she could run with such ease, no longer hindered by a long dress, crossed her mind only briefly before being swept away by her continued panic.

Finally, Triss could see light as the slope broke, and the trees ended in a grassy dell. *That was it, she was almost out of the forest and there were no Bandorians to be seen. She was free. She could leave. Go back to her life. Find her grandmother. Find someone she knew. It had to be better than this.*

Her panic calmed just as she came around the last tree, but the sight before her forced her to skid to her bum as she desperately tried to stop. Her panic returned, but only for a moment as surprise and shock replaced it.

What had appeared as a large boulder—when she'd glimpsed it through the trees—she could now see clearly. A massive sword, stuck deep into the earth with only the hilt and part of the blade visible as tall as four houses stacked upon one another.

She froze. Eyes wide and mouth open, she stared above the sword, straight up to the sky, at the colossal owner of the sword. She had exited the forest right under a behemoth. Its shadow engulfed her.

Its helmeted head pierced the sky higher than the tallest tree. The creature's base was so wide it took up most of the gulley. It looked human like, with armour, and flowing robes. It hunched forward, one hand grasped the hilt of its sword for support and the index finger on its other hand descended from the sky above her, pointing right at her.

She sat completely still on the ground, paralyzed with fear, unmoving, not making a sound. The creature was silent. It did not shift; it did nothing. Just pointed. Then, she noticed something odd about the titan; its flowing robes were not flowing. They didn't move an inch despite the breeze in the air. They were stone. The entire creature was stone.

It rested like a silent sentinel watching, guarding the gentle dell. Triss hesitantly stood as the terror subsided, replaced with childish wonder. The glen was silent except for the calm breeze twisting its way between the tree branches. A sense of tranquillity lay over the clearing, like a soft blanket floating upon a bed.

She approached the bottom of the outstretched finger; it hovered only feet above the ground. She raised a gentle hand to the air, cautiously wanting to touch it. *What was this thing?* Her delicate fingers traced the bottom of the finger just above her head, feeling the smoothness of the stone.

"An Ancient." A deep voice came from behind her in response to her unspoken question.

The voice startled her, and she pulled her hand back. She spun to see who intruded on her silent revery.

Axton sat on a stone, several paces away from her, by the treeline. His face was expressionless as he looked at her patiently.

"An Ancient?" Triss asked. She returned her gaze to the behemoth.

"Ancient, Titan, Colossus, Old Ones. They have many names, but the elves specifically call them a name that roughly translates to 'The Ancients'. They are stone now, and you can find them unmoving in every corner of Tal'am, but stories say that they once moved. The elves know the most about them. Their tales claim they walked this world before humans, or any of the other living races, for that matter."

Axton, turned away from her and looked up at the Ancient, then spoke in reverence.

Ay'uth en denha agwin
Those that walk before
awuth fwhenn, embar duath han
turned to stone when sun-touched

"These used to be alive?" Triss asked. "When? Will it come alive now?"

"More than an age ago. They have not moved since before the dawn of our time. You are quite safe here."

Triss let out a breath. "The sun turned them to stone?"

"Possibly," Axton said. He stood, looking up at the Colossus. "The tales are not clear. It may have been that, when the common races came to this world and felt the sun on them for the first time, the Ancients turned to stone. What few elves we have come across could not tell us the specifics."

"Are the elves real? You've actually met them?" Triss asked, her mind filled with disbelief. The tavern bards she had always listened to with rapt attention had spoken of the celestial beings of beauty and charm. Tricksters and enchanters, marvellous and perilous, living deep in the forests of the south, where few dared to venture.

"I have indeed, and you will too. There are very few elven Bandorians, but there are some. More commonly, we have half-elves among our people. There are even two among us in Clan Kaltor."

Triss felt her heart race at the thought of meeting these mythical creatures. *Could the bard's tales be true? Why not? After all, she had only recently discovered that minotaurs were not just fairy tales. Perhaps there was more to the world than she had imagined.*

She stood silently, her amazement giving way to the thoughts she had just before coming to this place. *Leave the Bandorians. Find her nana. Escape these people.*

As if reading her mind, Axton spoke.

"I meant what I said before."

Triss looked up at him quizzically.

"That you are free. You are not a slave. If you come with us, it is your choice. We do not force people to join us." He sat staring at her. His eyes looked soft. "You can leave if you wish. You do not have to come back with me."

Triss looked down away from his eyes, understanding his meaning; she could go. Escape this place. Return to her world and search for her nana. *Surely someone had survived the attack on her village. Most people had liked her. Someone would take her in, wouldn't they?*

But that possibility was not certain. She was just as likely to end up a starving orphan, sold into servitude. She was just relying on luck, and where had it landed her so far?

"Make your own luck," her nana had once told her.

These people offered to train her, share their knowledge, and give her a place to belong.

She could not forgive these people for what happened to her home, but they knew things she didn't. *Could she use them to grow? Gain the skills she needed to survive; to thrive even. She could take control of her life. Not rely on the charity of others.*

This was it. She had to make her choice. Did she go back to what she was used to. Cast her hopes with what she knew, what was familiar.

Or...

"You can take what you are given."

Axton's words came back to her. She could make the best of what he offered. Join the clan. Be fed, trained, and educated. Let them forge her into a self-sufficient person of strength.

Axton waited patiently for her to think it through.

Axton believed in her. He had extended her the only offer she had. *She would not run. She would accept it without complaint and see what the future held.*

"No," Triss said. "I want to go with you. I want to learn."

Axton nodded at her.

"Come, I will tell you more while we walk. We should get back to the others." Axton turned and hiked back.

Triss followed. She looked back, gazing at the Ancient as she gradually walked away.

CHAPTER 9
TALES FROM THE DRUNKEN OWL

"Did you guys hear about Creet?" Beacher leaned on the bar in the centre of the three friends. It had not been long since Lucius had seen his old friend. The trader was once again back in Crestwood and drinking at Lucius's bar in the Drunken Owl.

"Who hasn't heard about it?" said Ox. The farmer sat sideways on his bar stool and half-leaned against the counter. "Everyone is talking about it. Were you there? What happened?"

"Of course, he wasn't there," Marcus said. The Administrator stood sipping his glass of Car'athan wine. "Nobody was left alive when the army arrived. As to what happened, it was a simple Barbarian raid. They used to happen all the time hundreds of years ago, before the Imperial archons destroyed all the Barbarians."

"Not all of them, obviously."

"No, obviously not all of them." Marcus looked a bit annoyed by the interruption, but continued anyway. "The Empire knew the barbarian threat was growing. Evidently, they were too slow to act. Though they have confirmed that the army cut off their escape and wiped every one of them out. Not a single Barbarian survived."

"They apparently attacked at night, storming the town, and burning everything in sight. The monsters didn't even take anything. Not even any slaves. They just killed every single villager and burned down the whole town."

"Such senseless destruction," Ox said. "What even is the point?"

"I heard that as well," said Beacher. "Damn shame, Creet was decent business. Now, with the army checking every person coming and going, it is not worth travelling to the west. Trade will be better once things settle. Dirty savages ruining my business."

Lucius stood close by, washing a glass. He had not been commenting so far. He raised a cynical eyebrow. "Yes, your loss in profit is the most tragic consequence of this entire event."

Beacher said nothing but glowered at Lucius.

"That wasn't all I heard." Ox placed his mug down and leaned towards the others, then spoke in a conspiratorial tone. "My cousin, he has a friend, who is brothers with a guy in the army. He said that there are no barbarians. Said a mad wizard burned down the town. Said The Empire made it look like Barbarians. That way, they had someone to blame it on."

"Be careful friend." Lucius finally spoke up, in a serious tone, placing the glass he was cleaning on the bar. "I had an old friend in Creet. I would appreciate it if you showed some respect." He frowned at Ox. "I'll let this slide because you did not know."

"Oh. Sorry Lucius. It was just what I heard. I wasn't trying to say it was true. No disrespect meant."

"Lucius is right," Marcus said. "You should be careful. You don't want the guards to hear you talking like that. They'll arrest you for spreading false stories to folk. Just because you hear a story doesn't mean you should spread it."

"Sorry, you're right. I'll be more careful."

"So, Marcus, what is the Empire doing about this?" Beacher asked. "What are their plans now? Don't they have a dragon in the capital? Will they burn down the east?"

"No, no, nothing so extreme. As I hear it, they don't think the barbarians are still a threat. Most, if not all, the barbarians were killed. But the incident has helped the army in one respect: Support for the military is at an all-time high. They will not pass up this boost. It's not official yet, but they plan on using the extra ranks and finances to bolster the forces in the west. They are planning on sending several strike teams in to kill anyone they find in the Dead Hills. Inexperienced forces will benefit from the training, and they can advertise successes. They will stick close to the borders for now. The risk of wild animal and monster attacks is too high. But they will set up a garrison there and some watch posts, maybe towers. Give us extra support for expansion further west. They will probably send any extra recruits not sent west to the eastern shores to assist with naval conflicts across the Starlight Sea. Business in the west should be back to normal soon."

"Well, that is a relief," Beacher said. "I hate being stuck in one place. Goods are just burning a hole in my wagon. Luckily, just grains and nick-knacks. They should keep for some time still. Others I know are not so lucky."

"Hey, it's not all bad," Ox Said. "We get the chance to see you. At least if you must wait, the company is excellent."

"Haha, yeah, that is true." He raised his glass and clinked it with Ox.

CHAPTER 10
DRONOCH

Trisstiphina followed Axton once more as they walked through The Moving City of Dronoch. Their war-band had arrived less than an hour before, around midday and a procession of armed scouts had guided them down the hill into the valley. Lookouts waited, invisible in the surrounding forests.

They headed to the part of the city where others of his clan were camped. Those that didn't join the war effort. He promised her no more hiking, which lit up her eyes. It had been several days since she had woken in a new world after the destruction of Creet and the days of endless trekking had exhausted her.

She missed the softness of her old life; her comfortable bed and easy picking of apples. *No. That life was gone.*

Around her were functional house-like tents; the structures resembled handleless pots, with their circular shape, walls standing at the height of a man, and domed roofs resembling upside-down bowls. Bounded hides wrapped around an inner structure with rope. They seemed sturdier than a typical military tent and would weather a powerful winter storm. Yet, they had an appearance of versatility. The Bandorians could likely pack them up and move them if needed.

The entire city looked more like a semi permanent military camp than Trisstiphina's expectation of a city. It was nothing like Creet. Aspects of their culture shone through, with decorations like beads made of feathers or stones or benches and chairs that had large intricate carvings of animals, people, and battle scenes etched into them.

It was all so strange to her, like no place she had ever seen or heard of; she stared with eyes wide at her surroundings until a raised stone caught her toe and she stumbled forward, catching herself before she fell. She peeked up at Axton, hoping he had not noticed, but he snickered and was glancing down ever so slightly at her. "Don't let new things distract you."

Triss lowered her head with embarrassment and focused her eyes in front of her, determined not to make the same mistake twice.

After many twists and turns through the city, Axton led Triss down a road towards two dwellings with a fire pit between them. On a wooden stump sat a muscular Bandorian, wearing only short hide leggings. On top of him, facing him, with both legs straddling his waist, sat a gorgeous raven-haired Bandorian woman. Her hair covered both of their faces as their lips moved and pressed against one another. Her hands combed through his already messy hair, while his hands grasped her back and wrapped around her slim waist. The two were far too distracted to notice Axton or Triss approach.

"Brakan," Axton called to the two, as they writhed in a passionate embrace. The female's head, which had been moving back and forth between kisses, halted. The two faces separated, and the woman tossed her head, flipping her hair around out of her face, allowing them to both view their new company.

"Hi Axton," the female said as she looked at him with a big smile. She looked down at Triss with a curious expression, then gave her a smile.

"Good to see you, Bao," Axton said, returning the smile to the woman.

"Axton!" the man, Brakan, said as he helped Bao off him and stood up. "You're back!" A wide smile crossed his face.

Axton stood with his arms crossed and an eyebrow raised in Brakan's direction.

"Is this why you didn't join the war band? So you and Bao could just stay back and fornicate?"

Brakan gave a shrug and stood, looking slightly sheepish. Bao, though, placed a hand on Brakan's shoulder, and gave a mischievous smile, "Yeah, pretty much."

Axton gave a subtle laugh as he embraced Bao in a hug.

"I was sure this time they would do you in," Brakan said. "Attacking the entire town and western Garrison? I was starting to eye your stuff."

"You underestimate me, friend. I don't die that easily," Axton said.

He laughed and the two men embraced. As they separated, Axton turned serious.

"Though... our losses were significant. Only twenty of our clan mates made it back... And Gaer fell."

He let the comment hang, and Brakan did not immediately respond.

"Axton, I'm sorry," Bao finally broke the silence. "Was it a good death?"

Axton smirked a bit as he responded.

"Yes, it was glorious. When last I saw him, he had more than a dozen arrows sticking out of him. The town was burning around him, and he was standing on a pile of dead Venesterium soldiers and a wizard."

By the end of the description, Axton was wearing a smile on his face. The memory of that night brought a tear to Triss's face who stood relatively forgotten about a few feet behind Axton.

The sniffle from the unknown girl finally caught the attention of Brakan, and he gave a quizzical look at her and cocked his head slightly to the side. "Who's the girl?"

Triss tensed up as she realized she was being stared at. But eased as Axton spoke up.

"She was a resident of Creet. She lost her family, but I watched her attack a grown man three times her size, just because he threatened her pet. She is a fighter and a survivor; I am going to have her join the clan."

Triss perked up just slightly at Axton's words of approval.

Brakan's quizzical look turned to a smile, "Excellent! We will need to replenish our numbers. If she's as tough as you say, she'll be a great addition."

Bao grabbed a nearby blanket and approached Triss gently, "Poor child, you are probably terrified. Losing your town and being surrounded by strangers."

She wrapped the blanket over Trisstiphina's shoulders and enveloped her in a warm embrace. The sudden physical expression and tenderness confused Triss, but she did not resist; she'd not received comfort from a person in some time.

"Do not worry, little one," Bao said. "We'll make you feel at home here in no time."

"Thanks Bao," Axton said.

Bao's kind and welcoming words comforted Triss and helped her let her guard down further.

"Are you taking her to a pack?" Bao asked.

"Yes, probably Jaxon's pack."

Triss didn't know what it meant, but she remembered the boy, Jaxon, and didn't feel good about it.

"We actually need to get there pretty soon, and we need to report in. I heard the chieftains are gathering soon."

"Yeah. They'll be meeting in the council room in about a half hour," Brakan said.

"I will take the girl to the pack, then head there. Can you two gather information and meet me on the way?"

"Of course," Bao said. She turned to Triss. "Go on, little one. Go with Axton. They will take care of you and help you out. I'm always here if you need anyone."

Bao turned Triss around, gave her a smile, then took the blanket back and sent her along to follow Axton as he walked away.

Triss struggled, scurrying along, as she tried to match pace with the larger man through the city.

They rounded some more buildings and came upon a single-story structure with just one large room, made visible because missing the closest wall. The building opened into a small pavilion, where there were benches and log stumps for sitting, many of which formed a half circle around a dirt patch.

The building had a wooden frame made from huge hand cut logs wrapped in animal hides and a roof of thatch tightly packed to keep the rain out. Inside, there was a large table with writing utensils on it and many large shelves of books stood along the wall on the wooden planked floors. A cozy place for learning, with a welcoming atmosphere.

The sheer number of books shocked Triss. *It was a strange sight in a Barbarian city because she'd been told Barbarians could not read. No. She had to remember: these people differed significantly from the barbarians in stories.*

Inside the sparring ring, Triss saw Bullock, and Triss smiled; *at least she would know someone her age here. He had been nice to her.* He was clutching tightly in a strong grapple with another boy. The second boy was smaller than Bullock, but still muscular. The boys circled, and she recognized him as Jaxon, the obnoxious boy from before. *Great.* Her smile slipped away.

Bullock clearly had the advantage at this moment, but Jaxon jerked and twisted, forcing Bullock to overwork to keep his grip. Bullock was larger with a square build, but Jaxon was lean and agile; Jaxon appeared to have the energy to outmaneuver Bullock if they fought long enough.

The boys pushed back and forth. Swung from side to side. They held together as they tried to stay in the ring and gain an advantage over the other.

Finally, Triss noticed two other children with the boys; two girls, spectating from a wooden stump and bench. The girls seemed the same age as Triss, but to Trisstiphina's surprise, they were identical: exactly identical. Triss had heard of twins that looked the same, but hadn't seen any before.

They both had long red hair, so bright it seemed on fire, and they looked very fit, with lean muscle that looked much different from anything Triss had seen of eleven-year-old girls before. She suddenly felt intimidated and self-conscious; especially since she was wearing her new clothes, which showed her thin, gangly arms and legs. Triss reached her hands across herself, hiding what she thought they might consider a weakness. It was a feeble attempt.

Axton had walked off into the building now, and she was standing alone. As the sparring match continued, Triss could hear one twin yell out, "Come on, Bullock, finish Jax off."

"Yeah Bullock, finish him for me, and I'll give you a kiss on the cheek," the second sister said.

"Huh?" Bullock looked up in surprise; it distracted him for a second too long.

Jaxon used the opportunity to get an arm on the inside of Bullock's guard and bring a fist up to Bullock's jaw, stunning him, and he stumbled back. This gave Jaxon the opening he needed; he lunged forward at Bullock and put his right shoulder directly into Bullock's solar plexus. The hit lifted Bullock just barely off the ground before Jaxon slammed him down hard into the dirt.

For a moment Bullock lay there coughing and gasping for air; the wind knocked out of him. Jaxon reached his hand out to Bullock who sighed, before grasping the outstretched hand. Jaxon pulled him to his feet.

"Are you alright?" Jaxon asked.

"Ugh, yeah I'm good," Bullock said. "That was a good one;

though remind me not to get distracted next time. I think those girls are going to get me killed one day."

They both laughed and walked over to the girls. The sisters were only now picking themselves up from laughing too hard. When Bullock reached them, he looked at the one who had distracted him with her words. "You suck Kiva."

"I'm not Kiva. I'm Erika. Can't you even tell us apart?"

"Yeah Bullock, I'm Kiva. We can tell you and Jaxon apart well enough. We never mix you two up. Couldn't you care enough to remember us apart?"

Jaxon stifled a laugh as he took a seat on the bench beside Kiva.

"Oh, shut up, the both of you. You both suck. You are basically just the same person."

"No, we're not," both girls cried out in unison then giggled in unison.

Bullock just raised an eyebrow in a look that said, *"See? My point."*

At that moment, Jaxon looked past both girls and noticed Triss standing there, watching the spectacle. She caught a glance of his sky-blue eyes, and she could see a hint of mischievousness in them and determination.

Sitting on the bench beside Kiva, Jaxon hit her on the leg to get her attention and pointed directly at Triss. Kiva said, "Hey!" in response, so he hit her leg and pointed again, not breaking eye contact with Triss. Finally, Kiva and the rest turned to her. The bickering stopped.

While all four children still stared at Triss, Jaxon leaned into Kiva and Erika, "That's the new girl. I told you she looks different." He spoke in a whisper, but it was still audible.

Kiva tilted her head to Jaxon and whispered. Again, Triss could still hear. "She can hear you, dumbass."

All four kids huddled together, staring straight at Triss with fascination. She lifted her arm across her body, feeling even more self-conscious. She wanted to disappear.

Despite that, she spoke up, "I'm standing right here."

Just then, Axton returned from inside the building and an older man followed him. The man looked remarkably similar to Axton, but he had a bushy moustache and no beard.

"Triss, this is Rock," Axton said. "He will be your instructor. And I see you have already met the other four kids in your pack, your new family. I will be back later to check on you. I suggest you get to know them well and enjoy them. They might be the ones to watch your back one day."

Triss took a step forward while still looking down at her feet. "Axton Sir- I mean just Axton, I uh..." Her shoulders tensed. In an entirely new and terrifying life, Axton felt safe, and she was afraid for that to leave with him.

"What is it?" When she didn't respond, he crouched down and took her small hands. "Listen, Young One, these people are here to help you; help you get strong so that you can help them. You're a team. They will look out for you. You have nothing to fear from them." He looked into her eyes and let a smile creep onto his lips. "Besides, I'll still be here. You can find me and talk to me whenever you need. It was my decision to take you in, so it's my job to make sure you succeed. You can ask me anything anytime."

Triss looked at her hands in his. She could take his strength and protection with her. Finally, she looked up at him with her confidence returning, "I... um..." she said, but then launched herself at him and embraced him in a tight hug. It surprised him at first and he almost fell backwards, but then he slowly brought his hands around her and returned the hug. "Thank you, sir-" she cut herself off before finishing the title, "Thank you Axton, I could have died back there, or you could have sold me into slavery or anything really, but you took me in; you saved me. Thank you for what you did," she squeezed him tighter, then finally let go.

He grasped her reassuringly by the shoulders, "You will be alright. You are stronger than you know." Axton then rose and smiled at her one last time. He gave her a wink and walked back the way they had come.

Erika then leaned towards Jaxon and Kiva, while still staring at Triss. With one eye raised perplexed, she whispered, "You're right. She is weird."

Kiva gave Erika a quick jab in the ribs, and she fell from the log she was balancing precariously on.

Triss was looking down slightly, her eyes close to watering. Then she furrowed her brow, pursed her lips, and looked up, determined to make Axton proud and not regret his decision to rescue her. The four children, who had previously all hunched together staring at her, appeared to take her action as their cue; they all straightened up quickly and stopped staring at her.

Bullock immediately walked up to her, "Welcome, you are going to be in our pack. You already know Jaxon; this is Erika and Kiva... I think." He gestured at the two twins. "It doesn't really matter though, they are interchangeable."

"Hey!" the girls protested, and they crept over beside Triss and reached their arms over her, as if to claim her for their side of some contest. "She will tell us apart. We will teach her, and besides, she looks smart and caring. She won't have any trouble telling us apart," Erika said as she stuck her tongue out at Bullock.

Bullock just gave a sigh of defeat.

"We didn't catch your name before, though," Jaxon said. "What is your name, new girl?"

"I... I am called Trisstiphina."

"Trissti-what?" Jaxon twisted his face. "You start a new life, where you can have any name you want, and you choose that mouthful of a name?"

Triss was taken aback. She felt her back tense and her fists clench.

But Bullock cleared his throat, pulling Trisstiphina's attention to him. He gave her a caring smile.

"He didn't ask what you are called. He asked what your name is."

Triss was unsure what he meant, but she let the question bounce around in her mind. She heard a voice from memory; *her nana's voice? A memory of her nana calling her a name in the past.* The voice spoke up in her mind, and a name from somewhere in that memory came to the surface.

"My name is Fae."

CHAPTER II
THE GATHERING

Axton left the girl with the other children; he had not paused, not looked back. He returned to the main path headed for the centre of the city and he was glad to see Bao and Brakan on the route ahead of him. Brakan, with Axton's axe in hand, tossed it to him. Axton caught his axe and slung it over his shoulder as he walked, not slowing to greet them. They both kept pace with him.

"You took a little long," Brakan said.

"The girl needed some emotional support," Axton said. "She may be distraught for a while."

"Of course she will, Axton," Bao said. "She has lost everything, and they are not taught to deal with loss. This is new and overwhelming for her."

Axton grunted his agreement. They kept a fast pace, walking shoulder to shoulder.

"Did the clan choose a new chieftain? With Gaer gone, is there a new leader? I'm assuming I should show up to the Gathering, but is there someone else?" Axton asked, knowing he was a likely choice for the chieftain. He did not wish it, but he had a duty to be prepared if they chose him for the responsibility.

"Aye, the clan talked and agreed it's you. You and Gaer were the closest, and you knew his mind well," Brakan said.

"Were they certain? They considered Aisling and Gregor as well?"

He wished to be certain that the Clan had made a wise decision in choosing him.

"Yes," Bao said, "they were both considered, and either of them would have done a respectable job of it if we had lost you. We did not lose you, though, so the responsibility falls to you."

"Which means you get the joy of attending the Gathering Council," Brakan said.

Axton grunted and ignored the jibe. Gaer had always been the one to attend such meetings before, but Axton knew Bandorian council meetings were usually brief and to the point.

"What other clan leaders are here? Clan Blar and Eldur were with us, so I'm assuming they will be there; I also saw Clan Sterkt when we arrived. Has there been anyone else?"

"Yeah, they'll be there," Brakan said. "Filib from Clan Laidir will also be there. They arrived in Dronoch shortly after the war-band left. They were angry as a hungry vargr when they found out they missed the action. Probably less upset when they realized it didn't go too well, though."

"True. The imperials were more organized than we expected... and I think they were firing on their own people. We didn't expect that. Though we should have." Axton hung his head with a hint of guilt and regret. "I will urge the council to mobilize the rest of the clans. Gaer would say we should press the offensive."

Brakan grunted.

"But what would Axton say?" Bao asked.

Axton did not respond as they finally reached the Gathering Council building. It was larger than the other buildings, though it only had a single room inside. The supports were made of large timbers and walls from clay mud. Unlike the others, this building was permanent and could be reused after Dronoch moved on.

Axton paused outside the entrance and looked at his friends.

"Good luck," Brakan said.

Axton nodded and said nothing. He entered the building alone.

As he entered the room, he saw the four other chieftains standing round the central table, and it took his eyes a moment to adjust to the dim light. The table was an old oak tree, cut down exactly at standing height to make a relatively round table, and it had intricate etchings carved into the trunk; images of great battles, Bandorian origins, and other culturally significant illustrations.

Bandorians had placed wooden boards down to create the floor; they lifted the room above the roots so chieftains could gather about the table with ease. A hand-drawn map covered the table with Imperial settlements of Glenmor shown to the east, and the Craeg to the west. They laid small wooden pieces around the map to show their current location in the city of Dronoch, and more pieces laid close to where Creet had been; these represented the remains of the Imperial armies, and their movements.

"My scouts saw their troops moving north," Ulfar said. "There."

The burly dwarf of Clan Blar could look over the table just enough to point at a position north of Creet. He rested his arms on the top of his great axe as the handle was braced against the floor. His long braided blonde beard had enough weight to it that Axton wondered if he had ever used it like a club. *Probably.*

Filib of Clan Laidir, a human and the most senior of the chieftains present, reached a tightly muscled arm across the table to move a token representing a division of Imperial troops to the position indicated by Ulfar. He then returned to leaning over the table, his long grey braided hair running down over his shoulders.

Fionnula was the first to notice Axton. Even if she had the muscular bulk of any Bandorian, the half-elf of Clan Eldur had senses of the elves and their half-elven progeny.

"Good day Axton," Fionnula said. "It is good to see you."

Though her voice was youthful, and she looked younger than the rest with a face of a twenty something year old, Axton was relatively certain she was closer to seventy years old.

"Fionnula, good to see you again." Axton approached the table, "How is it looking?"

The others looked up at him, taking notice of him before returning their stares to the table.

"Our scouts tell us the Imperial troops have not advanced since the battle of Creet," Filib Said. "Their troops had spread out in search of any survivors to kill. We think they may even be killing their own people, anyone that made it out of Creet alive."

"Doesn't sound out of character for them," Igraine, the other human chieftain, said. "Likely to ensure no witnesses to the slaughter. Better to blame 'Barbarians' for the death of the entire town."

"Do we know if they intended to fire on their own town?" Axton asked. "Did they burn it on purpose?"

"You tell us. You were there," Igraine said.

"I cannot be sure. It seemed like it, but everything was very chaotic. We will have to assume that they are willing to sacrifice their own people."

"Cowardice," Ulfar said. The dwarf spat on the ground in disgust. Axton shared the sentiment.

"It was the biggest town in the region, was it not?" Igraine asked.

"It was," Filib Said. "And it also housed the entire western garrison. Their strength in the west is severely depleted."

"Exactly," Axton said. "Now is the time to strike them. If we rally the other clans, we can attack now while they are still regrouping. We have learned much about them, but they have learned little about us."

"Indeed," Filib said, "but as I understand, your forces have been reduced by almost half, have they not?"

Axton sighed, "That is correct. We can not lead an offensive as we once may have. We are no longer the largest clan... and as you know, Gaer is no longer with us."

"Understood," Filib said.

"We should pull back our forces and prepare for a counteroffensive," Igraine said, "If they rally the rest of their armies west of the capital, they could march on the Craeg. Do we have the numbers to hold them back if it comes to that?"

"We took a loss too," Ulfar said, "Doubt we could be of much help."

"You worry too much, Igraine," Fionnula said. A wry smile juxtaposed the half-elf's sharp features. "They are slow and unfamiliar with this rocky land. We can make them pay for every inch they take. Their losses will be too great to continue."

"Defence?" Axton protested. "You move so quickly to abandon our offensive? To let the plague of the Empire spread? You had promised Gaer your support. What would he have said to this?"

"Gaer is not here, Axton," Filib said. "And circumstances have changed since we last spoke. New decisions must be made. There is no reason to believe that the Empire is an urgent threat."

"Try telling that to the Horselords of Caelum," Axton said. "I'm not sure they would have agreed as they stampeded, in a panic from fear of murder, through our homes, before we were forced to cut them down in self defence."

Pain from the memory bubbled up in Axton and threatened to turn into anger. He saw the last centaur in the land die by his own axe, lying in a pool of its own blood as Axton felt it breathe its last breath.

"My friend, we feel your pain," Filib said.

Ulfar gave Axton a comforting pat on his back.

"Gaer believed more than any that this Empire was a blight," Filib said. "He was not wrong, and we will deal with them. But ask yourself, what is the best course to ensure our success in a prolonged war?"

"I'm not sure, but I know what Gaer would have said," Axton muttered, feeling his argument slip away.

No one spoke for a moment; Fionnula stood cleaning her fingernails with a dagger she held and Axton sighed and let the case rest for now. Finally, Filib looked around the room, ensuring the attention of the others, "On the topic of defending the Craeg; that will not likely be necessary, my friends. Our scouts tell us they are not advancing. Most of their army is marching back east."

Filib moved his gaze from chieftain to chieftain as he spoke, "Axton, Fionnula, Ulfar, you can each correct me if I am wrong, but from what I have been told, it sounds like once our forces were routed, the imperials would have thought us scattered or killed. They likely didn't get a good number on us, and they'll assume they killed most of us. If that is true, they will think us defeated, and if they believe us to just be barbarians, then they will have no reason to pursue us, since we will no longer pose a threat."

"That is an awful lot of ifs there, Filib," Fionnula stated.

"True, but if we speculate on the opposite outcome, we find it is even more unlikely," Filib said. "How likely is it that they took us for an organized group and not Barbarians, counted our exact numbers as we scattered back into the Craeg, rightly assumed that we only committed a fraction of our numbers..." Filib trailed off to let the point sink in.

Axton thought about this for a moment. "I suspect you are correct. Our retreat was under the cover of darkness and through the nearby forest. Even with the girl on my back, I wasn't seen. It's a reasonable assumption that they did not see the others either. The retreat was called silently. We realized the battle was lost and signalled each other to retreat. If what you say is true—that they are killing the witnesses—then our secret dies with them. The surviving army was outside of town. They did not see us flee. I say with regret that we certainly lost enough of our comrades to sell the ruse that they had defeated us entirely."

"If we are not regrouping to go on the offence, as Axton

suggested, then what?" Ulfar asked in a rugged voice after a moment of silence.

"Axton is free to still travel the Craeg and proposition the other clans," Filib said. "We all must decide for ourselves."

Axton frowned and furrowed his brow. He pressed his fists harder onto the table. *It was his choice then. He could travel to gather further forces, or he could give up the fight... for now.* He could not tell the others of his clan what they had to do, but they would likely follow his judgment.

Gaer had seen this as their time to right the wrongs of the Empire. Their time to destroy their power.

We all must decide for ourselves.

Filib was right. He had to lead the clan; he had to do what he thought was best for the clan, use his own best judgement. What he or Gaer wanted mattered little. He had to be who his clan needed.

"My Clan has been decimated," Axton said. "While once we were among the largest of the clans, almost three hundred strong, we now will be lucky if we are over a hundred and fifty Bandorians, many of which are not yet of age." Axton looked down at the table with a frown. "I am sorry, but you are right. My clan can not assist with any further offensives against the Empire."

"Clan Blar and Eldur suffered similar losses, and we other clans are not large enough to lead an offensive ourselves," Filib said. "But we have learned much about the enemy and what they are willing to do just to defeat us. This has also hurt them greatly. Their Creet garrison is gone, and they have lost a major food trade hub. We have stopped their expansion for now, and immediate military retribution is unlikely."

"They will eventually come back," Axton said. "Gaer was right about that. They are expansionists and will not stop."

"True, but it will take time," Filib said. "We need time to regain our strength, replenish our numbers, but so does the Empire. The next move of Dronoch will be to move further west into the Craeg. We should pull back from the borders and only post one or two clans on that edge. The Empire is unlikely to move into the Craeg and even if they do, this will give off the impression of unorganized barbarians, and not an entire group of people."

Igraine spoke up now. "My clan will move north and keep our skills sharp on the Fomorians in the Fangs of Abaddon."

Filib nodded, "That is wise. I will send some of our clan with yours; those that need it. The rest of us will move with Dronoch when it does so. We will carry news and welcome other clans that return to it."

Axton spoke up, "My clan will stay near the borders. The eastern side of the Craeg has less thistlebacks and other dangers. My clan needs rest and a quiet place to raise the young that we have. We will send the young north to join you, Igraine, when they are ready."

Filib nodded approval.

"But what council would you provide if the Empire assaults the Craeg?" Axton asked.

"This will be unlikely," Filib said. "If they do enter, though, try to avoid them as best you can. Whatever you do, don't let them know that we are organized."

"We will see them coming from a way off. We will move if they get close."

Fionnula nodded and smiled at Axton. "We will do the same as Axton and Clan Kaltor. We also need to replenish for now."

"And my clan and I will move with Dronoch for now," Ulfar said. "We will make further decisions when the time comes."

He clapped his hands together as his beard held up his axe. "We will each break camp at the end of the month when Dronoch moves once again. It is settled then."

"It would seem, my friend," Filib responded.

Igraine slapped Filib on the shoulder. "Good, now let's get some drinks and celebrate!" The others nodded their agreement and made their way to the exit. They each went their separate ways from the tent to gather their clans to meet that evening around the bonfire.

CHAPTER 12
FIRE LIGHT

The day had been exhausting but thrilling, with many new lessons Fae could barely understand, ones on reading and writing that she felt overwhelmed by but had learned a lot from, and fitness and fighting drills she'd never done before. They were now on their way back from a tree climbing exercise they had been performing just outside of town and were walking down the dirt road into the city. Fae's shoulders slumped, and she felt as though she could hardly lift her feet.

Bullock came alongside her as they walked. "Hey Fae, are you alright? You don't look too good." His voice was comforting to Fae, as she could hear the genuine concern for her in it.

"Of course, she is fine," Kiva said, or at least who Fae thought was Kiva; after the earlier comments by the twins, she was determined to tell them apart and she had noticed Kiva had a small feather and tooth charm tied to a braid at the side of her head.

Kiva skipped up to them. She then gave Fae a good slap on the behind, which shocked Fae, and by reflex, she jumped a step or two forward.

"See, she just needs a little bounce added to her step. Come on, sweetheart, we'll get some rest in our bunks, then get some food to re-energize you. You will feel right as rain in no time."

Fae's mind flooded with visions of a soft bed to sleep in, and the prospect of rest brought a new stride to her step that allowed her to keep up with the others once again. She had forgotten about sleep. *Where was she going to sleep? Axton had said she would sleep and live with the pack, but what did that mean? She knew she wasn't staying with him or Bao, or even Brakan, but would she have some sort of bedroom, or do they sleep in an enormous hall like an orphanage?* Her mind wandered, considering every possibility for so long she barely noticed the other children talking as they walked the streets back through the city.

She was shaken out of her mental speculation when they finally approached the education building that they had been learning in. *Why had they returned here?* She thought they had been heading to where they sleep. But curiosity replaced her confusion as the other children walked her right by the building and towards a taller tent out behind the building that she had not noticed before. It was like the other buildings she had seen, with a cylindrical shape making up the base, a cone shaped roof, and pulled fabric wrapped tight about the building. This building, however, was taller and much skinnier than the tents she had seen before.

They all approached the tent, and the others entered, but Fae paused a moment to look at it. The whole tent sat on a wooden plank base which lifted it half a foot off the ground.

Finally, she entered as well. Inside, it was a large bedroom. The floor had soft hide rugs on it, and large cushions made from animal's furs piled in corners. On the far wall, rounded because of the shape of the tent, was a large wooden set of four bunk beds—two above and two below—that appeared to be built into the supports of the wall.

Bullock climbed up a central ladder and into the left bunk, then Erika followed and took the bunk on the top right. Kiva picked a book up off a shelf, then sprawled out onto a pelt and cushions on the floor while Jaxon tossed his practice sword into the bed below Bullock's bunk and plopped himself down into an armchair.

Jaxon sat nonchalantly, leaning back and crooked so much that he could drape one leg over the small arm of the chair. Something about the way he sat seemed a bit forced, like he was doing it just to impress or intimidate her; she could not discern which one.

"So, you have never been in a fight before?" Jaxon asked. "Not even once?" He sounded confused about how that could be possible.

"Well, no," Fae responded, "I mean, not before the man attacked me the night that Axton found me."

"What if another kid challenged you, or attacked you, or just wanted to have some fun? What did you do when that happened?"

"Where I come from, girls do not get into fights, they don't fight at all. Boys are not allowed to hit a girl, ever."

"Never?"

"Never."

"Says who?"

"Says everyone. That is just the way it is. Everyone knows you cannot hit a girl."

Jaxon screwed up his face in confusion. Bullock lay awkwardly on his bed, dangling his arms and part of his torso off the edge beside Jaxon.

"Wait, what if a girl hits you first?" Bullock asked. "Then what can you do?" He looked satisfied with his question.

"Yeah, that's right. What could you do then?" Jaxon piped in.

"I suppose you could push her away, but you couldn't punch the girl." Fae expected she was about to receive several other questions. "I'm sorry, but it is not a situation that happens almost ever; women where I am from are not fighters. It just doesn't happen."

Bullock and Jaxon both nodded and had a look of acceptance on their faces.

"OK, that is fair enough," Jaxon said. "You'll learn to take a punch here. We learn everything here, how to fight, read and write, math, science, philosophy, logic, history, strategy, fitness, survival, art. We learn everything there is to learn, that's the point."

Fae gave him a funny look, "You seem to talk the most, don't you?"

The two twins burst into laughter, but Jaxon doubled down on his pride. "That's right, because I'm the leader," he boasted.

Bullock gave Jaxon's foot a shove off the arm of the chair. He half slumped into his seat and almost fell out of it. "There is no leader in a pack, and you are the youngest of us, anyway. You are no better than the rest of us."

Jaxon pulled himself up and gave a playful smile.

Kiva hopped up from her seat. "Stop asking her stupid questions." She put a hand on Fae's shoulder. "You can relax now, Fae. Welcome home." She gestured around the room. "Time to rest your feet for a bit and hop into bed. At least until we drag you to dinner."

Fae looked at the four beds, a bit confused, "Is there a bed that I can use?" She realized that there were clearly five of them and only four beds. She supposed they expected her to sleep on the floor, which made sense since they did not know that she would be coming.

"Of course, there is," said Kiva, and she gestured to the bottom right bed.

Fae had assumed that was Kiva's bed, so now she was utterly confused. "But... where do you sleep?"

Jaxon laughed, quickly understanding her confusion. "The twins sleep together. They were given two beds but have never slept apart. They do everything together. Just how it's always been." And just as Jaxon said, Kiva crawled into the top bed with Erika and laid down with her feet at the opposite end of the bed. It was big enough to fit the two of them, but not by much.

Erika took her big toe and poked Kiva in the ear. "The new girl doesn't know how twins work, sis."

Kiva let out a small giggle.

"I don't think you two know how twins work," Jaxon said. "I'm fairly sure not all twins do everything together, including sleeping in the same bed."

Bullock gave out a laugh and Kiva stuck out her tongue at the boys.

"Take a load off, Fae," Jaxon said. "It will be about an hour before dinner. Relax."

Fae looked at the bed and smiled. It looked wonderfully comfortable, raised about a foot off the ground with furs, blankets, and cushions on it. The whole tent looked cozy. Little shelves were cut into the bed structures with books, scrolls, and other items the children had collected. Cushions lay on the floors along the walls and there was a hammock for sitting and reading instead of sleeping. There were books and scrolls strewn around, carvings, forms of writing tools, and a few wooden weapons against the doorway. There were even spaces hidden beneath the beds that allowed them to store their personal clothes and effects. Overall, it was a home too small for adults but perfect for the small group of children; a place to read, socialize, and rest.

She did as Jaxon suggested, climbed into her bunk, laid her head back, and drifted off, listening to the other kids talking about their day and other topics she was only barely aware of.

"Fae!" she heard her name being called. She could sense the heat, the light flickered in her eyes and burst into reds and oranges of the flames all around her. Her feet shuffled on a dirt street; she was back in Creet, and everything around her was on fire. The flames climbed the nearby buildings on either side of the street. A familiar house to her left. She knew the owners. She could not remember the woman's name, but she had bought bread from her in the market a few times.

The doors to the house exploded outwards with a whoosh as the pressure and heat inside the house built up to the point of bursting.

Fae shrieked and shielded her face. She took a few steps back but tripped, stumbling to the dirt ground. Dust flew up around her, but she was uninjured.

The blank eyes of the dead body she had tripped over stared at her, and she screamed. She scrambled to her feet, almost falling again in her attempt to get away from it.

"Fae." She heard the voice again, calling to her as if trying to lead her to safety, leading her out of the burning town. She ran towards where she thought the voice was coming from, down the streets of Creet; but everywhere she turned were more burning buildings, more fire, with tongues of flame reaching out to her like long tendrils grasping. She jerked her arm away from a flash on her right, only to have more flames snap at her from the left. She kept running.

She reached the town hall, and it too was on fire. Doors smashed in and windows destroyed. The roof crackled and snapped under its own weight, losing support as the beams burned. It creaked once more, then finally she heard a large crack as a beam smashed and half of the roof came crashing down.

Fae shrieked again, and hot tears came down her face. She thought of all the people inside; she had known some of them, grown up with some of them. They were dead and there was nothing she could do. She dropped to her knees and sobbed; an uncontrollable cry wracked her body with tremors.

But something was off. She cried for the people. The people. But what people? She could not remember. Fae had seen one body, but where was the rest? She had seen no one else.

"Fae."

The voice came again, calm and reassuring. She had to get to the voice, but that too was wrong. No one had ever called her Fae in Creet. Except perhaps her grandmother, but this was a man's voice, or perhaps a boy. No, it was not real, she thought; it was a dream.

Fae opened her wet eyes and saw the blurry face of Jaxon through her tears. She was still in her bunk, and Jaxon had one knee on her bed, leaning over her, gently shaking her awake, "Fae, are you ok?"

There was obvious concern in his voice; none of the playful bravado he had had earlier. She was so happy to see him and escape from her dream that she flung her arms around him in a hug and pulled. He lost his balance and fell onto the bed, partially on top of her and partially beside her. It did not bother Fae, though, as she squeezed him and buried her head in his shoulder, letting her tears pour out.

They laid that way for a time. Jaxon said nothing and Fae was thankful, as she was not yet willing to let go. Once the tears stopped, Fae quickly released Jaxon, feeling a little embarrassed.

"Sorry."

"Fae, it's alright. That is what I'm here for." He gave her a genuine smile that quickly relaxed her. "Everyone went for dinner, but I said I would stay here and give you a bit more time to sleep. You started having a nightmare, and you were crying. You were tossing and turning, so I tried to wake you up. I hope that is ok."

"Yes, of course. Thanks, Jaxon. I'm ok now," Fae felt weak at first, but she perked up. "Did you say dinner?"

"Yeah, I bet you're hungry. Let's get going. There is always plenty of food, but let's move. I want to get the meat right off the spit."

Growing up, Fae had not been extremely fond of cooked meats, but in the last few days, with all the rigorous work and hiking, just the thought of warm, juicy meat made her mouth water. Jaxon stood up off her bunk and reached for her with a charming smile. "Let's go."

Fae grabbed his hand, letting him heave her off the bed and to her feet. She was glad that he did not force her to let go of his hand as they drew back the tent flaps and began their walk to the bonfire. Back home, boys would have been mortified to be seen holding hands with a girl, but Jaxon did not seem to care. Perhaps, even though this life would be full of toughness, pain, and hardships, there would still be places of comfort and kindness. The thought made her smile as she held this strange but caring boy's hand, and they made their way down the path.

Wood hissed, crackled, and snapped as the roar rose and fell with the flames. They grew and shrank, parts of wood becoming exposed and igniting. The sun was setting, and it cast long shadows that collided with the light from the fire, creating an orange glow throughout the area.

The roar of the fire was loud enough to be heard anywhere in the central gathering area, the space that other cities or towns would have considered a town square.

Fae sat on the ground with her back against a large log, arms wrapped around her legs, tucking them into her chest. She rested her head on her knees as she sat facing the fire.

Fae listened to the steady thump, repeating over and over again, creating a steady beat. A man with shaggy hair draped over his eyes was sitting on a wooden box and beating his hand against it to create the sound and a woman with a small vielle produced melodic vibrations rising and falling in pitch like rippling waves of the ocean. With one hand, she held the stringed instrument's hollow wooden body against herself and with the other hand, the musician drew a bow against the strings on the body, vibrating them, creating a haunting, invigorating melody that moved through the Fae's body.

Voices sung out complementing the music with changes in pitch and speed; not words exactly, just vowels. Like calling from distant woods. It came together, an ethereal sound, pulling you in. Almost seductive in its ability to remove Fae's mental defences and slide into her mind.

The flames and shadows mesmerized her, fixing her eyes on not just the music but the movements she saw. Men and women, and perhaps even children, ran, danced, and bounded around the fire. Faces flickering into focus then disappearing again as the light of the flames danced. Ribbons, jewellery, and long sleeves flowed with the music, seeming to slow time as they moved, then speed it up again.

The darkness crept closer around Fae as the day turned to night, but with the light of the fire in front of her, the music took away her worries, and with her new friends to either side, her fear was kept at bay.

Jaxon sat on the log above and to the right of her. His right leg was up on the log and the left one dangling down so it rested beside her. She could feel his leg brush against her from time to time; the feeling reassured her.

Bullock sat to the right of Jaxon on the bench, whittling a small piece of wood with a sharp knife he had. Fae could not yet tell what he was creating.

To Fae's left, Kiva sat on the ground as well, similarly watching the dancers and musicians.

Behind Kiva, Erika sat on the log, leaning forward, holding strands of Kiva's hair in her hands, and slowly working them over one another into a tight braid. There was an obvious closeness between the two that Fae had rarely seen before among siblings.

They sat unmoving for a long time. Since they'd finished their dinners and had no other tasks that needed doing, Fae could enjoy the night. Enjoy the energy of the gathering.

Finally, Bullock stopped his whittling, pulled out a small strop of leather, and drew his knife along it to clean and keep the knife sharp.

"Jaxon, we should get to bed. Fae will be exhausted, and she needs her rest."

"We should all get our rest. It is getting late for us, anyway," Kiva said.

"Hold still." Erika gave Kiva a jab with her knee. "Just let me tie this off then we can head out."

Bullock's words had shaken Fae out of a daze; she had been half asleep as she huddled against the felled tree trunk and Jaxon's left leg. She sat up straight and stretched out her arms and neck, then looked around, feeling lightheaded and a bit confused about where she was.

"Done. OK, you're good, sis." Erika gave her sister permission to get up and move. The boys were up off the log bench, waiting for the girls as Erika helped her sister up.

Kiva turned to Fae and stretched out her hand. "Come on, girly. Let's get you off to bed."

Fae's gaze lingered on the outstretched hand, a moment of hesitation gripping her. Sitting watching the fire had lulled her into a sense of comfort, momentarily obscuring the turmoil that had befallen her life. These children were so eager to make her feel like one of them that her mind struggled to reconcile them with the people from that terrible night in Creet. She felt a warmth towards them, though part of her was unnerved by how easily they could bring down her defences. But looking into the red-headed girl's comforting eyes, the unease faded away. She would remember her past, but for now, she would take what comfort she could.

Fae grabbed the outstretched hand and Kiva hefted her onto her feet. The flicker of firelight died down around them as they walked back towards their tent.

CHAPTER 13
THE BATH

Six Months Later
722: Year of the Second Era

It had been six months since Creet, but the dreams still troubled Captain Titus. The actions he had taken there haunted him, but at least here, in Ioshal it was tranquil. It helped him cope with the memories.

He sat on the large cut stone that had fallen into the river an age ago; a remnant of a civilization long passed. Now forgotten. It had created a dam, which narrowed the water flow into a large lake called Ioshalok; now the biggest in the region, it was a dropping off point for goods from the river leading to the Starlight Sea. The Town of Ioshal was created from the remains of the Ioshal ruins, but recently the size of the place had doubled; since the destruction of Creet, the Imperial garrison had made it a permanent camp.

It was a busy place, but at this time of morning it was peaceful; quiet and Sareen. Titus ate his porridge in silence and dangled his feet above the water. The morning sun reflected golden beams of the gently rocking water. Goslings followed their mother, drifting lazily through the reeds along the shore. The lake reminded him of Hadriana, and he wanted so badly to bring her here some day; it had been a long summer since he had seen his wife and their two-year-old son. But it was unlikely he would get the chance to show them this place, the ironworks and smelting were being built and would drain into the lake. It would make the water unpleasant to smell, and worse to bathe in.

"Captain."

"Deus spare me," Titus muttered. *He woke up this early for his breakfast, specifically to avoid other people.*

"Captain Titus."

Titus cursed under his breath as he set his bowl down and pushed off the ground to stand, turning to see a young officer running up to him. Probably from a patrician family, it was inevitable that this kid, with all the privileges and connections, would eventually outrank him, regardless of any incompetence. Titus had long abandoned any hope of being promoted beyond the rank of captain. He lacked the means to attend proper military school and instead relied solely on his on his old-fashioned experience.

"What is it, Officer?"

"Captain, you are being reassigned, sir. They sent me with orders for you."

"Papers?" Titus opened a hand to receive the paper orders.

"No sir. The orders were told to me directly, to give to you. You are to head out to the western borders for a new assignment."

"The west? But I just came from there. I am on assignment here. This doesn't make any sense."

Titus put his hand to his brow, in frustration, and rubbed his eyes. *What nonsense was this?* He let out an annoyed sigh, "I'll talk to commander Felix; get this sorted out. Find out what the abyss he is thinking. I'll have to change his mind. Send some other captain. I just got here."

Titus made to leave, but was cut off.

"The orders didn't come from commander Felix, Sir. They came from above him."

Titus tightened his fist, then stretched the fingers out. *Dammit.*

"You are to meet with a mage already on route to the west. He wants you to prepare your best platoon and meet him just north of the ruins of Creet. He will have more platoons for you to lead in a strike force against the butchers of Creet."

"Any reason I have to be the one to go?"

Titus still hoped he could find a way out of going west again. He looked out over the crystal water, watching it lap the shores of the lake.

"Not sure sir, but the mage requested you specifically.

"Me? By name?"

"Yes."

"Why?"

"Not sure, sir. My best guess is that he read your report on Vester Keep and Creet and deemed you the most experienced."

Titus hadn't fully realized the significance of his recent experience until now. As the most senior soldier who had witnessed the barbarians' tactics firsthand, he found himself in a unique position.

"Why go back, though? We have already scouted some of the dead hills. It turned up nothing. There was no one left alive. None of the attackers made it out. We couldn't find anyone."

"The mage said he can find them."

"That is one powerful mage, then." Titus was used to mages making ridiculous claims before.

He picked up his porridge bowl, frowned and dumped what was left into the water; the fish could eat it. His peaceful morning was ruined. *Time to get back to work.*

"Thank you, Officer."

The officer turned to leave.

"Officer?"

"Yes, Captain?"

"What was the name of the mage that requested me?"

"Damitus, sir."

Months after Fae's arrival in Dronoch, the clan relocated to a lush valley between Dronoch and the eastern edges of The Craeg. The campsite was located along a large river that flowed southeast from the highland hills deep into the valley before continuing east towards Glenmor. Hidden within the basin, Axton had deemed it the ideal location for their settlement.

After completing work on the camp, Fae's pack followed a large contingent of the clan down a game trail that wound northwest upriver through the trees to a nearby waterfall. Despite her hesitation, Fae welcomed the chance for a bath to wash away her own stench.

"They are your parents?" Fae exclaimed, abruptly halting in her tracks. Jaxon and Erika, who had been walking beside her, turned to look back at her in surprise.

"Bao and Brakan?" Jaxon asked, surprised by Fae's confusion. "Yeah, of course. What's surprising about that?"

"But when I first met them, they were sitting there..." Fae's discomfort came rushing back to her as she stumbled for the words, "Well they were sitting on the bench, on each other. And well, they... were... doing things that parents don't do." Fae's voice trailed off into a whisper as she finished her sentence.

Jaxon gave Fae a confused look, but Kiva spoke out, attempting to help Fae explain herself. "Were they fornicating?"

"What?" Fae asked, not recognizing the word.

"Fornicating? Swiving? Fucking? Loving? Humping?" Kiva threw the words out with an air of nonchalance like she did not understand what Fae was having trouble with.

Kiva would have continued, but Fae cut her off quickly once she caught on, "No! or I mean yeah, but not really. They still had clothes on." Fae made a squeamish face.

"That is a no to the swiving then."

"Why would that mean they are not parents?" Jaxon asked. "Do parents not do that where you are from?" he asked with a raised eyebrow.

"Well yes, I guess. But I don't think they like it, and they would never be intimate somewhere that other people could see them."

"Why not?" Jaxon asked.

"Don't ask her that," Erika said. "If you ask her that every time she describes something from her town, we'll be here all day. Didn't you pay attention when we studied the Empire? They find that sort of thing taboo."

"Oh yeah, we read they are really uncomfortable with that sort of thing. Weird." Jaxon gave a shrug, as if it were not that important. "Oh well. Yeah, Bao and Brakan are my parents" he turned and continued walking; Kiva and Fae followed. Bullock and Erika were now much further ahead with the rest of the travelling party.

Fae still found it strange to think of them as parents, but reminded herself that she was going to have to stop being surprised by things now that she was living with these people. Their way of life differed from what she was used to. She would have to adapt.

When they approached the end of the trail, the trees opened into a bright view of a wide, shallow pool at the base of a waterfall. The sight was beautiful, like nothing Fae had seen before. The sun shone from the north above the falls, its rays scattered through the mist that permeated the area, casting beams of gold that swung as she moved.

The water came from a cliff twenty feet above them on the northeast side of the pool. It poured over the edge and splashed as it ricocheted off lower edges or passed right by to spray the pool below.

Bright green was everywhere. The colour of life and growth flooded her view. Trees and plants grew all along the cliff as it gently stepped down along the wide sides of the waterfall, where the ground had not eroded; and where the cliff walls were too steep for plants, soft bright green moss clung to the walls, bathed in a constant spray of mist. Around the pool at the base, plant leaves wove down to the water like an animal trying to get a sip of the cool clear liquid, while larger tree's roots dipped into the translucent glass of the pool like someone dipping one toe in but not fully committing to it.

Fae could hear birds chirping, just before a flock of nightingales burst from the trees near the water and led her view across the way she had come. Hidden in the mist of the falls, she could make out the shapes of others that had made it there before her group, frolicking in the waters.

As the wonder of the view faded from her thoughts, she once again noticed those around her and that they were stripping down out of their clothes. Her friends and most of the others had only slipped their boots off, but Bao and Brakan were already down to their undergarments, though for most Bandorians there was little difference between that and their normal attire. Then, as Fae looked on in horror, Bao pulled off her top, exposing her naked breasts to everyone around them.

Others in Dronoch had danced naked around the fire before, which always made her uncomfortable, but it had always been in the dark. Or she had seen others naked in the distance, usually changing in other camps. She had not yet seen someone just strip in the middle of such a large crowd. Any time she had cleaned herself before, she had gone alone to a stream.

Fae threw her hands up to cover her eyes as she squeezed them shut. She peeked through her hands to see what the other women were doing with their eyes when the men also undressed. None of the others seemed to find this strange.

Bao was looking at Brakan with a mischievous smile and a glint in her eye. He was fully naked now, too. They were standing next to the pool now, and Bao turned away from him until he stepped towards her and gave her bum cheek a slap. He leaned back on his heels waiting for a response.

Bao did not disappoint; she turned around to look at him, then lunged forward and shoved him into the pool. He flopped in with a loud splash and sent water spraying the others. Bao, then not content to stay on dry land, jumped into the water beside him.

Fae kept her hand over her eyes, peaking through to watch the entire exchange. But now all around her she could see that the others were also undressing completely, even her friends. Then Bullock spoke up.

"Fae, you going to get undressed or just keep standing there with your eyes covered?"

"You know that just because you can't see us doesn't mean that we can't see you, right?" Kiva asked.

Of course, Fae knew that, and she threw her hands down quickly, embarrassed that she had panicked. She was still incredibly uncomfortable with all of this, but she was determined to stay calm.

But just as panic had faded from her mind, Bullock's words registered. *Did he just say get undressed?*

"Um... no, I think I'll just swim with what I'm wearing," she said, "Or I can just stay out here while you all swim. I think I'm fine."

"Oh no you don't sweetie. You stink just like the rest of us," Erika commented in a not uncaring tone. "You are pretty, hun, but not enough to make up for the smell."

"You could go in with your clothes, but it will be a wet, cold walk back," Bullock said. "Besides, why bother when you can just get undressed?" He asked the question innocently.

"They are weird about nudity, Bullock, remember? Imperial culture? We just talked about this." Erika answered for Fae.

"Oh, right." Bullock said.

"Fae, you can't go in with your clothes. Your walk back will be wet."

"Fine, I'll... I will climb in over there. I'll undress there too."

Fae pointed to a part of the pool along the far edge that had long tree branches hanging over the water, just enough to obscure the surface of the pool, so long as no one walked around to the southwest side.

Erika shrugged. "Suit yourself," she said, and she threw off her last article of clothing and launched herself into the pool.

Jaxon, Bullock, and Kiva all raced into the pool from a shallow entry and splashed down as the water got too deep to run. Water sprayed everywhere, and Fae had to admit it did look fun.

The rest of the members of the clan that were with them were now also in the pool, but paid her no attention. The other children, however, all watched as Fae made her way to the stream of water flowing out of the pool and began to climb awkwardly from rock to rock without falling into the water. She made it across, but not without a foot sliding off a rock at one point and splashing into the water. The rock scraped her hand, but she was more worried about the wet boot. She made a note to prop it up somewhere that would allow it to dry a bit.

Fae crawled onto the sheltered stone beneath the tree at the edge of the pool and began taking off her boots and clothes. Before she finally took off her undergarments, though, she looked out from beneath the tree branches and noticed the other kids were all staring at her. She was not sure if, from where they were standing, they could make out anything but her outline; the tree provided shade and cover, hopefully making it hard to make out anything beneath it.

"Stop looking at me," she called out to the other children, realizing that there was nothing she could do if they just ignored her command, but the other children simply shrugged and turned back to their frolicking. Fae was grateful for that. She removed her bottoms just before she slipped into the pool and then removed her top as she lowered herself completely into the pool. The motion was awkward, but she managed to keep her clothes from getting wet. The initial shock of the icy water hit her, but as she moved around and swung her arms, she warmed up. The water felt amazing on her skin, and she played with it as it flowed over her arms. The water was deep enough to submerge herself, but not so deep that she could not reach the bottom with her toes. The place was truly made to be enjoyed.

As she moved around, she relaxed, and while she was still nervous about venturing out from her safe little place, she did take note of the others having fun. She looked at the beauty of this place and thought to herself that there was something wonderful about it all. Maybe this life would be pleasant after all. They were supposed to be here for a long while now, setting down roots, with the intention of training the young ones. Her head was still full of so much uncertainty and confusion, but a moment of calm washed over her that brought the memories of the nicer recent moments to mind and made her smile.

After she felt she had washed off enough and enjoyed herself as much as she could while being alone in her hiding place, she climbed out of the water and tried to shake off the water as best as she could. She put on her clothes while she was still wet, which made them slightly wet, but it was much better than if she were sitting in drenched clothes. She climbed back across the stream and made her way to where the pool met the trail.

The others were still having fun, so she resigned to simply lying in the sun on a stone and enjoying its warmth. It had the added benefit of drying off her and her clothes. She laid on the stone with her eyes closed until she heard a noise beside her. She looked to her right and saw Bao lying on her back, naked, on a stone beside her. Sun caressing her body and evaporating the water droplets that remained on her skin. Fae could not help but think she was beautiful before snapping her eyes back to the sky. She still found it strange to see a naked woman beside her.

"It makes you uncomfortable, doesn't it?" Fae heard a voice come from Bao, though when she looked over at Bao, there was no sign that she had said anything.

Fae did not need to be told what Bao was referring to. "Yes," Fae said, "I have never seen people so comfortable being naked. I was always taught that it was shameful. We aren't allowed to be naked, almost ever. And definitely not around boys. Then they will see you," she said. But even as she spoke, the question came to her: *what does it even mean to "see you"?* She knew it was a dreadful thing, but could not verbalize a reason.

"I, I don't know. Everything is very different here." Fae sighed, as she realized that was just the way it would be.

"It will be ok Fae. Yes, everything is different, but you are strong, and you will get used to it. Others have been like you before and they adjusted just fine."

"Always?" Fae asked. "Has anyone ever not adjusted to it? What happens then?"

Fae's voice sounded stressed once again, and she looked at Bao, forgetting her discomfort. Bao also turned to look at Fae.

"Only once in the last decade have I seen someone not adjust," Bao said. "He was an orphan, being raised by a bitter uncle. His uncle did not want him, so the boy set off to explore the forest and live there. Gaer and Axton found the boy and agreed to train him when he asked for it."

"The boy was a great warrior, and he took to training in some of the magical arts: healing from Cairn, and the old elven craft from Fynnathias."

Bao noticed the confusion on Fae's face. "You have met Cairn, but Fynnathias is a half-elf, and he still knows some of the magic of the elves. They focus most of their magic studies on knowledge of nature."

"Anyway, the boy's interest in magic grew and he could not understand why we let the Empire have all the power with their magic. Why did we not study magic to defeat them? Gaer and Axton said that we would defeat them with our minds and bodies instead."

"They had a falling out, and when it came time for the boy to face the trials, he instead left the clan. We have not seen him since, but we think he travelled back to the Empire."

Bao finished and turned her head back to the sky.

"What if the same thing happens to me?" Fae asked. "If Axton found that boy and took him in, that's no different from my situation."

"I do not think it is likely," Bao said. "Axton chose you. If it was someone else, it would be hard to say. But Axton has made the mistake in the past, and he would be the least likely to repeat a mistake unless he saw something in you he knew would lead you down our path. You have a strong heart, even I can see that."

Bao sounded certain, but how could she know? Fae had lived through a devastating event, and even now was unsure if she wanted to follow the Bandorian way forever. She may have been more like this boy than they thought.

"You will be fine, Fae. Try not to worry," Bao said. She tilted her head towards Fae without opening her eyes and gave Fae a smile.

Fae relaxed and let herself sink back onto the flat stone. She closed her eyes once more and let the sun wash over her.

"And Fae," Bao said, "It is OK to see others naked. You don't have to cover your eyes." Fae had not realized that any of the adults had noticed her earlier shock. "It is just like seeing a naked animal. We are all just animals, it is our natural selves. Nothing wrong with it." Bao's words were calm and comforting, coercing Fae's tension to slip away onto the stone beneath her.

Eventually, the other children came out of the water and air dried for a time before putting their garments back on. Once everyone dried and dressed, they all began the walk back to camp. Bao's voice and words had felt soothing, but they still left much to think about, and left many doubts in Fae's mind.

But for now, she would learn. Axton had told her they would spend at least the next year in this valley. She liked this place, and she was glad they would not be moving anytime soon. It would give her time to adapt and grow. A comfortable place to get used to the strangeness of this life.

CHAPTER 14
THE STRIKE TEAM

Titus wiped the cool steel of his blade on the dead man's furs. Most of the blood came off with only a few passes. The thick tree canopy blocked out any moonlight and made viewing the face of the corpse challenging. The dead man seemed to be a young adult, heavily built and deadly. A Barbarian.

Despite how quiet Titus had been, the man had still heard him sneaking up behind him. The man had turned almost fast enough to avoid the quick blade. Almost.

"Damitus," Titus called in a whisper.

Titus spotted Damitus hunched over about fifteen paces away, having killed the other Barbarian lookout. Bandorian is what Damitus had called them, though Titus did not care what they called themselves; they had attacked Creet. Though he knew much of his anger was an attempt to redirect the guilt he felt.

Damitus's tight buckled cloak made him appear like a shade gliding through the trees. *How did the mage move so quietly?* Titus had military training for stealth, but they did not teach such things to mages.

"Captain," Damitus said. "The other guard is dead."

"How do you know there are not more guards?" Titus asked. "And how did you know where these two guards would be in the first place?"

"I know. They will have one or two guards posted on the other side of the camp, not more. More is usually unnecessary, and they do not fear a competent ambush."

Titus gave him an apprehensive look but did not question the wizard.

"Gather your men. We can prepare for the attack now."

Titus emerged from behind the tree, positioning himself as a silhouette against the distant Bandorian campfire's glow. Raising his hand to give the signal, he knew his men, strategically positioned far behind and out of sight, would see the gesture to move up. He glimpsed slight movement in the distance as his men began their stealthy approach; it would take them a few minutes to regroup at his position.

"You were in Creet, Captain, where you not?" Damitus asked.

"Yes, sir." Titus nodded.

"These are the so-called butchers of Creet?"

"They appear to be. They are dressed similarly. Clothes from animals, mostly, with better craftsmanship than I would have expected."

"What happened in Creet?"

Titus had rehearsed this story many times and told it many more, the doctored details of the event given to him by his superiors. He always hated telling it. He felt the muscles of his face wanting to tense, but he pushed the feeling down and forced a relaxed look.

"We arrived too late. They had already destroyed Creet and butchered its people. As the horde left the town, we were able to shoot them down with arrows. They quickly fled."

Titus could make out the mages skeptical look under his hood even in the darkness.

"I can see through that lie," Damitus said. "Even if I hadn't already known these people are not butcherers. Deadly warriors to be feared, certainly, but not murderers of children. I suggest you practice that lie a little more in the future. Your ability to lie may one day save your life. Or don't. It matters little to me."

Titus silently cursed the mage in his mind. *How had he seen through it so easily? No one else had ever questioned the story.*

Titus's men reached him and squatted behind bushes and trees, as Damitus and Titus were doing. His officer and three sergeants huddled closest to him, while the rest of the platoon spread out under cover. Titus had another two platoons farther east in the forest, but he knew he could not get more than one platoon up without the enemies noticing. Once the sounds of battle started, the other platoons would march forward and join. "Good. Hold here," Damitus said. "We are upwind so their beasts will not smell us, and this is as close as we can get before they detect us."

Titus stared through the trees; fifty paces still separated his men from the edge of the clearing. They could barely see the structures of the camp, but the fire from its centre flickered and provided enough light. The occasional dimming of the light from a barbarian passing in front was the only movement they could detect.

"Certainly, we can move up closer sir, we are still so far," Titus said.

"No," Damitus said. "They will know. They are more in tune with the forest than you are."

Titus was skeptical, but let it slide.

"Grierson. How many do you reckon there are?"

"Maybe two hundred, sir," Grierson said. "Can't be over sixty combatants, though, with the woman and children."

"One hundred," Damitus said.

"What?" Titus asked. He whirled his head at Damitus, confused by his sudden comment.

"There will be about one hundred combatants. There will be less than one hundred and fifty people, but besides the young children and five guardians at most, every member will be a combatant."

How could he know that? Who was this mage, sent from the

Magisterium to oversee this mission? He knew more than he should and barely seemed like a mage; he did not move or act like a mage, and he barely even dressed like a mage. His robes were pulled tight around him with leather belts and buckles instead of left loose and flowing and unlike other mages, the bottom of his robes was just below the knee, not hanging to the ground, and leather combat boots protected his feet instead of ornamental shoes.

"How could you possibly know..." Titus began to ask. The mage shot him a look. "Never mind."

The mage gave Titus a chill. It crawled up his back beneath his armour.

Even his age was unclear, his face covered in shadow and a clean-cut beard hiding the age that his face would normally reveal.

"I suggest that, once these men are ready to attack, you send a messenger to your other platoons to begin the march. We will need their reinforcements as quickly as possible."

"Of course, sir," Titus said. "Sergeant, head back to the other platoons and signal them to advance at pace and begin a charge once they hear signs of battle."

The sergeant gave him a nod and crept back east into the bush.

"Men, prepare yourselves. On my signal, we charge."

Axton stood back from the fire and watched the children nestled together against the flank of a vargr. Fae looked content, squeezed between the twins. He was impressed that she looked relaxed against the massive vargr. It had taken some time for her to stop panicking every time she saw them. Growing up with them from birth, her fear had seemed odd to him, but when he stared at the creature now, with its considerable size, wolf-like features but with thicker legs, he could now understand her fear.

He smiled to see her happy. The firelight shimmered in her deep blue eyes and her long blonde hair threaded into a Bandorian braid rolled over Kiva's shoulder while her head leaned against Kiva.

It would be good to stay put for a time. Fae was getting comfortable with her pack as well as around the others, and she was advancing well. It would give her some stability in a life that had completely changed on her.

Axton settled onto a nearby log, his gaze fixed on the children as they played. Eventually, Bao and Brakan finished their passionate dance with each other and took a seat beside him. Axton did not look at them, but Bao seemed to notice his focus.

"She is adjusting well. She is strong, smart, and adjustable."

"I know."

"But you still worry?"

"Yes." Axton still did not take his eyes off Fae, even as Bao stared caringly at him.

"That's not like you, Axton," Brakan said. "You are usually the one to tell us not to worry about things we can't control."

"I know. I suppose it is more correct to say I ponder. Ponder if there is an action I should take to avoid failure."

"Because of him?" Bao asked.

"Probably."

"He was different."

"But we didn't know that until afterwards."

"There were signs. He was never satisfied, and he had an anger in him."

"She has a rage in her as well. It helps her, but it's also dangerous if she cannot control it."

"She is learning to control it." Bao spoke in a soft and reassuring voice.

"I failed him. Gaer and I failed him. I worry I'll fail her too. Her rage is powerful." Axton drew his eyebrows together.

"Have you told her everything about Creet? Even your suspicions?"

"You mean that the Empire burned her town and murdered all the people?"

"Yes, that."

"No." Axton said. "I told her we did not come to destroy her town but said nothing of the Empire's involvement, though I think she holds them at least partially responsible. She already has enough fear and rage in her. I worry about making it worse."

"You have to tell her your suspicions, Axton," Brakan said.

"I will in time. I want to teach her to control her emotions first. This valley is good. She seemed to like the waterfall, and this is a safe place to focus on the young one's training. We have everything we need here."

For a moment, they stood in tranquil silence, their eyes fixed on the children sitting snug in the warm firelight. It was peaceful, and Axton savoured the moment.

A sudden bark shattered the calm. The sound was jarring, and the nearby dog's tense posture only added to their unease. Clearly, something was amiss. The three Bandorians quickly scanned the distance, trying to discern what had caught the dog's attention.

Another bark pierced the air, adding to the growing tension. It came from the western edge of the clearing. *Had the scouts let a bear pass into the camp just to give the clan a challenge?*

"I'll check it out." Axton said. Bao and Brakan nodded.

He picked up his axe and stepped along the dirt path to the eastern edge of the camp. He passed Farth to his left, moving something into his tent as he got ready for bed. Axton's eyes darted back and forth, tracing the edges where the firelight kept back the darkness. He couldn't hear or see anything in the forest beyond.

He couldn't hear anything. The crickets were silent.

"Farth," Axton called the question back to his friend, hoping he was there. He did not turn his eyes away from the darkness.

"Yeah?" Farth called back.

"Come here. Bring a weapon."

It took Farth less than thirty heartbeats to be beside Axton, and he heard a sound to his right and saw two other nearby Bandorians had looked up from what they were doing.

Crunch. Crunch.

Something was crashing through the forest, approaching them, and it was speeding up. Axton still could not make out anything in the tree's darkness.

Thwap.

The Bandorian on Axton's right dropped to his knee. A crossbow bolt lodged in his chest. They were under attack.

"Arm yourselves!"

Axton yelled as loud as his lungs would let him. He had to alert the entire camp.

He dropped into a ready stance with his battle axe ready. Armed men rushed out of the treeline directly at the downed Bandorian. The man coughed, choking on blood, but he still swung his sword at the first soldiers' leg, partially severing it. The next soldier impaled him on a spear.

The second Bandorian, Sara, disappeared in the rush of soldiers. The nearby flank of the charge approached Axton now. A maddened laugh burst from beside Axton as Farth prepared to engage.

Two men were closing in on Axton side-by-side, the left slightly ahead of the other. So, Axton changed his grip, prepared, and swung his axe hard from left to right. It bore through the first soldier and collided with the second soldier. They both collapsed to his right.

The thrill of battle flooded Axton's senses. *No. He was chief now. He had to lead. Think. Facilitate.*

This was what they had prepared for. These men were too well equipped for brigands. It was the Empire. Filib had warned him to not let the Empire discover them. They had failed. *Somehow, the Empire had gotten the jump on them. How could this have happened? Not important now. Could they kill all the Imperials? But what would be the consequences?*

There were not that many of the soldiers. Surely, they could defeat them. He used the shaft of his axe to block a sword swing, then pushed past the man's guard and smashed the axe against his helmet, denting it.

He was juggling with what to do when he heard more noise. More soldiers ran through the forest, metal armour clanging as it bounced along. *The second half of the assault? No. There was too much noise, it was much more than that. It was impossible to guarantee that no soldier got away to spread the news of the events here. And even if they did, the Empire would wonder what happened. They had to appear as a defeated rabble. They had to retreat.*

"Give ground." Axton yelled.

He had lost track of Farth. He had to hope that Farth and Sara could pull back. Another man charged him. Axton again blocked the sword swing, but the momentum pushed him off balance. Instead of simply falling, he reached forward and gripped the man's breastplate. Axton pulled and dragged the man into the ground beside him. They went down in a tumble, but his position surprised the guard and Axton pushed off of the man, forcing his face into the dirt, and got into a crouched position. He did not wait for other soldiers to reach him. Axton bolted off towards the centre of camp, all the while calling for others to give ground.

Moments later, he reached the campfire. Brakan was there, looking at Axton for direction.

"Empire?"

"Yes," Axton said. "The books? Supplies?"

"We heard your call. Rock is already packing the books and moving west with the children. Cairn is organizing the critical supplies just in case. He will meet us west of the clearing as well."

"Good."

Axton grabbed the non burning end of a log from the fire.

"Burn anything we leave behind. We need to make it appear as though we are disorganized and routed."

"Understood," Brakan said.

Brakan too grabbed a burning log and took off in the other direction through the camp, lighting tents on fire as he ran. Axton thought he saw Brakan reach Bao in the distance and update her. *Good.* Axton could still hear the clanging of metal throughout the camp and see other Bandorians, now all awake and ready for battle, causing chaos for the enemy.

Axton saw a nearby barrel of whisky-beer. He tested it for weight and thanked his luck that it was empty enough that he could lift it. The cork came off with one hit of his axe and he lifted it as best he could. He took four steps to build momentum and threw the barrel as far as he could down a row of tents. Ale sprayed in all directions as the barrel crashed and rolled.

The torch wood was still burning on the ground, so he grabbed it and threw it after the barrel. There was a loud *roar* as the ale caught fire and flames spewed wildly. The tents lit up, and Axton nodded to himself, deciding that would do.

He moved through the camp updating clan mates and continuing to call, "Give ground," to anyone that could hear. Smoke and darkness now made it difficult to see far.

Eventually, he came across Fae's pack. The young Jaxon, twelve now if Axton remembered correctly, approached first, leading his group. Fae stood on his left with her small axe at the ready. She had developed muscles in the half-year and appeared more up to the task of fighting with her pack mates. Her eyes were determined, fear barely visible, hidden behind her grim determination.

Bullock and the identical twins stood behind, all holding their own weapons. Bullock was wearing Farth's old head-butting helmet.

"Axton, we are ready. What is the plan, sir?" Jaxon asked.

"Retreat," Axton said. "Move west. You five need to get out of here. Find Rock in the forest beyond the clearing and report to him. He will move you farther to safety."

Jaxon's face sunk, and a look of shock grew on it.

"What? We are retreating? These guys don't look too tough. We can take them."

"Do what I said, boy. We need to convince them we are just a disorganized rabble. We don't want them returning with an army. Now go quickly."

Axton did not wait for another response from the kids. He continued moving through the camp and helped others pull back. Now that they had organized and moved back, it was time for them to regroup beyond the clearing. Gain back control of the situation.

"Retreat," he called.

He repeated the command every twenty heartbeats, fighting back soldiers as he went. With a shield in his left hand now, having picked one up as he went, he blocked attacking sword swings and pushed back advancing attackers, usually sending them into a tent or over a bench. The sounds of battle in the darkness became less frequent, likely the Imperials regrouping in the camp.

Seeing no more clan mates in his area, he turned to run, but before he had the chance, he heard a high-pitched cry pierce the darkness. *It sounded like a woman. No. A young girl's cry.* Then he heard the clanging of weapons and youthful voices yelling. His brain strained for a moment before concluding. Jaxon.

Dammit, child. Axton rushed towards the source of the cry. He came around a burning tent and saw what he expected. Jaxon, Fae, Bullock, Erika, and Kiva were there, and they were not alone.

Fae was lying on her back, seemingly having tripped over a log. Jaxon was trying to help her up. Bullock was holding up a shield, trying to block the sword swings of a tall soldier. Erika was trying to swing a small arming sword at the man, and Kiva was hanging on the man's back, trying to dig a dagger between the gaps in his armour.

On the other side of a small fire from the children, two more soldiers, seeing the young ones as little threat, were stalking towards them. Axton could see the deaths play out. The two men would likely run Erika through with a sword first before killing Kiva and then advancing on Jaxon and Fae. Lucky for the children, the two soldiers did not see Axton. He burst out of the shadows, swinging his axe down on one soldier and collapsing the man's neck guard and burying it in his throat.

The second soldier looked up at Axton in surprise, just in time for his swinging arm to be gripped by Axton at the wrist. Axton lunged forward, forcing the man's arm into an awkward position, hearing a satisfying cracking noise. The man howled in pain.

The soldier collapsed to the ground, holding his right arm. Before he could try to get back up, Axton stomped his foot down on the man's neck, bending armour and making it hard for the man to breathe.

Axton looked back to the kids, just in time to see the soldier attacking them, sink slowly to the ground, finally succumbing to Kiva's daggers buried deep in his neck.

Jaxon just looked up at Axton in shock, having not seen the other two soldiers, but knowing that Axton had saved their lives.

"Axton, we—"

"Damnation Jaxon. What were you thinking?

"We wanted to help. We thought we could take them."

"Well, you thought wrong. And you almost got your whole pack killed. Not to mention you are now a liability to me or any other member of the clan that has to save you five. I gave you a sensible order and you should have been smart enough to follow it."

Axton felt the heat in his face and realized he had to bring his temper down.

"All of you, get out of here. Get back to the forest and find Rock, like I said."

"Axton, I'm sorry," Jaxon said.

"Just go. Now."

His words came out harder than he meant to. The three children helped Fae and Kiva up and finally followed Axton's instructions, running as fast as their short legs would take them towards the western forest.

When the children disappeared into the darkness, guilt entered Axton's mind. *He should not have been so hard on Jaxon. The boy had bravery, but he was rash. Axton would have to sit down with him later and talk through all that had happened, remembering to not be harsh with the boy and use it as a learning opportunity.*

A clang of metal-covered boots caught his attention, just before a sword came down towards his face. Axton did not have time to block it, but he sidestepped the blow. His thoughts had left him open, and two soldiers were now bearing down on him.

A second blow came from the first soldier. Axton partially deflected it with his armoured arm, but the sword slid low and clipped his left leg. Pain shot up his body and he let out a strained grunt as his axe slipped from his fingers. Axton staggered backwards. He almost lost his footing, but years of training allowed him to stumble and still make the most of it. As he continued backwards, he narrowly evaded the fire pit, but he grabbed a burning stick log and swung it wide towards the two soldiers. They both leapt back, giving Axton the space he needed. He lunged forwards and picked up his axe. His leg still screamed in protest and warm blood ran down his leg.

With his axe in his left hand, Axton flung the burning piece of wood at the second guard's face. It collided with his helmet and burning embers sprayed into the gaps, burning his face and eyes.

The first guard paused before advancing again. It was enough space that Axton could grip his axe and swing it horizontally at him. The guard attempted to get his sword between the axe and his torso, but the weight of the axe was affected little by the feeble attempt. The axe batted the sword out of the way and collided with the man's armour, knocking him to the ground.

Axton limped forward. He switched grip on his axe, so that the sharp pole at the end of his axe was facing down. He brought it down quickly, piercing the man's chest armour and collapsing the metal down into his chest.

The second guard had tossed his helmet off and was still crying as he tried desperately to rub the burns out of his face. Axton switched grip on his axe again and swung it from the side, severing the man's head and putting him out of his misery.

Axton looked from side to side, listening for the sounds of any other of his clan struggling to pull back. He heard no more signs of battle, but he saw Imperial shadows and silhouettes in the darkness between the red flames licking the sky as their home burned. Ash and smoke billowed throughout the burning camp, making individual features hard to make out. But the shadows were closing in now. He could see the glistening blades in the glow of flame approaching him. He must be the last man still in camp.

He turned and ran.

CHAPTER 15
THAT WHICH WE CANNOT CONTROL

"We've regrouped now," Bao said.

Axton listened to her but continued to stare out from the cover of the forest at their old home, now destroyed.

"They are not moving forward; they are just setting up camp," Bao said. "By my count, we have not lost over ten so far. They have lost more than that. If we attack now, we could probably wipe them all out."

"You are probably right."

"We could salvage much and repair what we've lost. We wouldn't have to find a new site for our camp."

Axton rubbed his eyes with his thumb and index finger. She had a point, and he had to admit he would enjoy taking back their camp and wiping them out.

"They already think that we have run off. Look at them, they are not even posting guards; they think us defeated."

Think us defeated. Her words rekindled a memory. Something Filib, chieftain of Clan Laidir, had told him. "Don't be a hero, Axton. Run and make it look like we are just a rabble."

Axton had agreed with the reasoning before. *Did he still? He turned it over in his mind.* Yes, he admitted reluctantly. *It was a sound plan. Give ground to the Empire and pose as savages. They will not send all their forces after the remains of raiders in these harsh lands, but if they destroyed these people and the strike teams went missing, more men would come.*

Bao crouched beside him, her eyes intent on their attackers' actions, like Axton, trying to learn what she could of their opponent. The sun had risen now and the rest of Clan Kaltor's forces had pulled back deeper into the protection of the forest.

"No, Bao. I want to take them out as badly as you do, but we had agreed what we would do in this situation."

Bao just sighed and nodded her agreement.

"They think us a scattered rabble," Axton said. "That was our goal. Going in now would only put our goal in jeopardy."

Bao turned back to the camp, squinting her eyes to focus better on the men there.

"So, we watch and study them," Bao said, "and then we meet up with the clan shortly?"

Axton nodded.

Axton could see into their old camp, burned tents, and destroyed equipment scattered the ground. Little was still standing; the fire had run its course. Soldiers moved here and there. Some had picked up axes and were chopping down trees, others dug ditches or cleared refuse with shovels. *Bastards were going to set up an outpost in their old home.*

He was searching for the commander in charge. *Who were these people?* Finally, he spotted the man. His helmet was off, buckled to his belt out of the way, making it harder to distinguish him with the captain crest not easily visible. He stood out from the others with his segmented metal armour covering more of him instead of the single plate of metal covering his torso that the basic soldiers had.

The most obvious thing about the man, however, was how he stood and how others rushed to him, giving him reports, then carrying orders away. He held himself well, not visibly yelling or blustering to show power to his men. They seemed to respect him without such displays.

Axton continued to watch, while the captain gave out orders and oversaw the work of his men. Then a dark figure stepped out from behind a burnt tent and approached the captain. He was a large man, strength visible even beneath his robes. His hood was drawn up, making it difficult to make out anything about the man's face except that he had a short black beard.

A mage.

He stood, saying something to the captain. His presence seemed to darken the expression on the captain's face, looking uncomfortable at having the mage there. The captain walked away, out of sight of Axton, but the mage still stood there, looking out at his surroundings. The mage moved in the direction of Axton and Bao; out into the clearing, making it easier for Axton to see him, though he still could not glean more details about the man.

The mage stood there, almost as if he wanted Axton and the others to see him. *What was he doing?*

Then suddenly the mage whipped his head around towards Axton and he could have sworn the mage had seen him. Axton ducked down quickly behind the tree trunk he hid behind, a chill running down his spine. Something felt familiar about the feeling, like an uncomfortable feeling he had experienced before, but significantly more powerful.

"Bao, let's move."

It was time for them to leave.

"Sir," Titus said as he approached the dark wizard, "There is no sign of the barbarians. Our losses were significant, but we still have enough to hold the area. Their camp is destroyed. It seems they have fled into the hills."

"Does it?" Damitus responded quietly, but Titus heard him.

"My pardon, sir?" Titus asked.

"Never mind, Captain. They will be watching us, but we have accomplished our goal here."

"If you do not mind me asking, sir, how is it you know so much about these people?"

"I do mind you asking. My knowledge and how I gain it is my own."

"Of course, sir. Pardon my curiosity," Titus pulled himself up, trying to give off an air of professionalism. "I have set up guards to man the perimeter. The rest of our men are clearing the rubble to make space and gaining wood to begin construction. If the men work through the night, we should have basic defences established by the next morn.

"I would like to send scouts ahead to follow these Bandorians. They appear to me to be more organized than we expected and if more exist deeper in the dead hills, they may pose a threat to the Empire."

"Oh, you are certainly correct in your intuition, but no. We have accomplished our goal, and they will not attack now and risk showing their hand."

So, they are more than just small bands of barbarians. Titus wondered why they should not do something about this obvious threat.

"Damitus, if we follow them now, we may learn more about them and—"

"Captain, before you submit any report, I want you to show me what you intend to write. We report that this was just a rabble, easily scared off when we attacked. Do not provide any information or report regarding your intuition, only the things I have told you to report."

Titus grimaced as he understood Damitus' instructions. He hated all the lying that his role as captain was requiring him to do. *Why did Damitus want him to doctor his reports and comments? The machinations* of the magisterium's politics angered him. *Was this more Imperial propaganda like what they forced him to spread regarding the destruction of Creet?*

No, this seemed different. Damitus seemed too smart for petty propaganda, and he intended on lying to the military, not just the people. Titus would do as he was told. He belonged to this Empire, with its great strength, so he did not want his actions to lead to any dissension. He did not understand the objectives of the Magisterium, but he had a duty to uphold.

"As you wish, sir."

"I will be returning to the capital tomorrow afternoon once your report is ready, and I will take it to the capital for you. You are to remain here and oversee the construction of the outpost. Once it is complete, you are to inform me and the council and begin the journey back to the capital. Take only a small escort and leave the rest of your men to man the outpost."

"As you say."

His instructions were explicit, and as long as they did not come under attack by a bigger force, they would be simple enough to follow. Based on his observations and what Damitus had shared, he suspected the enemies would not return to attack them. It would reveal that they are bigger than the Empire suspects. *Didn't Damitus say something about them not wanting to reveal their hand yet?*

Still, he wondered if more lives would be spared if he shared the things he knew. *Were his lies being told to save the lives of his soldiers? He had to believe that they were, otherwise, what was he even doing in this army?*

CHAPTER 16
MACHINATIONS IN THE MAGISTERIUM

"Damitus is a problem, sir. He has been routing around in the library in the restricted section. He continues to manipulate the other acolytes not under his command, and he disrespects the edicts."

Damitus could hear the other mage complaining about his actions to the archon, unbeknownst to them. *Pathetic.* He paused outside the slightly ajar door to Archon Cicero's sanctum, eavesdropping on the conversation inside.

"Mage Vitus," Archon Cicero said, "you have raised these concerns about Damitus before. I worry you are making the very foolish mistake of wasting my time."

"Sir, he has been sighted in places far from his assignments, sneaking to parts of the Empire that he is not assigned, coming and going as he pleases. My contacts saw him on the eastern coast just this month, inquiring about passage across the Starlight Sea all while he was assigned to the western reaches. We do not even know where he is from. He appeared at our academy years ago, demanding to be trained with no history and no past that anyone can corroborate. We do not even know if he was born of the Empire. He could be a spy from—"

Mage Vitus froze mid-sentence. He stood before the archon, not moving, not even a shiver. He was frozen as stone, with his lips parted mid speech and a stupid expression locked on his face. *It suited him.* A handy spell Damitus had picked up; *good for shutting up people who run their mouths too much.*

As Damitus strutted into the room, he smirked at the shocked look on the archon's face. With his mouth hanging open, the archon stared at Mage Vitus, frozen before him. The chaos a simple spell, implemented at the right moment on an unsuspecting victim, could inflict was amusing.

When the archon finally noticed Damitus, he slowly closed his mouth and replaced his shocked expression with a smug look at Damitus.

"Quite the dramatic entrance you managed there, Damitus," the archon said. "I take it you heard Vitus's accusations and have something worthwhile to say."

"I heard Vitus whining to a senior wizard—an archon—and wasting his time. I will do no such thing," Damitus said. "It was a favour I did you by silencing the prattling cretin. I will not dally with overly long details."

Damitus had reached the two speakers now but turned to only face the archon.

"The raids on the dead hills went as expected. A simple raid scattered the Barbarians. I also have a proposal for you. I would not waste your time with a proposal without doing the needed research beforehand, which is why his men saw me on the east coast gathering information. Perhaps if Vitus wasted less time on tracking me and spent it on his own studies, he would be competent, and not need to drag down other wizards such as myself."

Archon Cicero's eyes narrowed and looked at Damitus with curiosity.

"Unlike the other fools here that waste time on political games and sucking up to other archons, I have been researching history and reports of the borders. I aim to know the enemies of our Empire, for they are greater than we suspect. I have studied our history, known the stories of our lord Deus. Looked into what we once knew of the greater world. I have had my people pour over the trade reports with the pirates and free merchants of the east, those that have crossed the Starlight Sea. I have even met with some of these people myself."

"What people do you have?" the archon asked.

Damitus bristled at the interruption, but he did not let it show. He still needed this man to grant his requests.

"I have my own people. Just as the archons each have their own resources."

"There are none that should be yours exclusively. They should belong to the Magisterium, not you."

"Do not mistake me for such a fool as to think that those that succeed do not find their own advantages to use."

This comment did not gain a response by the archon. He just stood back, looking bemused by Damitus's tenacity.

"The brigand raiding parties of the starlight sea to the east, which we regularly skirmish with, are more than they seem. I suspect they are just a proxy of a much larger threat that is hiding beyond the far shores. We have not advanced further because they seem to have no useful resources, but I believe they hide what information reaches us. There is a threat there, and our Empire is not as strong as it thinks it is."

Damitus waited a moment for the archon to pour over this information. But as he saw the archon's face sour—likely from his comment on the overconfidence of the Empire—he continued to speak. He had the archon's ear and would not waste the opportunity.

"These barbarians to the west are also a threat and have shown us that our power over magic does not make us immortal. With magic, we are unmatched, but we are still susceptible to blades and force. I was not in Creet, but even when we strip out the ridiculous lie told in the capital that the barbarians killed everyone in the town, a wizard from the garrison was still killed by them."

Damitus watched for the archon's reaction as he spoke. He saw what he was watching for.; the archon's eyes flinched, only the smallest amount, when Damitus mentioned the lie of Creet. He knew, and he was surprised that Damitus knew. *Good.* He continued.

"You must have seen the body. He was one of the strongest wizards and still he had been cut down by blades. We are not untouchable. We train the mind but not the body. Only if we master both can we overtake every enemy."

"You have talked much, but I am yet to hear this proposal you speak of," the archon said.

"Two actually," Damitus said.

"Pardon?"

"I bring to you two proposals. I request we search through our army for some of the best fighters and test them for potential in the ability to use magic. You allow me to teach a regiment of men, even women, if I can find any. I will train them to master mind and body. These will become our most elite wizards in battle. I need only a few people to prove the concept."

The archon made a move as if to speak, but Damitus did not give him pause.

"Second, once their training has started and is stable, I will lead an expedition of experienced merchants and spies east over the Starlight Sea to infiltrate and learn more about other threats to the Empire. These tasks will take me, I suspect, the better part of the next five years. It will allow us to grow our understanding of power and our understanding of the greater world."

Damitus ended his speech now. He prepared himself; he had laid his powerful cards on the table and readied his arguments to the possible objections. This archon he considered wiser that most of the others; constantly too concerned with politics and overconfident in the system that had brought them to power.

But no immediate objections came. Archon Cicero stared at him, and his smug look of disdain returned to his face.

"Damitus, while you are correct that Vitus is a fool, you have been flaunting your power and disregard for our authority. You've had our leniency in the past and freedom to roam as you please, but that ends today. You are not born of a respectable family, nor do not have a family history of payments in donation to the Magisterium. The fact is that we do not know where you come from, and the lies you have told about your past have been overlooked because of your skill."

The Archon was confident and pompous in his piety. His long robes laced with gold and jewels, elegantly flowing to the floor. *How could the man not see the need for his proposals? Even one of them would have allowed Damitus to further his plans. He did not expect his request for a unit that he could train to be accepted the first time he proposed it, but he expected to have his request for an expedition east to be at least considered.*

"Not only am I going to refuse your proposals, but from this day on, you will report to Vitus. He, at least, is highborn and understands his station and he is dedicated to the magisterium. He knows how to succeed through Imperial law while you simply ignore it."

Report to Vitus? No, he was less than a peer to Damitus. He tensed as he felt his plan quickly beginning to backfire on him.

"You will go nowhere without logging it with the Venesterium as new wizards are supposed to, and Vitus will be required to approve any trips or assignments you take. Perhaps this will teach you the respect for the Empire and the system that you live within. Teach you to respect the archons and magic above all else."

Damitus grimaced at the threatened leash to be thrown about his neck. *It was a mistake coming to Cicero. How could he have been foolish enough not to see the man as a powerful zealot?*

He had to turn this situation around, and quickly. Only three of them were in the archon's Sanctum, one of which was frozen and did not even know Damitus was there. Only he and the archon were aware of this conversation.

"If you will not consider my proposals and are not open to discussing them, then I will bring them to a wiser Archon," Damitus said.

The archon looked as if he was close to laughing at Damitus's suggestion.

"You will do no such thing. I will inform the other archons of your transgressions and insolence to ensure your assignment to Vitus is respected."

Damitus tensed his muscles as he prepared his next comment.

"You will be unable to do that if you are dead…"

The condescension and annoyance vanished from the archon. His eyes darkened and lip curled as his face took on a cold deadly glare.

Damitus could feel the energy in the room charge. He knew he stood little chance against a full archon, even with his considerable control over magic.

Before the archon had time to go on the offensive, he began the swing of his arm across his body, as he spoke his spell and poured his emotions into it.

"Li'ali awyr," Damitus said.

Fire. Air.

"Tavyan thwur," Cicero said.

Protection. Water.

"Awyr," Damitus said.

Air.

They spoke their spells in less than a heartbeat, both at the same moment. Fire erupted from the palm of Damitus, air blowing it forth as he swung his arm across his body.

A barrier of water and energy sprung up in front of the archon, extinguishing the fire and blocking anything from entering it.

No magic that Damitus could throw at the archon would penetrate the shield the man controlled.

As the archon stared at Damitus, his look of confidence and contempt returned. He looked about to snicker. Damitus showed a defeated face, but the expression became deceptive as he turned his lips into a grin.

The archon made a motion as if to laugh, but no sound left his mouth. Instead, there was a strangled coughing noise, followed by a gurgle. Then blood sprayed from the archon's mouth and his eyes looked forth in terror.

A blade protruded from the archon's upper chest.

Damitus knew the fire would never have engulfed the archon, nor would have the thrown blade he had flung from within his sleeve as he enacted the spell. But the blade, with a spell to push it forward, would pierce the shield. Strength of mind and body.

He smiled at his ability to prove the exact point he had been trying to make to the archon.

Archon Cicero's eyes rolled back, and he crumpled as he fell to a heap on the floor. A pool of blood formed beside the man's body. Damitus admired his work.

Damitus pulled the blade from the chest of the corpse, then he approached the still frozen Vitus. He took the blood from the knife and smeared it on Vitus's frozen robe. Lastly, he placed the blade hilt in the hand of Vitus that was opened just enough to fit it. Vitus had not even known Damitus had been there. He smiled at the thought of the shock the man was about to experience when Damitus left, and the spell wore off.

Damitus would take his proposal to another archon. Besides, a spot had just opened on the council for a new archon, and if it could not be him, he would ensure it was a wizard that would be receptive to his plans.

He walked to the door of the sanctum, quietly opened it, and passed out of the room, walking down the stone hall. Before he was gone, he heard Vitus's shrill scream of terror from far behind him.

CHAPTER 17
MISTAKES

Three Years Later
725: Year of the Second Era

There was a ringing sound in Fae's ears, and the taste of blood, sand, and dirt all mixed in her mouth. She tried moving her tongue around to build up enough saliva to clear it. She felt the hard-packed ground of the training arena as it pressed against her face. Her skull throbbed from the recent blow she had received. Kiva stood above her in full combat gear, grinning as she opened and closed the hand that had just pummeled Fae's face.

"Get up, princess. That was only one punch. You can do better than that," Kiva said.

Kiva was usually the nicest one to Fae, watching over her like she was a sister too; but in the ring, she was ruthless. She became a different person, the kind version of Kiva transformed into a cruel and taunting opponent, saying terrible things and playing with her adversary; never ending the fight as quickly as she could. Fae wondered if it wasn't really Erika that stood over her in the ring right then.

"She's doing it to help you," Jaxon had told her. "You are easily provoked, and she is teaching you to control your emotions. Your anger is powerful, but you have to control it. Channel it."

Fae had a hard time believing Jaxon at the moment.

"Come on Fae. Get up," she heard Jaxon say.

He called from the sidelines, watching the fight from a broken log. Bullock and Erika had headed off elsewhere for some free time, but Jaxon had talked Fae into getting some more practice in. Part of his ongoing attempt to help train her.

Fae looked at her arm and the leather bracer upon it. Her nana's green gem of the amulet glistened in it. Once Fae had finally trusted Sara enough to part with the amulet for a day, Sara had built a small crown in her bracer to house the pendant. It was now with her always but did not have a risk of getting caught on anything in a fight. It encouraged her to get back up.

Fae pressed her palms against the soil and pushed, heaving herself to her knees and then quickly up to a crouch. She scooped up her dropped training sword. Kiva stood over her, waiting for her to stand back up.

Fae had learned to face the others, using her strengths to her advantage, and trying to avoid her weaknesses. The other three pack members had strength over Fae, but she had learned to be faster. Fae had won almost half of the fights with Erika, Jaxon, or Bullock lately.

But with Kiva, it was different. A part of her loved Kiva because Kiva had been the one to take Fae under her wing besides Jaxon. Kiva had taught Fae a fighting style that used speed over strength, but that had no advantage against Kiva. Fae was fast, Kiva was faster. Fae was nimble, Kiva was nimbler. Kiva may be weaker than the others in the pack, but Fae was weaker still.

Kiva knew better how to use her advantages and hide her disadvantages than Fae did which only added to Fae's frustration.

As Fae rose to her feet, she glared at Kiva, standing there taunting her.

"Why don't you just stay laying down," Kiva said. "That's what they teach you Imperial brats, isn't it?"

Anger surged through Fae, and she lunged for Kiva with abandon. She swung her sword wildly as she moved; anything to penetrate Kiva's guard. Back and forth, executing combinations she had learned.

Fae's pressure mounted, forcing Kiva back as she continued the assault. Just as she broke through Kiva's guard, she hesitated. Barely noticeable, but she felt it in her mind.

Like a swan beating a wing, Kiva brought her sword up to deflect Fae's away. Kiva sidestepped Fae's charge, drawing Fae closer. She swung her fist around as she turned and connected with Fae's skull. Right in the same spot Fae had taken the previous hit.

Fae saw a flash of light and pain and, as she was crumpling forward, Kiva brought her sword back down in a hard strike to Fae's side. She gasped in pain and collided with the ground, winded. She squirmed there coughing and trying not to sob as her eyes watered.

Kiva laughed at Fae. "You are not even thinking now, just flailing about like a fish out of water. What did you expect would happen?"

Fury flashed across her mind again and she remembered Jaxon's words. "Use the anger. Do not let it use you. Do not let it control you but focus rage into clarity and determination." Fae couldn't help but feel frustrated by how easy Jaxon made it seem, however, she recalled the story he had once shared with her about how he had also struggled with managing his emotions. As a young boy, an older, stronger girl had taunted him. Her aim had been to teach him to control his emotions. Now, he spoke of her fondly for helping him learn to use his anger instead of letting it use him.

She found Jaxon's words often annoying, but she would try. Fae slowed her breathing to a calm tempo and cleared her mind, bringing herself back under control. She rose from the ground again to the same crouching position. *Could she use her anger, channel it, to break through her fear and hesitancy?*

"Maybe Axton should have just left you there to die, like the rest of your worthless people," Kiva said.

"Kiva, you're supposed to be taunting her, not emotionally crippling her," Jaxon said, but Fae did not hear him.

She wanted to scream at Kiva, rip her to pieces. But she tried to control it. Fae envisioned her rage as a ball inside her. She wrapped it, rolled it, held it in reserve.

This time, when she lunged forward in the same manner, she had a measure of control. She swung her sword forward once more. Kiva deflected it away, but instead of being redirected herself, Fae let go of her sword. She had a stronger weapon; her controlled ball of rage. She unleashed it.

The move surprised Kiva and Fae crashed into her chest hard. The two girls went down together in a tackle, and Fae let loose. Kiva tried to lift her head from the ground after the fall, but Fae's fist knocked it back down, once again colliding with the ground. The redhead tried to bring her fists up to protect herself, but Fae, straddling her, continued to bring down a barrage of fists. Kiva blocked some, but she could not stop every hit.

Fae punched harder and harder. Over and over. An alarm rang in Fae's mind.

Kiva went limp, but Fae didn't stop. Her mind screamed in horror at what she was doing, but her fists carried on. Just as her punches started to slow, she felt something large hit her in the side.

Jaxon tackled her, pulling her off Kiva. They tumbled, and he rolled on top of her. He pinned her arms to the ground.

Fae's rage peaked once more, anger at Kiva, anger at Jaxon, and most of all, anger at herself. Fae screamed a horrid scream in Jaxon's face, but he remained impassive with only a look of sadness. Her scream transitioned into a wail, and finally a cry as sobs crashed over her body. Jaxon released her arms and she curled into the fetal position and wept.

From her position on her side, she could see Kiva's body, lying limp, her facial features hard to make out after all the blood blended in with her red hair. She tried to yell out, but only sobs came from her now.

Fae could hear Jaxon's low voice yelling something, but it was dulled like she was listening to the world through a cushion. Her focus was solely on Kiva's motionless body. Footsteps thumped around her, and she heard more calls from other people.

After some time, Fae felt large hands pick her up. The person was big, probably Rock or Axton, but Fae did not care who it was at that moment. The world was blurry when she opened her eyes, her vision obstructed by tears. She closed her eyes once more, too distraught to keep them open.

The pace of the footsteps of the person who carried her was soothing, but she felt unworthy of any comfort. *Who was she becoming?*

Finally, the person placed her down on a soft bed of furs, then walked away. Just for a moment, she opened her eyes. She was not in her pack's tent; it was a tent of a single occupant. She saw an axe in the corner with a familiar filigree and a braided ribbon on it; Axton's axe. He must have carried her to his tent to get her away.

She closed eyes once more and just laid there, crying. She sobbed for what felt like an eternity, the pit in her stomach aching so much that she almost choked on her cries. Part of her wished she could die. Eventually, with her body so wracked with guilt and fatigue, she fell asleep.

Twenty-four hours had passed since she had put Kiva in Cairn's medical tent and Fae was once again in the sparring ring. Cairn and his apprentice had seen to Kiva, setting her nose, and bandaging her with medical salves in cloth. Cairn said Kiva could still count fingers so there was no damage to her brain, and she should heal up in time.

They allowed Fae to see Kiva. She had been asleep, but Cairn had said she was awake earlier and was not upset as long as she would still look identical to Erika, so they could still carry out their mischievous pranks.

That would have made Fae laugh, had it not been for the pain and fear inside her. Fear wrapped with many more complicated emotions. She wanted to be as strong as the others, but what had happened terrified her.

Jaxon and Erika had been distant since the incident but Axton had talked to her when she woke in his tent and told her not to sulk when she had cried that she could have killed Kiva.

"But you didn't kill Kiva," Axton had said, "and that was what Jaxon was there for. He did his job and Kiva will learn not to let her guard down when she thinks she has control of the battle."

Their calmness made Fae uncomfortable; they acted as if it was just something that happened. She suspected that she would have felt better if she had been yelled at.

"Do not sulk, Fae," Axton had said. "Your guilt does not help you. You lost control of your anger. You let it control you. It happens. You need to keep working on it, but it happens. Just learn from this and don't let it happen again. But don't sulk. You need to get your head together and get back to it."

Now she stared across the combat ring at Bullock. Rock and Jaxon sat on a bench nearby, likely ready to carry out their duties like Jaxon had yesterday. Jaxon was still watching her strangely, like he was watching to better understand something. It unnerved Fae.

Her stomach ached with the guilt she felt from the previous day, and fear grasped her as she worried they would banish her from the Clan if she could not *get her head back together,* as Axton had put it.

She knew it was affecting her; her legs felt weak and not spread out very well. Fae held her arms too close to her sides and didn't shield herself adequately. She heard Jaxon's voice from their practices together, pointing out things for her to improve. She could hear his voice and knew what to fix, but everything felt off and wrong.

Bullock stood facing her with a quizzical look on his face, likely noticing her poor form. He seemed to make up his mind about something and focus replaced his previous expression. He charged her.

They were both unarmed. He charged in for a tackle. Her muscle memory kicked in and her body dodged to the side. Bullock's body passed by her without making contact.

It was a feeble charge by Bullock. Fae realized he was going easy on her, but it had shaken her out of her stupor.

Bullock had turned back around to face her now and was throwing weak, slow punches and hooks, harassing her more than actually posing a threat. Fae slid from side to side and under the punches, but she found it hard to gather her strength to throw attacks herself.

A low kick, she raised her own leg to block. Back-step. Duck a punch. Duck another. Back-step to build space.

Bullock said nothing, just looked focused and continued his weak assaults. Leaving her plenty of places to land a counter. But she didn't.

Finally, Bullock sped up. He swung his left. Fae threw an arm to block. Then he came in with the right. This one hit. But again, it was not hard. She had only been hit because she herself was slow today.

More attacks. Another fist connected, this time against her shoulder. Finally, one hit the side of her head, annoying her more than anything. He was egging her on.

More punches and kicks. Finally, Fae tossed off a punch then parried the next, then got inside his fists and connected with Bullock's right temple. Not hard, but it was enough for him to ease the assault for a moment.

"Bullock," Fae said, "I'm not in the mood today. We should just fight another day."

"No can do, Fae. Axton gave me specific orders to take you through the paces."

"Since when can a Bandorian give out a direct order like that?" Fae asked.

"He can't. It was more like guidance, but right now, between you and him, I figure he is the one thinking more clearly right now. Probably not a bad idea to listen to him."

Fae got under another punch, slid to Bullock's side, and delivered a hard punch to the side of his ribs. He staggered.

"Good Fae," Bullock said. "That is looking better. Another one now."

It was working. Her mind was clearing as she fought. They continued back and forth. She remained on the defence as they sparred, only delivering hits when she countered a punch he threw.

Her mind stopped focusing on her mistake from the previous day and she began to feel better. She finally went on the offensive; punches, jabs, hooks. She pushed Bullock back. He was back to fighting her with his full skills, using his strength to block her hits, trying to keep up with her speed.

Finally, Fae saw an opening. Bullock had been a fraction of a second too slow, bringing his guard back up after he had thrown a punch. She saw the space open to his face. She swung her fist, putting all of her strength behind it.

Her energy and channeled rage flickered to life again and helped her strength. But then an image of Kiva's bloody face flashed in her mind. Terror came with it. Crashing over her and making her heart hurt. She was inches away from connecting with Bullock's face. She hesitated. The punch never landed as she held it back.

Wrong move.

Bullock's counterpunch connected. Hard.

Everything went hazy.

It had been two weeks since Fae had injured Kiva. Kiva was recovering nicely, but Fae was unable to finish a fight since that day. She could not make herself fully engage any time she trained. Every time she tried to tap into her emotions and control them, she pulled back, not putting strength into her attacks.

She had scared herself that day. Something in her mind had put up a barrier. She wanted so badly to be a member of the clan, but something about being a Bandorian scared her. When she met Axton, she told herself she would join them, she would learn from them and become strong enough to survive, then she would figure out if she wanted to continue or leave for another life. But she had not thought about another life for some time. She had almost forgotten that she had once had another plan. These people had destroyed her home, and she had not intended on loving them and calling them family.

She had hoped that losing today's sparring match again Erika would help her feel better, having let Erika get some revenge for her sister. Erika did not seem to be into revenge as much as just keeping Fae on her toes, but her body had taken a thrashing and still there was no relief from her emotional turmoil.

She had also felt nervous and shameful; Axton had been there to watch the match. She did not know why he was there, but presumed it had something to do with whether they should continue to bother training her.

Fae was wiping her face dry after the failed sparring match when she heard Axton call out.

"Fae."

She had been ready to go pack it in for the day at her bunk, but she turned to look back at Axton and saw him standing off by himself. The others had picked up their equipment and headed back into the school building.

"Sit," Axton said.

He motioned to a log bench beside himself, indicating that she should join him, and dread grew inside her. Fae approached, and Axton sat himself down. She took her seat beside him.

"Fae, I know you are..." Axton paused, appearing to search for the correct word, "conflicted. You have come to love your family here, but you also have a rage for the Bandorian people for what happened to your town, family, and old life. And, at times, a rage for the Empire as well."

Fae did not speak but hung her head and rested it in her palms.

"Firstly, what you are feeling... It's real, and it's understandable. I have not spoken of that night to you since I found you, only because I did not feel a need to excuse our actions. We did what we did because it was the best choice for us to make at the time. I will say, because it may help you, that we did not intend on burning your town. We will destroy an outpost or military keep, but we will not burn helpless villages. There is no honour or challenge in attacking those that cannot defend themselves. But that night, things got out of control. The wizard unleashed an inferno, and it spread without mercy. We don't burn towns, but our actions led to that result.

"For what it is worth, I am sorry that we have hurt you. But I cannot regret any action that has led to you being here with us. Your pack loves you and so do the rest of us."

"You will have to deal with this conflict in you forever, but you can either fight against it, or accept it as part of yourself. You fear losing control, becoming too much like the part of us you hate. But that is why we teach control. Your emotions are powerful, but only until they take control of you. Then they are a weakness."

Axton put his arm around Fae.

"Axton. What I did to Kiva... I... She could have..."

"It is behind us now. You cannot change the past, but you can learn from it."

"But..." The objection died on her lips as she looked up at his grizzled face. "Control? How do you... how do the others control it?"

"With practice. Jaxon has struggled before as well. Look to him for help. Now get some rest. And get back at it tomorrow."

Axton got up and walked away, leaving her there, alone with her thoughts.

Was Axton callous? He had no profound or simple solutions but expected her to deal with her problems. But he was not uncaring. He understood her conflict, as well as she understood it herself. How did he do that?

A thought resurfaced within her, one that had lain dormant since her arrival. *She had joined the Bandorians because they were the best option, but was it who she wanted to become? She was not sure. But for now, she would learn how they could control their emotions. She would practice and grow.*

That night, Axton leaned against a tree, arms crossed, one hand stroking his beard. In the distance, Jaxon, Fae, and their pack chased each other around the fire and between the tents. He had made the right decision. Fae had seemed more confident since he had spoken with her.

Axton heard someone approach him from behind.

"Did you tell her?" Brakan asked Axton.

"I told her enough. I told her what I know." Axton said.

"But not what you suspect?"

Axton didn't reply immediately. *Should he have told Fae everything? Told her that the Venesterium burned the town on purpose and killed the witnesses? No. It was only speculation, anyway.*

"No." Axton took a deep breath. "She has enough rage in her, we saw that when she put Kiva down. I told her what would help her control her emotions, that we did not intend for her town to be destroyed. Telling her everything would just increase her anger. She already must live with her grief; I don't want to poke the wound."

That was only half of the truth. He also feared her rage. Feared it consuming her. He had seen it before, in his first apprentice. He needed delicacy and patience to avoid a similar outcome.

"You are going to have to tell her, eventually."

Axton sighed.

"I will, when she is older."

Brakan did not push the issue further. They stood together and watched the children dance around the fire light together for a time before they moved to the circle and joined the others.

CHAPTER 18
THE NEW ASSIGNMENT

*C*runch.

Captain Titus's metal greave covered foot stepped down on the darkened earth, a cloud of ash and soot swirled up from his step, lit in firelight from the nearby flames shimmering in the dark of night. He kept up his pace, searching for something still living or at the very least not destroyed in all the burning rubble. Houses all around him had collapsed into ash.

Titus reached an armoured hand to a collapsed roof and grasped a wooden beam with his hand. Protected by the fitted glove on his hand, he pulled it back to reveal the inside of the building. Nothing. Only more charred furniture, burning rooms, and two skeletons. The smell of burned meat hit like the heat of an oven first opened with his face not pulled back enough.

Nothing but the dead.

How long had he been searching this town? Everything was destroyed. Burned. No one lived, only the empty eye sockets of skeletons tormented his desperate search. He stepped back from the burned building and tossed the beam to the side. The roof caved in just a little more.

He turned to the road to continue his search. A gangly boy with eyes of black stared back at him.

The sight gave Titus a start. He stumbled back and fell into a seat against the remains of the burning building he had just searched. Sparks flew at him from the impact, but they did not burn where they contacted his skin.

The boy's hair seemed to have burned off, black scorch marks covered his skin, and what was left of his clothes seemed to have mostly been burned away. His skin was further covered in dark red burns. It surprised Titus that the boy was still alive. Though his eyes were black and dark, like the haunting look of the skeletons. Tears ran down the young boy's cheeks. An arrow was also embedded in the boy's left side, which forced the boy to stand with a hunch to his left.

"Why did you do this to us?" the boy asked. "Mr. Titus, we thought you would protect us. You were supposed to save us. But you murdered everyone I loved. Shot them down where they stood and allowed them to burn in the fire instead of dying quickly by blade."

"I didn't... I didn't..." Titus tried to speak.

"Titus. You murdered them. You slaughtered all of them." The boy looked around and more tears poured down his burned and cracked face. "You murdered me, sir. Condemned us all to death and damnation."

Titus could not speak. He just looked around at the hellish landscape surrounding him. He recognized it now. Titus was back in the remains of Creet.

"No!" Titus bellowed.

His yell started out dulled, like it was not quite real, before his panic forced it louder until he could hear it in his own ears. He was ripped awake, and he bit down on his voice. His scream had broken out of his dream into the waking world; he had been yelling in his sleep.

His sheets were covered in sweat and he could feel the slick moisture covering his face. In a panic, Titus looked to his side, hoping he had not woken up Hadriana.

He breathed a sigh of relief when he saw his wife was still sleeping soundly beside him in his bed, her soft brown hair framing her face perfectly on her pillow.

It had been months since he'd had this dream and he had hoped it would fade away. After all, it had been four years since the destruction of Creet and he had told himself many times that it was not his fault; he had followed orders. If he had not done it, they would have just found someone else to have done it.

The boy in his dream had not been real, but he knew that in some ways the boy had been more than real. It had not been one child that died that day in Creet, but hundreds. He had seen the skeletons when they entered the town. They haunted his dreams, and he deserved it.

What was worse was the lies they had forced him to tell. That the atrocities committed there had been done by barbarians. That they had arrived too late, and the only arrows fired by them were into the chests of the fleeing barbarians.

Titus reached for a firestick to light a candle. His ignited it and held it out to the candle but his hand shook. Rage grew in him as he tried to force it to steady. *Why couldn't he make his hand stay still?* Guilt, anger, and frustration mingled together. It did not make the hand any less shaky.

Finally, he lit the candle and sat on the edge of his bed. With his elbows perched on his knees, he leaned forward and buried his head in his hands.

When he pulled his hands away, they had tears in them. His hands had stopped shaking, but his knee was vibrating. *Dammit.*

Titus turned his head to look at his wife. She was beautiful in her own way, especially now that she was sleeping and not angry with him. It seemed she was always angry with him, unless she was disappointed with him.

They had grown apart in the last few years. He wanted to blame her; she had no compassion for him anymore; she did not seem to care for him like she once had. *But was that her fault?* He had changed since Creet. He could not tell her what had happened. Instead, he distanced himself, became a weaker man, less confident and, most importantly, he did not have the playful spirit he once had. The spirit that she had fallen in love with. *Why couldn't she love him now when he needed it the most? How could she love him the way he needed, when she did not even know what troubled him? Dammit all. He could not burden her with the knowledge that he held.*

He could tough it out. For her sake. That is what she would want him to do, wasn't it?

No. Yes? He wasn't sure.

She had loved him once, and he had loved her. It had been so strong. But how could he get back to that? They had shared their burdens once. All of them. Until Creet. He would have to share this burden with her. He would tell her first thing in the morning while their son played in his room.

It would be hard, but she was suffering from what had happened anyway, she just did not know why. It was only right that she understood her own suffering. Their relationship might not survive this, but if he did not tell her, it was a certainty that it would not survive.

As soon as they woke in the morning, he would tell her.

He did not have any more dreams that night. In fact, he hardly slept at all.

The whistle of the kettle made Titus grimace, hoping it had not woken up Hadriana. Quickly, he grabbed the cloth to protect his strong, callused hands and lifted the pot off its hook above the fire.

He carried it to the counter and poured it into the teapot to steep beside two teacups. Then, he returned the pot to its place and leaned over the counter, looking out the window. The aroma from the tea wafted up to his nose and helped him relax. He was afraid of what he knew he had to do.

He heard a noise through the door of his son's room off the kitchen. A soft clack and a muted grunt. The six-year-old was playing with the wooden sword that Titus had made for him during the time off last month. He had a stable position now as instructor, training younger recruits to merge their units into cohesive platoons and battalions. Titus would have much time still in the capital and at home before he would have to be sent for duty once more. He would need the time to work on his relationship with his wife once he shared this with her. She was beautiful and charming, and Titus knew other men would take her hand if he let his marriage fall apart.

Yes, now was the time to do it, to tell his wife. His son was playing in the room. The sun was coming up over the city and shining through the kitchen window. Things were right. Titus poured some of the now steeped tea into both cups.

Titus lifted the one cup to his mouth. He let the warm liquid pass between his lips and fill his soul like a glow that spread through his body. The tea was relaxing.

Titus grabbed the second cup to make his way to his and Hadriana's room.

Rap, rap, rap.

Three hard knocks at the door.

Titus paused. He waffled between continuing to the bedroom and turning to address the person at the door. He had been prepared to talk to Hadriana, but the fear of the task and the curiosity of the visitor tipped him back.

It is probably just a messenger.

He moved to ignore the door and continue to the bedroom when the knock came again. He put the two teacups back down, crossed the room to the door, and began unlatching it.

The large wooden door swung easily on its well-oiled hinges to reveal an outfitted soldier, with a proud draw to his shoulders, golden filigree on his segmented plates of armour, and an ornamental cape draped over his back.

"Commander Augustus," Titus said.

He stammered and could not hide his surprise at seeing his reporting officer at his door. Titus opened the door further to avoid being rude.

"Please, sir, come in. I just put on some tea."

"Not now, Titus. I have other tasks to accomplish, yet this morning. I don't have time for niceties."

"Of course, sir. What can I do for you?"

"Titus, your current assignment as an instructor at the academy has come to a close. You are to ship out immediately."

"Wha... What? Ship out where?"

Titus strained to keep his composure and not let his voice crack. It was still early in the morning, and he had not been up long.

"You will be helping set up an outpost just a few hours' march east of Southshore."

"An outpost? Surely, they could send anyone to do that. Why would they want me to take that assignment when I am doing important work with the recruits here?"

The commander did not give an immediate answer. The air between them felt uncomfortable suddenly.

"Commander," Titus said, "Why are you here? Why did they not simply send a messenger here to tell me of this?"

The commander let out a sigh. Titus had just reached the heart of an issue.

"Titus, we have watched you over the last few weeks and we do not feel you are ready to take on the assignment of instructor at the academy. You have consistently failed to meet military objectives."

"Well, sure, but we usually solve the overall problem given to the units. I have done my duty to keep my men safe and cohesive."

The commander ignored his protests. Instead, he made a pinched expression, grimaced, and gave a heavy sigh.

"We worry you lack what it takes to be an instructor and perhaps even what is required to be a captain."

"What? But I have been a captain for years now. And how can you judge my skills as an instructor? I have just started. Sure, my platoon has performed subpar on a few drills, but they have picked it up and are adequate. How is that different from other new instructors?"

"We rarely start an instructor here in the capital. They selected you to start here as opposed to gaining the experience elsewhere."

"And you judge me by the first few weeks?"

"We judge you by how you instruct. You are lenient with your men. They are free to raise opinions and bring up troubles with you with no form of consequence for their interruption."

Titus was at a loss for words. *He was being stripped of the assignment for what? For treating his men with respect?*

"Titus, you are too... nice."

Commander Augustus said the word nice with a sound of derision, like it was a pathetic quality to have. It made Titus feel ashamed, but also enraged. Sweat collected under his armpits as he tensed his muscles to control his anger and keep a calm face. He feared showing a loss of emotional control to his superior.

"What?" Titus asked. "Commander, I don't think kindness is making my troops underperform."

"Titus, yesterday when you were off, we had Captain Remulus take command of your platoons at the academy."

"But my platoons had the day off. So did I."

"That was easy enough to remedy since they all sleep in the dorms in the academy. We woke them and got them to training with Remulus."

Titus clenched his hand ever so subtly and forced himself to breathe slowly, almost shaking. Rage filled him at the thought of Remulus and the commanders going behind his back to test his men when he was not there. Especially on a day that his men were supposed to have off.

"The lack of obedience and discipline in your men was atrocious. They immediately questioned Remulus and were slow to follow his commands. Remulus saw some improvements when he expelled the worst recruit from the army and submitted the second worst recruit to ten lashes to make examples."

Titus wanted to scream at the commander. He had doomed the man they had expelled. The military was likely the man's only hope of being able to afford food and shelter. He would starve to death. If he was lucky, he might sell several years into servitude.

Titus had to use all his willpower to keep control of his rage. His body wanted to clench his fists and flare his nostrils, but he had to remain dutiful, in control. Titus hoped his commander would burn in the Abyss.

Titus did not want to hear any more. Arguing further would just hurt his cause with this man, as they had shown by expelling his platoon trainee. He could not afford to be expelled from the army; his son would starve and his wife would end in another man's bed, whether from marriage or forced prostitution.

"What are my orders, sir?"

"You are to grab your essentials and come with me. You will then pack equipment from the barracks and join a company making their way to Southshore where you will be escorted to the outpost."

"Right now? I can't report to the barracks later today? My wife is not even up yet."

"Titus, you need to figure out where your loyalties lie. Show some commitment for Deus's sake. We would have expelled you from service if it were not for your long years of service so far, but that does not mean that we will not. We are more than comfortable having a conversation with you about finding a place where you will be a better fit."

No. Titus could not lose his position, he could not afford it.

"Sorry, sir. Of course."

"Good. Now I recommend you write a note to your wife and grab your bag. I will give you five minutes, but if you get tied up in a conversation with your wife, I will not wait, and it will be a different discussion that we have when you see me next."

Titus gritted his teeth but forced himself not to let anything show on his face.

"Of course, sir. Thank you. I will be back shortly."

He turned back to the kitchen, grabbed a scrap of parchment and some charcoal. He scribbled a quick note, then he grabbed a few essentials and was out the door.

CHAPTER 19
COUNCIL OF ARCHONS

Two Years Later
727: Year of the Second Era

Damitus stood in the antechamber of the Magisterium's Hall of Archons, staring out the window, down on Emor, the seat of the Empire. The Golden City. He thought the name was self-serving as he looked at it. The Inner Palace and the Autumn Court were indeed golden, with pillars and statues of ivory and marble capped with gold. Even the inner city was a display of the opulence of the Empire, with its mansions spreading to the inner wall. No shortage of wealth was on display in the architecture of those that lived there.

But beyond the inner city to the outer city and the suburbs, poverty was visible. The stone buildings ranged from simple grey colors, some looking acceptable, to the ghettos where many of its inhabitants were born and had never ventured beyond the neighbourhood their birth had trapped them in. The dirt and much of the roads blended with the bodies of the starving. Beyond the outer walls, people were more mobile but equally poor, with only small scatterings of towns that had something to sell, making them profitable enough to keep the poor out.

So much potential, wasted on an Empire blinded by its own greatness.

The council of archons made him wait. *They would make him wait for hours if it was of convenience to them, his time being meaningless to them, but Damitus had what they did not; patience.* After what was likely close to an hour of waiting, the door finally opened and a lean-looking servant dressed in upper class clothing, he likely could not afford himself, popped out.

"Master Damitus?"

"That I am."

"The council will see you now."

The servant opened the door further and held it to allow Damitus to enter.

"Thank you," Damitus said.

Damitus walked through the archway into a large circular central area of a vast hall. Like an amphitheatre, stairs covered the outside of the circle leading up and away from him towards the outside walls. Several feet above his head on the outer edges were the twelve daises of the archons of the Magisterium Council. All were occupied save one. Each of the archons looked down upon him, waiting for him to begin.

"Council members," Damitus said. "I thank you for this audience. I have come with information and with counsel…" He let his words hang, wanting to pull on their attention just enough. "And to take my rightful seat as an archon on this council."

There were rustles around the court at his statement. Council members looked between each other, some covering their faces with sheets of parchment as they whispered to colleagues.

Finally, one archon spoke up, "Settle please."

He waited for the other archons to quiet down.

"Damitus," Archon Marcellus said. "You come to us and demand the rank of archon? We elect our own and take counsel on this from no one. What case do you have for this demand?"

"I have done more and accomplished more than any other non-archon in the entire Magisterium," Damitus said. "While other mages, magi, and acolytes waste time studying the exact information we already know to master what you have already mastered, I have learned about the very nature of magic. I have studied the history of the universe and pushed the boundaries of our understanding of magic. These would sound like nothing but empty platitudes if stated by other mages, but you know... you know the truth of what I speak. Many of you yourselves fear how much I know and the powers I wield."

"I know more about our enemies than any on this court. I have found our enemies to the east, and we will need to deal with them in time. But they are not what threatens you now. As we speak, an army grows on our western border, hidden in the vastness of the dead hills that you have no sight into and have made small expanses into. You think the forts and outposts recently created, pushing into the dead hills, will stop them, but they are an enemy like no other you have ever faced. They have tricked you before, posing as mindless barbarians, you have faced less than a tenth of their forces, and they allowed you to think them defeated. They were just testing you."

More rustling about the court, until Marcellus raised his hand for silence. "Even if there are more of them, what threat do men pose to Gods such as us that wield the forces of nature?"

"You call yourself a God, but these barbarians have already killed the High Wizard of Creet, and that was less significant. They have also killed an archon."

More whispers of shock and confusion as the archons looked from left to right, attempting to see if an archon was missing. None were.

"No archon has ever been killed by an enemy," Archon Marcellus said.

"Hasn't one?" Damitus asked.

More confusion.

"Tell me then, who killed Archon Cicero?"

"Archon Cicero was killed by Mage Vitus. They found him standing over his master with the murder weapon in his hand."

"Again, they fool you. Why would Vitus stand there in shock after killing his master? He could not have killed him with a simple dagger, and where had the dagger even come from? They reported they did not know its making or origin."

The auditorium was silent, archon's hanging on his words. *Good.*

"I am not telling you this because I am speculating. I tell you because I know these things. This enemy does exist, and they have the skills to kill archons. You have magic but have no power of might. They have power of might and no magic. They will evenly match you unless you make me an archon and follow my counsel."

Damitus thrust his fist forward. "Give me the title. That I might access the entirety of our knowledge, including that which is restricted to all but the archons. I will help you overcome these coming threats." He punctuated his points and let them echo throughout the hall, then let the hall fall silent.

He waited patiently as the archons whispered to one another and notes of paper were passed back and forth. After more whispers, he received a response.

"Damitus," Archon Marcellus said. "We expected this bid from you. We deny your request for the rank of archon."

"What foolishness is this? Did you not hear what I just said?"

"You are unpredictable, and you do as you wish. Often accomplishing assignments you should not have been able to succeed at."

"Surely this only strengthens my case."

"But mystery and uncertainty surround you at every step. You hide much. We admit you are among the best of our wizards, but we cannot grant you full access to the restricted texts until you have earned our trust."

Damitus had to suppress a smile at the comment. They did not know; he had played his part well. He had gained access to the restricted texts years ago. Combinations of assisting certain archons while simultaneously blackmailing them had allowed him to compromise members of the council already, but he knew the value of playing the part of the person your enemies thought you to be. *He had to continue the ruse.*

Damitus looked around the council at the eyes of the members. He saw the awareness in those that he had under his thumb already. Them knowing the falsity of the statements made by the archon.

"Your lack of trust in me does not negate the genuine threat at your doorstep. What plan do you have for that?"

"Damitus, do not assume that you know everything. You are not the only mage studying the nature of magic and what boundaries have yet to be tested. We have other ways to defend against enemies, weapons that have never been used or seen."

"What ways are those?"

Damitus had been assured he knew all that was discussed among the council. He looked around the council, watching their eyes. His eyes went to the weakest archon and saw him suppress a nervous look when their gazes met; he had not told Damitus everything. There was something they were hiding.

He knew that, more important than the words being spoken, were the messages hidden in the faces of the council members. If he stayed perceptive to the hidden cues, they may allude to that which he did not know.

He had not expected that they would grant him the title of archon, nor did he actually need it. He already had everything he required and had thought he knew all that was essential; until this. *What was this weapon they spoke of; he did not know, but he soon would.*

Archon Marcellus did not give an answer to his question.

"But of course, my archons," Damitus said, "you have your ways. I thank you for your time and I pray to Deus that some information I provide today can be of use to you. I thank you all for your time.

Damitus looked up at Marcellus and gave a smile, then dipped low in a deep bow. He swept his cloak and walked out the door before they had time to stop him from leaving.

"Thank you, Felix," Damitus said. "That will be all."

The porter left the papers Damitus had requested on his large oak desk, bowed his head, and then turned to leave his sanctum. Felix pulled the door closed, and the room fell silent. The only movement was the dancing shadows on the stone wall cast by collections of lit candles perching on Damitus's desk, illuminating the parchment he looked at.

Damitus finished reading the paragraph he had, then began leafing through the following pages for a reference to the ancient magics. He heard a sound like the smallest of pebbles sliding across dust.

"Tiberius," Damitus said. He did not look up from the parchment he was reading. "You have something for me?"

"Master Damitus," Tiberius said as he slinked out of the shadows behind a bookcase. "How is it you always hear me? Of all my clients, you are the only one that I cannot creep up on."

The slim man had a voice like smooth wine, charming enough to make people forget it is poison.

"And I pay you specifically to ensure no one else knows anything about me, either. I also pay you well to ensure that I am one step ahead of the council and the others of the Empire."

"Ah yes, you pay me well. The only mage that can afford my services. I am obliged to tell you that while your propensity to not waste your money on temptations of the Empire, as your colleagues do, affords you the wealth to pay for my services, it does not endear you to those same colleagues that surround you day to day."

"Tiberius, I hope you have not come here just to tell me I would have more friends if I wasted my money on the events and brothels, as the other mages do."

"Haha. Certainly not my friend. I have come to tell you that whatever your goal in meeting with the council today was, it succeeded in stirring them into a panic after you left. Though I doubt they showed it in the meeting with them."

"They held themselves together quite successfully during the meeting, though I was able to gleam that they were nervous when I mentioned the threats on the borders. They also let slip that they have some sort of magic that they are studying that I am not aware of. I need to know what."

"Oh, my friend. That is excellent to hear. This means I have brought you a very timely present."

While Tiberius's games, to get to the point and play at things, could slow down Damitus' acquisition of knowledge, it did remind him of the playful banter of his youth with the clan. He would play the reluctant patron for now.

"Do tell, my friend," Damitus said.

"Well, I must give credit where credit is due. I learned of this because you clearly put the council into a panic. They usually take more precautions with their information, but a hasty discussion was overheard by one of my spies when agents of the council failed to ensure that no one else was around."

"Excellent."

"He could not hear the entire conversation, but he could determine that the archons were angry at Marcellus for talking about their research. That research seems to be performed as a joint effort between the magi here and the magi in Southshore, with what sounds like most of the effort being taken on by the latter. He also gleaned that they were looking into the magic of life from death. They called it Necrotic magic."

Damitus froze on the words.

"Damitus? Do you know what this is about?"

Damitus did not answer. He just sat in his chair and rubbed his beard with his hand.

"Damitus?"

Finally, Tiberius shook him out of his trance, and Damitus cleared his throat before talking, "I cannot tell anything for certain from what little information this is, but it definitely gives us a great place to start. Necrotic magic can be powerful, but the cost of using it is so high that none have used it in a practical sense."

His fingers curled into a fist, "What are they thinking? How could they even have thought of this? There is only one book in the entire royal library that even references it. They could not have found it somewhere else and how did they even notice it was there?"

He had been through that entire section, and no one had looked through the books in decades. *What recent factor could have convinced them to look through it now? The only new factor would have been... would have been him. Damnation. Did he leave the book out, something to clue them into other powers?*

"It was me."

"What?" Tiberius's eyebrows pressed together. "Damitus?"

"Never mind, it is not important. Thank you for bringing me this. This is exactly the sort of information I need."

His mind was racing. Tiberius seemed to notice and give him a moment.

"Tiberius. I want you to expand our network. We need more spies, but mostly in Southshore. I need to know everything that is going on there. Especially about the necrotic sorcery."

"It will take more funds, my friend."

"Yes, of course. I have a few leads on how to solve that problem. You do what you need to in order to get started and I will gain the funds we need. We must try to take advantage of the panic I have caused. And I want to know who is the next candidate for promotion to archon if they will not allow it to be me. I want to ensure I own whoever they choose."

"Very wise, my friend."

"And Tiberius?"

"Yes, sir?"

"Thank you."

Tiberius settled back in his stance, happy to have served well.

"Of course, my friend." He gave that charming smile once more. "We will next speak once these plans are set in motion."

Tiberius silently opened the window in the back of the sanctum, slipped out and once again closed it behind himself.

CHAPTER 20
PREPARATION

"Are you scared?"

Jaxon's voice was soft and comforting to Fae as she sat facing him on the end of a fallen log by the bonfire.

The sun had long since set, leaving the encampment bathed in flickering firelight. The flames danced majestically, casting an ethereal glow on the walls of the tents and the clan members gathered at the centre of the camp. Shadows and silhouettes of friends and family danced around her, all enjoying the carousing and merriment of the evening bonfire.

The night was cool, but the crackling warmth of the fire kept any thoughts of cold at bay. She couldn't help but cherish the warmth of Jaxon's hands pressed against hers and she gazed down at their entwined fingers.

Both would face the trials the following day and Fae could not hide her fear. Certainly not from him.

"A little," she said hesitantly, then asked in a soft voice, "Are you?"

"A little," Jaxon said.

They both giggled. She appreciated that they could be honest with each other.

She could see the firelight dancing across his handsome face, revealing his soft smile, then hiding it once more. It was nights like this that she marveled at how soft and caring his eyes were, a contrast to his strong, well-defined frame.

She knew that this did not differ from herself, though. The twins had told her frequently that she had a gentle beauty to her, though her body had hardened to a toned physique instead of the awkward and somewhat lanky young girl she had been when she first met her pack six years ago.

They also liked to make her blush by pointing out how, even though she was still the smallest of the five close friends, her body had developed some very noticeable curves. Jaxon and, to a lesser extent, Bullock would occasionally stare her up and down with none of what she would have once called shame. She had learned long ago that none of them had any form of discomfort with bodies.

Fae had butted heads with Jaxon when they first met, his confidence had annoyed her so much back then; *when had things changed?* His compassion had surprised her before, but now it seemed natural. She felt a pull towards him that she did not completely understand.

Fae now looked up into his eyes and she could see the reflection of the fire glisten in them.

He flashed his charming smile back and a flutter of emotions stirred within her. She could not help but notice how much he had grown in the years since the two of them had met. He had shed his former small and scrappy appearance, now standing at the same height as the other men in camp, except Bullock, who had surpassed the height of almost every other member of the clan. Jaxon's frame had broadened, showcasing newfound muscles in his arms and legs. Fae couldn't deny her growing admiration for him, his confident demeanor and increasing stature making him all the more captivating. Yet, she sensed that there was still more growth ahead of him, both physically and, she hoped, intimately with her. It was a silent longing that she kept hidden, knowing that time would reveal what the future held for them both.

"It should be fine, though," Jaxon said. "Mostly, I'm just excited. You should be excited as well. You have trained for this, and you know what you are doing." His words carried a welcome encouragement.

The children had spent several years growing, training, and learning, even returning to Dronoch for a time; though it was never where they had left it. They had stayed through several of the city's migrations, but now they travelled the Craeg with their clan, waiting for their time to become adults in the eyes of their people.

Fae smiled back at Jaxon; she appreciated the reassurance.

"Yes... I'm excited too."

She turned her head to the fire for a moment, then back to his gaze. "I feel like everything that we have done until now is to prepare us for this, so it feels more like a chance to confirm what I already know."

"That's how I feel too."

He spoke quietly to her. She drew her hand gently over his, letting the tip of her finger trace his hand up to his forearm, enjoying the sensation and feel of him. The breeze shifted, and the fire crackled. She felt an ache. She would do anything to survive the trial, even if just for another day to see him again.

Jaxon gave her hands a squeeze and released them as he turned towards where Bullock sat. He was on a tree stump just outside of earshot of their whispers.

Bullock had one twin on each knee, though he looked extremely uncomfortable and like he was not overly pleased with it. He had been sitting there trying to enjoy his ale and socialize with the twins, when they had decided that they needed to get much closer than they knew Bullock was comfortable with. Bullock liked both girls but was so confused by both of their advances that he did not know what he was supposed to do. His cheeks would often turn red, and he could never figure out if they were sincerely interested in him or if they were always just using him as the butt of their jokes. Fae was certain they were doing both.

It seemed to entertain the twins to no end, and Fae found the whole situation beyond amusing. Jaxon also seemed to have it figured out and would often giggle about it with her.

"Besides, if this oaf can pass his trials, then I'm sure any of us can." Jaxon raised his voice so the other three could hear as well. "And the only reason the twins had any trouble with theirs is because they forced them to take the trials separately. They couldn't handle doing anything without the other for the first time."

"It was a mean trick, separating the two of us," Erika said in a pouty voice.

"We do everything together," Kiva continued, mimicking her sister's pout.

"You can't do everything together," Bullock said, as if stating the obvious fact.

The two twins turned their eyes back on Bullock and gave mischievous grins. Kiva replied to him in a sultry suggestive tone, "Can't we?" Both girls then leaned in closer to Bullock. His cheeks immediately turned bright red, and he looked like he was going to die of embarrassment. When the two girls buried their heads in his chest, he looked over at Jaxon with a look that said, 'You have to save me!' Jaxon just shrugged. Bullock was on his own.

Fae covered her mouth with her hand as she giggled, and Jaxon let out a soft laugh at Bullock. *All of them found it entertaining except poor Bullock.*

Fae knew that there were a few interesting romantic arrangements among some of the different clans of Bandor, but she had never heard of two twins being involved with a single person. She was sure there were no rules against it, though. The people of Bandor seemed to encourage whatever romantic relations members wanted to have if those involved agreed to it and no one ever felt lied to or betrayed.

Fae thought more about it. On one hand, it could work well for Bullock since he often could not tell which of the two was which. Even Jaxon could not always tell them apart. Fae seemed to be the only person in the clan that could always tell which was which.

So, at least Bullock would not have to choose between them. But on the flip side, he clearly did not know what to do with this newly found attention he was receiving, and he seemed out of his element with the girls.

This, however, was one issue Bullock would have to figure out himself; or the girls would eventually just tell him what to do. The thought made Fae smirk once more.

Kiva got up and walked over to where Fae was sitting on her log. She plopped down beside Fae, wrapped her arm around Fae, and gave a squeeze.

"You will do great, girl. It is normal to be nervous the night before your trial. Just remember to have fun."

She squeezed Fae's body into hers and Fae rested her head against the taller girl's soft chest and shoulder.

"Thanks, love," Fae whispered to Kiva. "You've helped me so much. I still can't believe you forgave me for—"

"Shh. We don't dwell on things. Besides, if it hadn't happened, we might not have grown as close."

It was true. Though it had taken years for Fae to let go of her guilt over how she had injured Kiva, and even now it was not completely gone, Kiva had fought tirelessly to help Fae overcome it, and in the end, their struggle had forged an unbreakable bond between them.

"You're right," Fae said and gave a smile.

Even though she was trying to put forth a strong face about the situation, she was sure others could tell she was worried about the trials, probably much more worried that any of the others had been. She had not been a Bandorian all her life like they had. *They had been Bandorians from birth, but she had come to them at eleven years old. Eleven years they had on her; was she one of them?*

She had hurt them before. Made mistakes the others did not. She still struggled with the control over her emotions that the others maintained so easily, and still felt lost about who she was sometimes.

She knew Jaxon did not understand how she felt. He tried, but empathy cannot replace the experience of a thing.

Fae wrapped her arms around Kiva's waist, feeling a tight squeeze in return. It felt good to be held in an embrace. She loved her small pack, her family, so much, and she never wanted to be without them. But she was not born of Bandor, and she wondered if the trials would expose her as un-true. She knew of others who had not been born into the culture that had passed the trials and were true Bandorians, but she was the only one of her pack that was not born of Bandorian blood, and she was afraid of failing them.

The other four had been born through selective breeding, with their parents carefully chosen and approved for their physical and mental strength. Fae was the product of chance, an accident in comparison. Her birth lacked the same intentional design as the others, making her feel like an outsider among her own people. She had always been aware of that fact. If she passed the trial, would she still feel that way? She did not know, but being surrounded by the ones she loved, her family, she knew she had to succeed; could accept nothing else. She cared for them too much to let them down, or not come back to them.

The friends spent the rest of that night laughing, talking, singing, and enjoying the revelry until they were tired enough to get the sleep Fae and Jaxon would certainly need.

"Coming to bed?" Sara asked.

"In a moment," Axton said. "Go ahead."

Axton stood back from the bonfire, watching Fae and the two twins dancing by the fire. The girls were trying to convince Bullock to join them, saying something about his dancing prowess.

Jaxon sat on a nearby log, appearing relaxed and content to watch his friends. Lost in a serene daze, he didn't notice Axton approach and take a seat next to him. Startled at first, Jaxon quickly recognized his mentor and a look of familiarity appeared in his eyes. Axton placed a reassuring palm on Jaxon's knee, wanting to provide support even if the boy likely didn't need it.

"So, you ready for your day tomorrow?" Axton asked.

Jaxon looked at his friends dancing and smiled.

"I am."

"That's good to hear, lad."

Axton followed Jaxon's gaze over to where Fae was dancing by the fire. "What about Fae? Is she ready for tomorrow?" Jaxon furrowed his brows, revealing his concern.

"How do you think she will do?" Axon asked.

He unintentionally let a note of concern carry on his voice. It seemed to surprise Jaxon as he turned to stare back at Axton.

"I think she'll be good," Jaxon said. "I know she is capable enough that she should have nothing to fear." He paused for only a moment. "But... I'm certain something is bothering her, or she is afraid. I don't know why, though; she may not even understand it herself."

"Hmm." Axton's reply was non-verbal, but his emotion was thinly veiled within it.

"You care, don't you? You care about her and how she does," Jaxon said.

Axton had over the years realized he, the chieftain of the clan, did indeed have one he cared for specifically. Jaxon had somehow noticed, too.

"Aye lad, you got me. I was the one that found her, saw the potential in her, and brought her into our clan."

A slight smile grew on his face as he looked on to watch her dancing in the firelight; she had an amazing grace to her while also having great strength.

"I watch over her from time to time as a father might do, and I have been immensely proud of how much she has grown. The five of you have helped each other grow much over the years. I will be there to see you both off tomorrow, but as Bao and Brakan will be there wishing you well and proud to see you come back after your time away, I will do the same for Fae, and my heart will feel pride when she returns."

Jaxon seemed to understand. He smiled again, clapped a hand on the larger man's shoulder.

"She will come back, I know it. We both will."

"Aye, I know you both will, lad. It is natural for a father to feel a tinge of worry, but you are right, and I will not dwell on it. I just wanted to come over and make sure she was in good spirits. You will both need your strength and your wits about you."

Fae stood, facing the forest just beyond Clan Kaltor's encampment. Before today, the trees had always been a welcome place of fun and play, but as she looked at them, she feared they would consume her, keeping her from returning to those she called family. They looked darker and more foreboding than usual, but she knew this was just in her mind.

A shiver crawled across her skin as the cool morning wind brushed over her breasts and buttocks, which were not used to being completely exposed. Having just removed the last layer of clothing, she now stood there completely naked, utterly exposed to nature. Many other Bandorians opted to go without clothing when it suited them. As a culture, they had no stigma about nudity, so no one cared when one went naked.

Kiva and Erika would regularly tease the boys, flashing their naked bodies at them, or dancing around naked, but not Fae. She had never become completely comfortable with this aspect of their culture, though no one had ever forced her to go naked until this day. The thought occurred to her that perhaps this aspect of the trial was intended for just that: to ensure she could be comfortable enough with her own body to exist in only it and still have the confidence she would need. She had waited until this moment to go naked in front of others, and now it was taken to the extreme. Every single member of the clan could see her now, but she was determined to not feel any shame. She was a Bandorian, and this was how she would prove it.

She forced herself to take on a confident posture. She clenched her toes in, pulling at the dirt beneath her feet to help ground her; it made her feel tough and strong. The shiver abated as she channeled her fear into excitement instead, gaining a small release of animalistic energy; enough to get her blood pumping and keep out the cold.

Two outcomes were likely: she would return victorious, or the wilderness would consume her, and she would find a new life if she survived. Nothing she could do in this moment would change which outcome would become real. Everything that would affect the days to come had already happened, in her physical training, her learning, in the character she had become. "Trust yourself," she thought to herself, "Trust your training. All you can do now is trust that the person you are is the person who will pass the trial." It sounded like Jaxon's voice in her mind. She stepped outside of herself for a moment to think about the person who was about to take the trial. She was a person who Fae could be proud of, someone she already knew was worthy.

She thought back to Jaxon as well now and knew that they were both worthy. She tensed her body, refocused, full of excitement, and waited for the command to start.

She was ready.

Axton raised his voice loud enough for all to hear.

"You have both been raised in the way of the wise warrior, the way of Bandor. You have learned our teachings and shared our culture. You have been treated as Bandorians until this moment. Now prove that you are worthy of the title. Leave now into the world to choose your own path, be that a path of the others, a path to your death, or if you return on your own with the body of a wild Craeg boar, having survived the hardships of nature alone, you will have chosen the path of Bandor. Now go, and we hope to see you return as grown children of Bandor."

Fae took off at a jog, ensuring she did not waste time, but also ensuring that she could conserve her energy; she would need it in the days to come.

Fae bounded through the forest. She had to find the stream and set up a small camp for the course of the trial. She moved gracefully, like a deer gliding between bushes; years of practice had changed the way her body moved. She flew over stone and log, slipped under branches, and darted around the foliage. It was like a dance in the way she could shift her weight and pivot her momentum.

She made good speed, having travelled the forests many times before. Until she bounded around a tree and stopped dead.

In front of her was a bush of berries, identical to the ones she had once picked with her nana on the farm as a child. She had seen berry bushes since that day, but something about these...

The memory flashed across her vision, and a wave of nostalgia hit her. Fae missed her grandmother terribly, but where would she even be? She knew nothing of who her nana was, and it had been so long. *Was she even still alive?*

Six years had passed since Fae's life had changed forever and the pack had met their last member. Sometimes Fae felt as though memories of her old life had faded like old dreams that had never really happened. She could still feel pain inside when she thought back to that fateful night and what had befallen the townspeople, those she had known growing up. Fae had never borne them an abundance of love, but she still felt sadness. *Did she miss her parents?* She could not remember them; their memories had faded and conflicted with a family she now cares for. A sliver of guilt crept through her thoughts, though she had been taught not to feel such. She felt more of a sort of sorrow at the memories; a sense of pity for the lives they had led, and their subsequent fate.

She felt the hair on her arm stand up on end and a charge run up her spine. The world around her darkened; bright greens turning dark, while flowers seemed to brighten. She looked through the tree cover to see if a dark cloud had rolled over them. But what she saw made little sense to her. The sky was night, and the stars were out, but it had been midday just a moment before. She spun around, trying to sort out what was going on; panic crept into her mind, despite the years of training she had received from the teachers of the clan.

Fae remembered her lessons and paused long enough to take some deep breaths. She would need her wits to get through whatever was happening. *Where in her training had she heard of this effect?*

Her mind raced through every lesson she had learned for a plausible explanation for her current situation. *Loss of consciousness? A blow to the head might explain the strange sense of colours. But no, she should remember hitting her head or at least getting back up. Being transported somewhere else in Tal'am? That would not explain the colour oddities. She was here, but not here, in her world, but also in another world.*

Otherworld. Elfame. The realm of Faerie.

She remembered studying about the realm of Faerie; another world interwoven with the natural world; a conjoining of the two. There were places where the veil between the two realms was weaker, and aspects of Faerie could drift into theirs. Perhaps it was possible for people to wander into Elfame as well. Her surroundings appeared most similar to descriptions of the realm of Faerie.

She centred her mind, heightening her senses, waiting for what might come next.

Fae did not have to wait long. The tree in front of her slowly twisted and turned so that the side that faced away from her became visible. As it did, a human shaped creature stepped out of the tree. It was the height of Fae, thin and in the shape of an adult female. Her skin was a smooth olive brown, and her hair was an earthy green and appeared to be made from soft vines. Flowers bloomed from her hair with more wrapped around her forearms and legs. Other than that, she stood there naked in front of Fae.

Oddly, Fae felt comforted by the fact that they were both naked, as if it was something they at least shared.

Though Fae should have been afraid, she felt a calm, soothing feeling that made the fear feel distant, like someone calling from far away. The tension in her body melted away, like the first drink of a strong alcohol hitting her system.

The lady, with an innocent smile on her face, glided down to where Fae stood paralyzed by her beauty.

"I have heard of you, young one. The others call you the outsider."

Her voice was sweet and childlike, though her tone and mannerisms were clearly womanly. She moved on bare feet around Fae, gracefully placing each foot as she went. She drew her soft hand across Fae's bare shoulder and chest and looked her up and down as she wrapped around Fae.

"I heard you were beautiful."

The lady crossed back around in front of Fae and gave another look up and down her body, lingering on her breasts; it made Fae feel odd. "You *are* developing *very* nicely. What a treat." She produced a sweet giggle that echoed in Fae's mind. "A sweet little specimen. I'm sure the boys are constantly chasing after you," she gave a sly smile, "and possibly the girls."

Fae felt the blood rushing to her cheeks. She had a sense of what this forest spirit was saying and felt embarrassment. It occurred to her that her feelings of shame came from her earlier life in the Empire, but that did not make her feel them less.

She let the feelings float away and centred herself once more. Whatever this creature was, it was not human, but she did not feel it was a threat to her either, though she readied her muscles as best as she could, just in case.

The spirit noticed her tense, "Ah yes, but your beauty is just the distraction. Your body and your mind are your tools. You have learned much since you came to the forest. You will become powerful... *very* powerful."

"You know much about me, but who or what are you?" Fae asked. Her voice was cautious, but kind and had wonder in it.

"Hehe," her laugh was like honey and echoed inside Fae's mind again. "Just a friend, little one, just a friend. Right now, we only watch, but we will be there for you when you need us. We are in many places, and we watch you when we can. You are our favourite, but that should not be a surprise."

So distracted was Fae that she almost did not notice another woman form. A drop of water fell from a rose petal. It landed on a leaf below and when it splashed; it sprayed unnaturally into a large mist of clear water. The water spray grew and swirled until it coalesced and formed into a small, beautiful woman with clear blue skin like the colour of a crystal azure mountain lake. Her hair flowed over her shoulders like running liquid. Drops of water would fall from her, then reabsorb into her as they fell.

"Dryads, I assume?" she tried to sound confident and friendly. Her question took on a charming, youthful tone, something she had learned from Jaxon.

The dryads took notice. "Oh, I like her, sister. She is wise,"

"And quick."

"And controls her fear well."

"Very delightful." They had an odd way of speaking in which they seemed to carry on each other's sentences without pause.

"What do you want with me?" Fae asked.

They ignored the question. The blue dryad began their speech, "You are a special one,"

"The boy may command, but you will lead."

"He will help you."

"Yes, he has helped in your training."

"Helped give you purpose,"

"Belonging."

"You grow strong with him and the others."

Fae's mind raced to keep up. Trying to listen and decode their meaning as they went. *Were they talking about Jaxon?*

"Blooming love."

"A flower cared for."

"Beauty."

Fae was getting dizzy from their circling.

"You did not answer my question. What do you want with me?" she asked.

"She is a silly girl."

"She expects straight answers from the Seelie."

"From dryads."

"Not now young one."

"We will be watching."

"My little Fae."

My little Fae

The name made her whole body tingle with a memory; the name her nana had called her.

"What did you just call me?" Her voice cracked slightly. "What do you know about my nana?"

"Such a cute name it is."

"Like the name of our world."

"We like that."

She rarely thought of the fact that she shared her name with the realm of the Fae. *Did her grandmother have something to do with that world? Why did they call her that?*

"Do you know my nana?" Fae asked.

"No more time, sister," the first dryad said.

"Yes, you are right. This one is busy."

"Much to do."

"We mustn't keep her from her tasks."

"Goodbye, pretty little girl."

"No. Don't go," Fae said.

Then there was a flash, and the spirit disappeared. Fae dropped to her knees and looked at the ground. She was back in the forest she had been running through.

"Don't go..." Her voice was a pleading whisper. She cupped her head in her hands and sat there, unmoving for a time. Emotions welled up inside of her, but she was able to push them down before tears formed.

She had to think.

The Seelie were known to be mischievous so, she did not know if anything they said could be trusted. Fae couldn't rule out the possibility that they could delve into people's minds and extract information. She resolved to approach what she heard from them with a healthy dose of skepticism, tucking it away for future reference but refusing to fixate on it.

Still, they had reminded her of her nana, reminded her of a life she was not living, and that there were other lives out there besides this Bandorian life. She shook her head to clear it. Nothing had happened that changed what her current goal was. She still had a boar to catch.

She heard the far-off sound of trickling water from a stream and took off towards it at a sprint.

CHAPTER 21
THE TRIALS

Fae stalked through the forest, spear in hand, eyes tracking the foliage for any surprises while keeping her focus on her target.

It had been several days since the trial began and her encounter with the dryads. She had seen no other sign of magic since then.

She had spent the first evening creating a small camp, lighting a fire, gathering sticks, sharp rocks, and long weeds. She recalled the feeling of the warm fire on her naked body the first night once she had gotten it started; the contrast of cold and warmth as the heat danced over her skin, exciting the nerves. It had kept away both the animals and the chill.

The faint smell of her prey and its lair hung in the air. Animal mixed with damp crushed foliage. She placed a hand on the hoof prints in front of her; only one type of print. *Good, she had the right lair.*

Her thoughts were interrupted as she shifted in her squat to adjust her outfit. It chaffed and itched, being the best thing she could create for the time being.

She had spent the first few days crafting her tools and fashioning makeshift clothing. She'd wrapped plant material around her torso to keep her breasts from getting in the way, then her bottom to protect her nethers from scrapes or infections. They were far from comfortable. But they would have to suffice until she returned to camp.

Thankfully, she was not hungry enough for her stomach to be growling. She had lucked out and found a berry bush full of ripe berries that she knew were safe to eat from her studies.

A day before, she had picked up the trail of a Craeg boar and had followed it to this spot. Ahead, she could see the animal's lair down the path.

It had taken her much longer to find a boar than she had expected, but now she had it and she would not lose it. She was sure that it had not taken Jaxon nearly as long to pick out a trail; he was always the best tracker. She tiptoed along the subtle trail, through the underbrush, her bare feet able to avoid any sticks that might snap as she moved, and her arms carefully brushed branches out of her way.

She had followed the trail from a small pool of water, just off a flowing creek which had many tracks from the boar. It was clearly an area it frequented, which meant it must have a lair close by, probably built into some underbrush it had cleared out and patted down. Now she was approaching such an area and as she snuck without making a noise, she could hear rustling up ahead in the brush. Then she heard it, the unmistakable snort of a Craeg boar. *This was it.*

As she drew nearer, she could see the boar stomping the ground and moving around to get into a comfortable position to lie down in its den. She felt for the small rocks she had prepared, grabbed the first one she found, took aim, and threw with well-trained precision. It hit the boar but only on the right side of the shoulder; it deflected off and the boar only let out a grunt and turned to see if something was beside it. "Dammit," she cursed under her breath.

She reached again for the rocks she had brought. Her fingers searched for the one with the perfect weight and grip. With keen focus, she fixated on the boar's nose, honing in on it with a hunter's precision. She drew her arm back, coiled like a spring, and released the rock in a smooth, fluid motion.

The missile flew through the air in a graceful arc, striking the boar square on the nose. The animal howled in pain and fury.

Fae waved her hands and made enough racket to get its attention. It pawed the ground, ready to charge at her. Fae remained unfazed. *She had it now.*

She leaned back in her crouch and braced the spear against the ground behind her. The boar let loose a wild growl, saw her crouch as a sign of fear, and charged. Boar tusks tore through the underbrush, making a loud racket.

Then, as the boar neared Fae, she shifted out of the way so that only the spear lay in its path. The spear plunged into the boar, creaking and groaning as it pierced flesh.

Crack!

The sound of the spear snapping echoed like a whip.

Fae realized too late that the boar was larger than she had expected. It collided with her, knocking her off her feet and to the side of the path.

The boar's hooves came down on her, but quick reflexes allowed her to use her right forearm to redirect them away from her as she rolled away.

Pain shot up her arm. She winced and wondered if she had broken something. Her right arm hung uselessly at her side, but she had redirected the boar's assault.

As she lay on her back, she seized a sharp rock with her left hand and drove it deep into the boar's underside, where it is most vulnerable.

The boar let out a howl and brought his tusks and snout into her right shoulder. It broke the skin, but she rolled with the impact and absorbed some of the brunt force, moving her farther away from the boar.

She nimbly continued her momentum up to her feet and took off down the path at a sprint. She felt warm blood trickling down from her shoulder but ignored the pain.

As the sound of the charging boar grew louder, Fae's heart raced in her chest. She sprinted down the path, her feet pounding against the ground. Just in time, she spotted the four spears stuck in the earth. Without slowing down, Fae deftly dodged to the side, her reflexes honed from years of training, and narrowly avoided impaling herself on the sharp points.

The boar was not as nimble. It collided with the spears, impaling it right through the throat and killing it instantly.

She grinned at her handiwork. She had whittled the wood to sharp points and firmly embedded them there when she had discovered the lair as a back-up plan.

Fae lay on the ground, chest heaving as she caught her breath. Her honey-colored hair sat disheveled over her face, but she puffed out a breath of air to blow it away. The ground felt comforting against her body as the surge of energy faded.

She slapped her hand down against the earth and grinned widely, excited by a sense of accomplishment. *She could rest. It was done.*

As she lay there, she looked up at the tree canopy. She watched the leaves dance in the small breeze, sunlight flickering through them as they moved.

Eventually, she got up and began wrapping her bleeding arm. When she finished, she gutted the animal with a sharpened stone; the extra weight would have just been unnecessary. She then tied it with rope made of bark fibers and ivy and began the march back to the encampment. Fae was eager to see pride and acceptance on everyone's faces when she returned.

Her journey back was exhausting. The boar was very heavy, her muscles ached, but they were well trained, and she had pulled heavy weights before. She was grateful for the non-stop physical training she had once complained about. All those annoying lectures from Axton had contained wisdom in them, after all.

"When you lose all you have, you still have your body. If you lose that, you still have your mind, and if you lose that, well then you are not you any longer."

Axton had once told her that, and the saying had always made her snicker. She was not snickering now. *Your mind and body affect your quality of life, so you must work on them, always.*

Finally, Fae broke through the treeline and came into the clearing surrounding the camp, still towing the Craeg boar over her uninjured left shoulder. One clansman gave a holler to alert the others of her return. Many members of her clan came running to the clearing as she dragged the large beast closer to them.

She smiled to see Bullock, Erika, and Kiva's excited faces as they quickly approached her. Behind some of the crowd, she could see Axton standing tall with his arms crossed and a smile on his face. He did not have the same look of excitement, but simply a look of pride and knowing. There was no surprise in his eyes. He had always been confident in her abilities.

She released the boar's rope, gathered her strength, and stood as tall as she could. She could hear joints cracking as she did so. Her long blonde locks stuck to her face with sweat, so she lifted her hand and brushed them back. She felt strength and confidence exuding from her. In her minimal outfit made of only grass, she felt like quite the warrior woman.

While staring straight at her clan as they watched her, she pulled a sharpened rock from the loop on her loincloth. She took the rock up in her hand to show the others, then slid it between her skin and the grass straps holding her bottoms on and slit the grass. She did the same to her top, and both small articles of clothing fell to the ground, exposing her completely naked body.

She met Axton's eyes and, knowing she had always been uncomfortable with nudity, he cracked a smile at the gesture. He then dipped his head in a subtle nod of respect. Fae nodded back. She appreciated his support.

Her pack stopped their full-on charge as they reached her, and Bullock lifted her off her feet in a great hug, which shot a pain through her injured arm, but she did not care. The twins also wrapped their arms around her as Bullock's embrace kept her raised off the ground. Their embrace warmed and comforted her. Her sore body turned to putty as the tension just slipped out of her. Bullock leaned his head back so he could look into her face, and she could see his beaming smile. He pulled her closer again and gave her a caring kiss on her forehead.

Finally, he let her down. She was lightheaded and felt like tipping, but Kiva and Erika braced her. They pulled her arms over both of their shoulders to help her keep balance and walk towards camp. She only now realized how tired her legs were. Erika gave her a big kiss on the cheek and Kiva tousled her hair as they made their way towards the centre of the encampment to celebrate.

After walking for only a moment, a sharp realization ripped into her mind. Abruptly, she stopped and asked, "Where is Jaxon?"

The girls stopped their walk and Bullock turned to face her. He had a smile, but Fae could tell it was an attempt to hide a hint of concern he felt.

Jaxon was likely the best trained hunter of the five of them, and certainly the best tracker. He should have been the first back, no matter which one of them had gone at the same time as him. Fae had even had trouble finding a Craeg boar, which meant that she had taken longer than she should have, and Jaxon should certainly have been back by now.

Something must have happened, but that was why they were trained the way they were; to ensure they could adapt when something went wrong.

Bullock hesitated before responding. "He is not back yet, but he should be back soon. He is probably already on his way. I am sure we will see him later tonight. Knowing him, he'll get back just in time for the ale and celebration."

Bullock's comment did not settle Fae's heart, but she accepted it for now.

Despite her concern, the evening was wonderful, and she looked at the other members of her clan with fresh eyes. They had always made her feel a part of the Clan, as if she had been born one of them, and she knew that many clan members had joined the clan instead of being born into it, but for the first time in her life as a Bandorian she did not doubt her right to be there with the others.

The worry for Jaxon did not disappear, but her knowledge that there was nothing she could do for him that night, and knowing that he would want her to be proud of herself, let her place that worry aside. Either he would return this night, or there would be plenty of time to worry tomorrow, but it would do no good to dwell on it.

They drank, they ate, they sang, and they danced. For the first time in her life, when others removed their clothes to dance naked around the bonfire, she removed hers too and joined in. She felt free and powerful. Invigorated. As if her body were the most powerful tool she had. She could feel every muscle flex and release, every inch of skin accepting the cool flashes of breeze and dancing heat of the flames; it was exhilarating and freeing. When the evening finally wound down, she was too exhausted to let worry bother her and sleep took her the moment her body hit her bunk.

CHAPTER 22
EMPTY BUNK

The next morning, Fae woke up and left the pack's tent, hoping to hear that Jaxon was back. But there was still no word. Morning turned to afternoon, afternoon turned to evening, and still nothing. The worry creeped like vines through her mind.

That night, she set up a bedroll and some cushions on the edge of the encampment so that she could watch for Jaxon to return. She had a fire started and sat beside it, looking into the darkness for any sign of movement. Fae gave a small start when she felt a large hand on her shoulder; she had been focusing so intently that even Bullock had caught her by surprise.

"Fae..." he said. "You can't make him appear, not any better from here than you can from back in camp. Why don't you-"

"I know, Bullock, I know." Her voice was kind but firm. She paused for a moment. "I know it is not our way, and I know I can't control what happens, I just... I just..." her voice wavered but Bullock squeezed her shoulder harder, and she placed her hand on his, leaning her head against his hand.

"It's OK Fae, I understand." She lifted her head back up and released his hand, having received the comfort she needed. He let go of her shoulder and she heard his footsteps as he made his way back into camp.

She did not mind sitting there watching by herself, as long as no one forced her to return to the camp centre. *She would wait alone.*

Not too long after Bullock had walked away, she saw Kiva approach from the corner of her eye. Kiva said nothing to her, but simply spread out a bedroll and laid down. A brief time later, Erika also appeared and said nothing. She set up her bedroll and sat cross-legged on it, staring at the fire.

Eventually, Bullock appeared with several skewers, each with a piece of some bird meat on it. He passed one to each of the girls, then passed around a water skin to wash it down. The last skewer he had was uncooked, so he dragged a log over to the fire, sat down, and roasted it over the fire. Like both girls, he also said nothing. The simple presence of her family there with her made some of the tension melt away from her and helped the time pass much more quickly.

At some point, Fae rested her head in Erika's lap and Erika hummed a soft tune, stroking Fae's hair. Eventually, as the fire flickered, Fae fell asleep.

The next morning, when the twins had gone back into camp to carry out their chores, Bullock still sat with Fae. As Fae sat staring out into the forest, she heard footsteps behind her, heavy with a larger gait; Axton.

Once he reached her, she felt him place his large hand on her shoulder and take in a breath to speak. Before he could, Fae, without turning her head, spoke, "I know Axton. I know."

Axton paused, then drew back his hand.

"It is time," Fae said. "Sitting here isn't making him come back any faster. Either he will return, or he will not. Nothing I can do to affect the outcome."

Axton said nothing at first, then said, "You are correct."

"Thanks Axton, I appreciate you coming. Bullock, you can go with him. I will be along soon. Just give me a moment."

Her voice was steady but had an obvious note of sadness in it. She could not see it, but she imagined Axton's empathetic look. After a moment, she heard the dwindling sound of footsteps as Axton and Bullock both made their way back into camp.

She sat there a while longer. Sitting on her knees and with her hands in her lap, tears dropped onto the backs of her palms.

Finally, she pushed herself back onto the balls of her feet and stood up. She took one last look at the forest before turning and walking back to camp.

Bullock still stood there at the edge of the camp, patiently waiting for her and she was glad to not be alone. She reached him and he put an arm over her, comforting her as they walked back.

After they had taken only ten steps, they heard a humorous but strained voice call out from behind them.

"Oh, come on. I know I stink, but it can't be that bad. You don't need to walk away from me."

Fae's body froze, and a feeling of complete shock washed over her. A single soft word brushed her lips as it escaped from her mouth.

"Jaxon."

She was so terrified that she was imagining his voice. She resisted turning around at first, just wanting to live in that moment of hope in case she turned around to see nothing.

She stayed frozen in place. She felt Bullock's hands on her shoulders, encouraging her to turn, and his voice was ever so gentle, "Fae, turn around." She finally turned to look the way they had come.

There, shuffling towards them, was a half naked, bruised, and bloody Jaxon.

He wore only scraps of animal hide wrapped around his feet, waist, and shoulders. A large cut traced down the front of his left shoulder, the beginning of which was hidden under the fur and leather. The rest of his body had dark black bruises, some of which had yellow tinges around them. His face and most of his body had patches of dried blood on them, but Fae was pleased to see that there were no open wounds on his head. Over Jaxon's right shoulder was a string made of dried animal skin that continued behind him towards the ground where a medium-sized Craeg boar was being dragged.

Fae's head exploded with emotion, first a massive relief of joy at seeing him alive, then anger, furious at him for making her hurt.

"Where have you been?" she asked so aggressively that it made Jaxon stumble back and even knocked that cocky grin off his face. He tried to bring it back, but Fae could see now that there was a hard pain in his expression he was trying to hide, and the anger faded from her.

Her face turned to a look of concern, and she bolted forward towards him. Bullock was just a step behind her, and they reached Jaxon at the same time just as he collapsed. Bullock caught him with a firm hand, and Fae lowered his head into her lap as they all sat together.

"What happened? Are you ok?" she asked, this time with a softer tone of affection instead of anger.

Jaxon grimaced but seemed to have the strength to respond without difficulty. "I think I'll be fine. Just need some rest and perhaps to see the shaman."

Bullock lifted the hide scrap covering Jaxon's shoulder to inspect the wound. Fae was relieved to notice there was no acrid smell of infection, as she had first feared.

"You look rough, brother," Bullock said, even as a relieved smile grew on his face.

Jaxon took a breath, looked up at them from Fae's lap, and cracked a smile.

Fae repeated her question, "What happened?"

"Things didn't go exactly as planned. First day was fine, water, supplies, and so on. I thought I got lucky, actually. The second day, I found the trail of a boar, heading north along the stream."

Jaxon was the best tracker of the pack.

"I followed it, and after not too long, I found where it was resting. Up a high bank on the west side of the stream. Prepped my sharpened staves and had him charge me. Impaled him first try."

The cocky bastard almost looked proud of himself with his half grin.

"Everything was great, but when I was prepping the boar, another rotten boar charged out of nowhere. Its mate probably. I moved so the dead boar took the brunt of the attack, but it knocked all three of us over the edge. We tumbled down the bank together. I swear we hit every boulder or hard root on the way down."

Fae glanced over Jaxon's red and black body. The bruising made her believe it.

"When I hit the bottom, I felt cold and wet. I thought it was blood at first, but I was lying in the stream, pinned under a dead boar, and with another beside me. It was banged up enough that it was not long for this world. Unfortunately, I was so battered that I could not lift the boar off me; probably couldn't have moved even if the boar had not been on top of me."

"Did you break something?" Fae asked. "Why did it take so many days to come back?"

"Sprains maybe, but no breaks. I had to lay in the freezing water for far too long. When I finally got the strength to crawl out from under the boar and out of the water, the sun was out and warm enough to dry me off, but the damage was already done. I could feel a fever setting in. I wasn't strong enough to carry the boar back."

"Oh, you bluntaxe," Fae said, using a Bandorian curse even as she stroked Jaxon's hair. "You could have crawled back. Called for help or something. Anything."

"No good. Had to get the boar back. On my own."

An exasperated sigh escaped Fae's lips.

"On the plus side, the water was cold enough and flowing fast enough that I didn't seem to get an infection before the cut could seal itself up."

"Things became hazy. I was cold, then I was hot. I had to lie there for what I think was a few days waiting for the fever to break. I could reach the dying boar, and I pulled it close, gutted it using the carcass as shelter to block any cool air when I was cold, and I used the cool water on my head to keep the fever from getting too hot. Finally, the fever broke, and my body recovered enough to move. I grabbed the other boar, only recently dead, tied him up, grabbed the tusks from the first boar, and dragged it back here."

Bullock and Fae looked over at the dead boar; the tusks of the other boar were tied to it. Bullock cocked an eyebrow at Jaxon. "You were worried we would think you were lying?"

Jaxon gave a weak shrug. "I imagined enough crazy shit while I was lying there. I think I wanted to make sure I didn't imagine the whole thing."

"Ha, fair enough."

Fae leaned down into Jaxon, wrapped his head in her arms and hugged him closely. "Jaxon," she said with care as she held him.

"If I get this kind of reception when I half die, maybe I should do it more often."

Fae gave a low growl at him. Then the grin disappeared from his face and his eyes turned softly to her. "I missed you too, Fae."

She just held him there for a time, as if worried he might disappear. Bullock left to take the boar to Sara, who would use the unique hide for Jaxon's adult armour. Fae knew he would also bring back some water and the shaman, Cairn, to tend to Jaxon.

"Fae, I just thought about you while I lay there, knew I had to survive, so I could see you again. I don't know what it means, but I kept seeing your face and that got me through. I... I..."

"Shh," Fae cut him off. "It's ok, Jax. I know... I know. You're OK now."

Bullock came running back carrying a canteen with Cairn not far behind him. Jaxon had a few gulps of water from the canteen and, by the time the shaman got to him, he felt rested enough to try standing. The shaman helped Jaxon up, put his hands on Jaxon and inspected for any permanent damage.

"Well, you look awful, but I think you'll be fine, lad. Let's get you to my tent, where we can patch you up. Then you can go celebrate," Cairn said. Bullock and he helped Jaxon away to the shaman's tent.

Fae stared after the boy that was once her best friend, now perhaps something more. A gentle tear crept down her cheek, and she did not bother to brush it away. She decided then, if they were to live Bandorian lives and accept that they may not last, then she would not take it for granted that he would be there the next day. She would enjoy every moment she had with him until the day came that there were no longer any moments left.

She thought of the old Bandorian saying: *in order to enjoy those you care about, you must accept that they will not always be there*. She smiled at the thought and finally brushed the tear off her cheek.

She ran for the encampment centre to ensure the others were told, but by the time she got there, the word had already spread. Bullock had made enough commotion as he ran to get the shaman; people pieced together what was happening. So, when Fae arrived, she found they were already setting-up to celebrate the success of the two of them.

The Bandorians did not have many formal traditions around celebrations, they simply celebrated when the mood struck them. Every evening was a celebration, some being larger than others.

That night, after Jaxon had returned from being tended to by the shaman, they enjoyed dancing, drinking, singing and general revelry with their dearest friends and the rest of the Clan. It was a good night of celebrating, and when Fae found she was not dancing around the fire with the others, she was curled up in Jaxon's embrace, muscular arms wrapping her tight, pulling her close, and her head pressed against his powerful chest.

She had done it. Had passed the trials. She had feared for so long that she would not be able to. She was a Bandorian now. A full member of Clan Kaltor.

What was next?

Fae thought back to the little girl that had first gone with the Bandorians. *What had she told herself then?* That it had been the best path laid out in front of her. She had been determined to learn what she could and told herself she could run away if she wanted to. Go find her nana or start a new life.

It had been so long since she had thought about that. What had happened to those thoughts? She had become distracted, by family, by fear of failure, by life.

Fae shivered, and Jaxon squeezed her tighter, misinterpreting it for a chill.

The thoughts and fears of an eleven-year-old girl returned to her. *These people had killed her family and butchered her people; burned down her town when she was young. She didn't hold it against Jaxon, he hadn't done it, but Axton had.*

Her pseudo adopted father had destroyed her old life. *Sure, he had given her a good new life, but these people, her people, had destroyed her old people. She was a Bandorian now, but was that what she wanted?*

There was good here, she knew that, but she still struggled to justify everything that they were and what they had done.

CHAPTER 23
THE ASSAULT

Two Years Later
729: Year of the Second Era

Fae smelled the burning earth around her. She peered out from the cover of the trees and saw a field riddled with scorched patches. She inhaled, steadying her breathing to its natural rhythm. *In and out, in and out.* With her back against an old oak tree, she pressed the side of her head to the trunk, and turned slightly, just enough to get a view of the other side and identify her enemy.

Beyond the treeline lay open ground with corpses littering the recent battlefield. She immediately spotted four cloaked figures spread out, slowly creeping forward through the grasses.

Great. Acolytes.

Moving cautiously, they scanned the area for hidden traps or any surviving enemies. A gully ran parallel to the tree line, separating Fae from the wizards. Fae noted the terrain, then withdrew her head and huddled behind the tree, keeping herself out of sight. She pressed her hands against the trunk, took a deep breath to steady herself, then moved.

She rushed from the tree line with a fury of speed. Her feet beat against the ground as they hastily propelled her towards the lip of the gully.

Her eyes briefly met those of her enemies on the other side and, in that moment, she could see the utter surprise on their faces. But their shock was quickly replaced by hatred.

She unleashed a cluster of bolts at the closest acolyte, firing in rapid succession from her wrist mounted crossbow. But she did not see the bolts tear through her enemy. She had already dropped into the gully and pressed herself against the opposite wall.

Not a moment too soon either, for just as her head dropped below the horizon, a burst of fire scorched the air above the ditch. She felt the heat burn the top of her head, and she patted it quickly to make sure none of her long, golden locks had been singed.

"It's about damn time you got here," said a friendly voice from beside her against the gully wall. "What took you so long?" The strapping man had a mischievous twinkle in his eye as he teased Fae.

Fae gave a disapproving glare, "Nice to see you too, dear. I was held back by the foot soldiers you left behind in the trees. Someone had to clear them out."

"Those guys are fodder. The fun ones are out here with us." Jaxon responded with a playful smile.

After a moment, Fae's disapproving look was replaced by a barely held back smile.

"Also, I took out the wizard. You need to be more careful; he was almost on top of you."

"I would have had him; he didn't even know I was here." Jaxon gave a wry smile, probably catching the pinch of concern in her voice.

"You might be right," Fae conceded with a smile. "The look of surprise on his face when I came out of the treeline was amusing."

"Yeah, I bet it was." Jaxon gave a laugh, and it made Fae smile.

His carefree grin was infectious, and no matter what happened, he always seemed to find a reason to smile.

Fae swiftly handed her shield to Jaxon, realizing that there was no time to waste on reminiscing.

"Hold this. I am going to take a peek at our remaining friends over there."

She crept up to the edge without her shield to weigh her down. She knew that Jaxon's gaze followed her as she gracefully pulled herself up to the ledge and peeked over.

Her eyes were over the rim for only a moment, then she dropped back down, crouched a bit, and said, "Yeah, that seems about right. Duck."

"What?" Jaxon asked in surprise, but he crouched anyway as a large roar erupted above them, and again she felt the heat of fire on her head.

"I see three more acolytes approaching," Fae said. "Not too scary, but they do love their fire. Luckily, they cannot lob anything at us."

"That's nice, but do you have a plan? Cause I got nothing."

"Not a plan exactly," she said, "but I wasn't the only one in the treeline when I left, and I figure us sitting here as bait should get those wizards to cluster nice and close for the others."

Jaxon grinned as they huddled together against the gully wall. They did not have to wait long. Grass swished, as the three robed men beyond the gully cautiously stepped closer to Fae and Jaxon's position, and closer to each other. Each slow step they took, wary of any counterattack, grouped them more and more closely.

Just then, a round object not much bigger than an adult's fist came arcing out of the forest. It passed over the gully and landed beside the wizards.

Fae snuck another peek. The wizards had only a moment to look towards it before it erupted in an explosion and flames engulfed the first wizard.

He dropped to the ground in a pile of burnt cloth and flesh. The second wizard howled, shrapnel embedded in his leg, and fell to the ground writhing. The remaining wizard scrambled backwards, then turned to bolt in the opposite direction.

The explosion had caused enough of a distraction for a figure to sprint from the treeline, far to the flank of the last wizard. The figure advanced on them before the wizards could notice. With a flash of blades, the last enemy dropped to the ground and the second wizard stopped squirming. It was over in only moments.

Erika came sauntering out of the woods, from where she had thrown the bomb, and over to Fae and Jaxon.

"You two can come out now," she said.

She reached out a hand to the two of them to help them out of the gully. They took her hand, and she heaved them out one at a time.

"Thanks. Nice timing Erika, and you too, Kiva," Fae said as she turned around to see Kiva cleaning off her blades on the dead wizard's robes.

"Any sign of Bullock?" Jaxon asked.

He looked around to survey their surroundings, searching for his best friend.

"He will be along shortly," Kiva said with a grin.

Fae looked back into the trees and noticed she could hear some noises that sounded like grunting and the clanging of steel.

A figure then came into view. An Imperial soldier was hurled from the forest with the sound of a shield crunching against face and helmet. The soldier came toppling to the ground and behind it came a beast of a young man charging forward with a shield in one hand and the throat of another soldier in the other. Bullock threw the wriggling body directly at the first soldier as he was attempting to get back up, knocking them both into a sprawling heap.

As one soldier rose, Bullock altered his grip on his shield, so he was holding it with both hands as someone might hold a serving tray. After lifting the shield, he swung it against the soldier's head. The man went down in a crumple of limbs and armour. He didn't get back up.

Erika stepped up beside Bullock and gestured to the soldier that had not tried to get back up. "You going to kill this one, or...?"

Bullock turned over his shoulder to look at the soldier she was referring to.

"Him? Nah, I broke his leg earlier in the fight. Even if he isn't dead, he won't be fighting anytime soon. There'd be no challenge."

Bullock wandered back to the treeline as the others continued to talk.

"So, Jax, what do you think?" Kiva asked. "Where next?"

Bullock was rummaging around in the bush for his misplaced battle axe.

Jaxon surveyed the battlefield they now stood on; they had not been there when the actual battle had happened; the five friends had been called back from the far north only a fortnight earlier and missed the conflict.

Fae thought back to that last time they had seen the rest of their clan. *How long had it been? Six months? More? Maybe even a year?*

On the stony foothills, they had battled the Fomorians and Giants in the long shadow of the Fangs of Abaddon, the largest mountain range in the known lands. On the craggy stone hills, they had sharpened their skills in battle against foes much larger and stronger than themselves.

Fae remembered they had been standing in their clan's camp, watching others disassemble it around them. Fae had been resting next to a loaded wagon, with her pack resting behind her. Jaxon was talking with Axton.

"Axton, if a war is brewing, we want to come with you. You are going to need us. We are one of the fastest packs in the clan. We can cover more ground than anyone in less time."

Fae and the others had talked through their reasoning with Jaxon carefully beforehand, but she could tell now, as he spoke with Axton, Jaxon was just letting the arguments fall out in a jumble. *He was usually smoother than that.*

Fae was thankful Axton was kind enough to respond in a slow and calm tone. He seemed to take their comments seriously.

"Aye, I know that boy, I know. The five of you are impressive. It is true. You fight with a keen mind and strong body, but this will be good for ye. You need the experience. The Fomorians are excellent teachers."

"Excellent fodder is more like it," Bullock jibed.

"Shut it," Kiva hissed, elbowing him in the ribs.

"We have fought Fomorians for over a year now. What more can we learn here?" Jaxon asked Axton.

"You can learn patience, for one," Axton said.

He plunked a bag of blacksmith tools down on the cart he was packing.

"You have all more than proven yourselves in combat, yes, even against the largest of Fomorians. But..." he heaved a large iron mallet onto the cart before continuing, "But you have always had your clan to fall back on. Spend a few months living in the wilds by yourselves, with Fomorians behind every shadow. You will need your wits and your cunning to survive, not just your speed and strength. You will need to play the long game, make decisions while behind enemy lines, knowing you will have to live with those decisions for months to follow."

Jaxon and the pack did not speak. They knew to listen and learn from the words Axton spoke.

"You have stayed for long bouts in the wild before. It is true, but this will be different. With the clan not here any longer, you will be alone, cut off, and with only your pack to help keep you alive. You may find yourself in this situation in the coming war, especially for a group like you that can move so quickly and flank the enemy.

"Do not make the mistake of thinking we keep you behind because you are not ready for war. It is because you are ready that we feel you will need a greater challenge." Axton had stopped loading packs onto the wagon and was talking directly to all of them.

His demeanour, while before somewhat stern, now relaxed as he spoke.

"Besides, the war will take time before it even starts. We will do recon and scouting for months before there is any real action. When it is time for the fighting to begin, we will send a rider on vargr-back to get you. We need you all sharp instead of letting your skills dull in the time before the fighting."

Jaxon turned to look at the others. They had chosen him to speak for them and bring up the topic with Axton. Fae nodded at Jaxon. He had done as they asked, and Axton's reasons were sound. He had presented the arguments and learned from it; she was satisfied with the outcome.

"Well then, we'll miss you, Axton."

Jaxon turned back to Axton and reached out his hand.

"Aye, I'll miss the lot of you as well, but we'll see each other soon."

Fae pushed past Jaxon and threw her arms around the Bandorian chieftain. He rested his hands on her, then she stepped back and nodded at him.

Nothing else was said, nothing else was needed. The pack had already said their goodbyes to the rest of the clan. Axton patted the side of the vargr attached to the cart and started south; the vargr followed beside. They watched as Axton and the rest of the clan marched off to the south, leaving them all alone, with nothing but the tall, gnarled trees, and the monsters that hid in their shadows.

That had been the better part of a year ago, and they had learned much, as Axton had said. They had learned their patience.

Now they stood amongst the remains of the battlefield.

Signs of the conflict and the work of their clan were all around them, but no sign of their clan in sight. Jaxon crouched in the grass, focusing.

He pressed his hand against the charred ground and inspected the scorch mark found there. Then, as he often did with them, he spoke out loud as he thought.

"The direction of the burned grass mark on the ground. Spread out from the point of impact. It wasn't a wizard's fire; it came from the Bandorian side. Gnomish fire flasks."

Fae observed the bodies strewn around the scorch; they were clumped together but all had fallen away from it.

"The enemy formed a phalanx," Jaxon continued. "They assumed their tactics would easily overwhelm us; made excellent targets for the flasks."

Jaxon walked in a crouch along the battle lines, noting the placement of bodies with his hands.

While some bodies were Bandorian, the majority were Imperial. The centre of the attack was the site of the most burned corpses, but those who weren't in the centre were scattered sparsely around the area.

"They didn't know how to deal with our weapons," Jaxon said. "They spread out and engaged our troops one on one."

"Ha, that was a mistake," Bullock said. He had made it back from the treeline now, battle axe in hand, and he gave a good chuckle at the enemy's plight. "They give a bunch of farm-boys a few months of training and then send them to be fodder in the Empire's wars. Idiots."

Jaxon looked up at his friend and responded, "In their defence, that is usually sufficient to secure a victory."

The bodies were riddled with punctures and slashes, indicating that many had been cut down by steel. But there were also many that were burned, flayed, or peppered with metal pieces. It was not a scene of normal death on a battlefield.

Fae had once found Bandorian weapons strange and foreign, but now she couldn't imagine living without them. As she surveyed the bodies, she noticed that many of the wounds were only possible with the weapon machinations of gnome and dwarven weapon smiths and tinkerers.

Since the formation of Bandor they had allowed and encouraged other races to join their culture, and if not join, they at least showed a mutual level of respect for other races, which garnered them a level of respect from those subsequent races. Those strong relationships had led to a prominent level of trade of both goods and technologies.

Jaxon reached an arm out and pointed to where the bodies spread out closer to the tree lines.

"They broke rank and fled to the forest for protection over there."

All the bodies here were facing the trees, and ones with arrows in them all had them in the back.

"Our people hacked them down as they ran."

Jaxon stood fully upright. It appeared he had all the information he could gather.

"They ran for the trees and are likely forming up again beyond the forest there. The ones we found here must have just been scavenging the battlefield."

Bullock stepped up beside Jaxon to stare at the thicket of trees to the east.

"We go east then?"

Fae stepped up to where Bullock and Jaxon were both standing. Then, without a look at either, she took another step beyond the both of them.

"We go east."

She said it with confidence and determination, and began walking off in that direction.

"You heard her," Jaxon said. "Let's get moving."

With the sun directly overhead, they made their way across the wide meadow, stepping carefully to avoid fallen bodies obscured by the tall light grasses that came to their hips in places. They walked quietly but at a steady pace, wary of any ambush that might wait for them as they approached the woods. Fae knew they would find none but was also wise enough to not be hasty.

As the five friends reached the bush that marked the start of the woods, Fae looked back at the field of death behind her. Carrion birds already picked at the remains. Bodies, equipment, and battle standards strewn about the region, but for the moment, it saw peace. A cool breeze brushed the tall grass, then it was still.

She turned back towards the forest and led her friends forward.

There was no sound to break the relative silence of the forest floor; it was dark and what animals were around had decided it was best to stay quiet. A gentle ravine flowed quietly from the north, and while it must have been larger centuries ago, to have worn down the twenty-foot banks that marked out the ravine, the actual flow of water was far diminished from the roaring stream it had once been.

Fae silently cursed as the sound of her leather boots finally broke the calm, sliding on gravel as part of the ravine bank fell away. It was a subtle noise, but in the forest's stillness, it could have been a loud crash. A small creature scurried away.

Fae pulled herself over the ledge of the ravine, her fingers digging into the damp dirt, a bit of mud getting under the already weathered nails. She stood before turning back and reaching her hand out back the way she came. Jaxon clasped her hand, and she heaved him out of the ravine. Despite his considerable bulk, she lifted him out gracefully.

A few feet away, Bullock was giving Kiva a boost up the side of the ravine while Erika waited patiently beside him. Unlike Fae, Kiva's foot slipped on the soft mud of the side of the slope. She momentarily fell, but Fae saw it coming and sidestepped to grab her hand and pull her up.

Erika came up next, and as the twins reached down to pull up Bullock, a deep voice bellowed from a hidden place in the trees beyond.

"Nobody move. State your business."

The soft creaking of bowstrings being drawn came from more hidden locations in the trees. Fae's keen eyes could just barely make out human shapes hidden by the leaves and shadows. They were surrounded and their light armour would not protect them from arrow fire. Only Bullock carried a shield, and he was clinging to the side of the ravine.

"Our business is our own," Jaxon called back.

"Not if you want to live longer than the next few heartbeats."

Jaxon drifted his hand to a hidden throwing dagger in his belt, and Fae did the same.

"Hands off the weapons."

"Axton? Is that you?" Fae relaxed her shoulders and dropped her tense arms. "Ashes Axton, if you don't tell them to lower their bows, I'll come over there and whoop your arse."

A loud bellow of a laugh echoed from the trees, and the shadowed outlines lowered their bows. The large muscle-bound adoptive father Fae knew so well came striding out from behind the trees, followed by the other lightly armoured Bandorians. Cairn stepped out as well and went to the lip of the ravine to help the twins pull Bullock out.

"Whoop my arse?" Axton asked as he approached Fae.

Fae jumped at Axton, wrapping her arms around him, and squeezing tight.

"It's good to see you too, lass."

Finally, she let go of the big warrior. Jaxon had a beaming smile, and the twins, with Cairn's help, had Bullock out of the ravine and beside them.

Axton stepped back and peered at the five of them. He looked the same to Fae, but they probably seemed different to him. She felt different. Older. More confident.

Axton smiled and nodded his head at them.

"This way," he said, then gestured to the west and began walking.

As Axton led the group back to the Clan's camp, he updated them on the progress of the war. Clan Kaltor had travelled south while the main Bandorian force engaged with the forces of the Imperial capital.

"The intention is for us to sever the connection between Southshore and Emor, the capital," Axton explained.

"The south is heavily forested and hilly, which gives us the advantage, even with fewer numbers. We've been harassing their army, striking from the cover of the forests."

Fae smiled as she kept pace with Axton and listened. It felt good to hear his voice again. It felt natural to listen to his briefing about the situation, like he had before they had separated.

"They have been trying to regroup, but every time enough of them gather, we attack them at night, scattering them once again. They have lost all of their supplies and equipment and those still alive have run back to Southshore. Bao and Brakan have been identifying the best places to harass their supply lines between the two major cities."

Jaxon's eyes brightened. "They are well then?" he asked, relief clear in his voice. While he was closer to his pack, it was clear to see he was glad to hear his birth parents were still alive.

Axton slowed his walk to a stop and turned to face them, seriousness likely showing in his face; the others stopped as well.

"They are well, but Farth is not. He was killed yesterday in the skirmish. Bullock, I'm sorry."

No. Not Farth. Bullock had always been close to his adopted father. He had told Fae stories about the man often. She stood tentatively, watching Bullock for his reaction.

Bullock looked at Axton and let out a deep sigh. He raised his axe high and brought it down hard on a nearby fallen tree. *Crack.* It stuck in the tree and Bullock let it go.

He dropped to one knee, made a fist, and punched the ground hard. Dust plumed around his knuckles. He stared down at the ground for a moment in silence, not moving, like a statue.

The others watched but did not speak.

Still frozen, Bullock asked, "Did he die a good death?"

"Aye lad he did," Axton said. "He cleaved a path through the enemy. We found him dead, surrounded by enemy bodies, some on top of him. I was told that they stabbed him many times. He killed his killer and two others before finally falling."

Bullock let out a solemn chuckle, "Aye, that sounds like Farth."

"We burned him in a warrior's pyre last night."

Bullock finally moved from his pose and stood. He pulled his axe out of the tree with one heave. "Tonight, I'll drink for him. Tomorrow I'll kill for him." He took a step forward and slapped his hand down on Axton's shoulder. Axton did the same to him. "Thanks Axton. I'm good. Let's move."

A smile cracked Axton's stern expression; he was proud of the young man. They all were. Bullock handled the loss well and with honour. They had all grown so much, and Bullock had matured from the young foolish boy to a wise adult.

They were not kids any longer, nor had they been since the trials. But, even so, something about them was different. Now, standing together, they appeared confident and independent. They had learned to rely on one another to survive. Important lessons for any Bandorian pack.

They continued their march to the camp. Axton left them to settle in once they got there. The clan would move west soon.

CHAPTER 24
TALES FROM THE DRUNKEN OWL

"War? What the hell are you talking about?"

Ox, blurted out the question, shaking his head in disbelief. As the farmer swung his hands emphatically, he nearly knocked his pint of beer off the bar. Lucius tensed and dropped his cleaning rag, ready to catch a pint if it flew off the counter.

The trader, Beacher, had brought up the conversation, and now seemed surprised that Ox had not been aware.

Marcus's mouth tilted up in a smirk and he crossed his arms over his administrator's vest, amused by his friend's ignorance of the current affairs in the Empire.

"Just that," Beacher said, "Those barbarians are at it again." The trader lifted his mug of ale to point at Ox. "That is why I have been in town so much lately. Why did you think I could drag you to The Drunken Owl today?"

"Well, yes, er, no," Ox said. He rubbed the back of his neck. "I just thought that the trouble on the borders was frontiersmen rising up and complaining about taxes or something again."

Marcus sighed. "Yes, well, that was what the Empire was first saying." The administrator's tone was informative without being condescending, and Ox turned to him with an attentive stare. "Information was unclear and inconsistent even within the Empire's institutions and army," Marcus clarified. "They broadcasted the simplest version of the truth until they knew more."

Lucius lowered his hands and relaxed now that Ox was no longer waving his arms in danger of knocking over glasses. Instead, the farmer scrunched his face, thinking.

"But it has been years since we have heard anything of those barbarians."

"Yes. Eight," Marcus said. "And apparently they call themselves Bandorians."

"I thought they were wiped out back then."

Lucius stood again, having picked up his dropped rag. He raised a skeptical eyebrow at Marcus. "That's what the Empire told us, when they took all those conscripts and moved them to the far east, instead of sending them back home."

"Apparently they were wrong," Marcus said.

"Careful who hears you say that," Lucius said with a warning look. "You don't want to be overheard, especially in your line of work."

Marcus let out a brief sigh, and his shoulders sank almost imperceptibly. He gave Lucius a defeated look.

"Yes, well... Apparently, it was only a small force that was defeated those years ago. Barely over a hundred were killed in Creet."

"It sounds like the numbers were slightly exaggerated back when it happened," Lucius said.

Marcus gave no argument.

"The force that is attacking now is estimated to be in the thousands, maybe tens of thousands. Barely a tenth of the size of our army. But they are fast and mobile, and they have been attacking and destroying important supply lines and resources. They are spread across a long western front. But they will not let us draw them out into an open confrontation, so our numbers are not helping us much."

"Is it a serious threat?" Lucius asked.

"Yeah, am I going to get back out to the frontier anytime soon?" Beacher asked. "I know grabbing ale is usually my idea, but I'm going to run out of beer money soon, and Lucius does not give me free drinks."

The trader tapped his mug on the bar, and the bit of ale left barely sloshed around. He reached a hand into his jacket, searching for more coins.

Lucius waited for the payment, but his eyes locked in a dark stare with Marcus.

"How far does the Empire think the Bandorians can push into our borders?" the bartender asked. "Crestwood? The capital?"

Ox laughed, but it was not loud and had a flat note to it. "They can't reach Crestwood. Our army would destroy them." The farmer said, though he did not look confident.

"Ox is probably right," Marcus said. "I'm sure there is nothing to fear."

Marcus, agreeing with Ox, made both Lucius and Beacher give skeptical looks. Marcus lowered his eyes to avoid the stare.

"What is the Magisterium doing about it? Any word from the Autumn Court?" Lucius asked.

"They are handling the situation. Already, wizards have been sent to the front line with the army. They will push them back. And the magisterium has announced that they are preparing powerful magics that can protect the Empire, a new ritual that they can use if needed to bolster the ranks of the armies."

"Not sure that makes me more comfortable," Lucius said. He leaned forward over the bar to make sure no one else could hear him. "I don't trust their magics."

"Lucius, you are too paranoid," Beacher said, laughing off

Lucius's concern. "Every comfort we have is thanks to their magics. Have you seen how people live beyond the Empire? Not great."

Lucius frowned. "Scholars at the college have warned it could have consequences playing with magics we don't fully understand."

"Like what?" Marcus asked.

"Like... I don't know. I just hear talk and know who to listen to. I'm not a scholar, but you should ask them."

"Nah, everyone knows they are a bunch of quacks. Paranoid bunch of nuts. The Empire only keeps them around because they are occasionally useful. Definitely not experts in magic."

"I heard my trader friends say that they get in the way more than they help," said Beacher.

"Well, that much is unlikely," said Marcus. "The senate would have gotten rid of them if that were the case, but they are almost as much trouble as they are worth, though barely. That is why the senate keeps them on a short leash."

Ox gave a short yawn.

"The Bandorians. Guys, why are they attacking us, anyway? What do we know about them? Do we even know anything?"

"Of course, we do," Marcus said.

"I heard we captured a small group of them," the barkeep said.

He stepped away when he saw another patron place a mug down on the bar, empty.

"Just two. Captured last week. In the north, by Dorst," the administrator said. He scratched his chin and stared at the roof, trying to remember what all he had heard. "I was told they were half mad. A human man, and a female half-orc. They were both interrogated. Laughed a lot, apparently. Had no interest in torture and just answered every question the interrogators had. Officially, it was said they talked because of a fear of us, but people I trust—closer to the interrogation—said they just didn't seem to care if we knew everything they knew. In any case, they come across as quite peculiar individuals, whichever way you look at it."

"Who are they? What do they want?" Ox asked.

"Well, apparently, they are not just humans, or even humans and half-orcs. They can be any species at all. They are a massive collection of barbaric tribes. Their culture is archaic and savage. They live outside or in tents. Nothing even close to our advancements. Although..." he paused, remembering something he had heard.

"Although what?" Ox blurted out. He leaned forward in his seat, eager to know more. His eyes were bug-like with annoyance at Marcus leaving the words hanging.

"Although, I also heard much of their weapons and equipment, at least that which we've found are way more advanced than our own. A contradiction of sorts."

Marcus's eyes stared off into the distance, thinking once more, but he shook his head and looked back at the attentive friends.

"As to what they want, they want to stop our ability to expand, apparently. They despise our way of life and want to crush our military and government. Evidently, we had quietly moved much of our forces back west and had pushed into the dead hills. The Empire was looking to expand into there and figured we would find little resistance. The men we captured said they wanted to stop us. Apparently, we woke the sleeping bear."

"When asked why they didn't negotiate with us, they told us they knew they could not find common ground with our leaders, so it would be a waste of time. Our people believe they just did not want to show their cards until they were in the best possible military position to strengthen their claims."

"Either way, they ended up telling us everything they could, which was not much, as they seem to operate in small groups and lack a large military organization. They were both killed immediately after the interrogation. When they laughed at their execution, we knew they were mad."

"An enemy without fear is a danger indeed," Lucius put in, as he stepped back from filling up the other patron's mug. "I just worry about how successful they were at their initial gains and how much of a threat they might actually be, even if the Empire doesn't yet recognize it." He wrinkled his brow. "But more importantly, with their successes, I worry what measures our Empire might take."

None had a suitable answer to this concern. None that had not already been discussed. They all stood and sat there, thinking about what this threat might mean.

CHAPTER 25
FLASHES IN THE DARK

Leaves ruffled under foot, silent enough to be drowned by a gentle breeze, as Axton crept between trees, leading his people through the forest. The darkness enveloped them and shrouded them from sight.

Clan Kaltor made their way through the dense foliage of the forest on their way to Car'athan. Two carts of their equipment accompanied the clan, following the less dense routes through the trees, each pulled by a single vargr. The clan moved, wary of any signs of an ambush. Scouts were out in front of the main column, sweeping the area for enemy placements and movement. They had reported back that the way appeared clear, but it was difficult to be certain. A well-hidden ambush, by enemies with enough patience, can be missed in a sweep.

Axton stepped hesitantly out of the deep brush and into an open space with only a few trees. Fae, Jaxon, and their pack were just behind him, and the elders were spread out to his left.

They were more exposed here, but it would take too long to divert south or north around the large clearing, and the Bandorians deemed it unnecessary. It was late evening, and the sun had set, so their movements should not be easy to see. Still, Axton had a wary feeling. He looked to his right and saw Jaxon fingering his sword hilt, also on edge.

The feeling only grew as he moved on. They were a third of the way across the more exposed area when Axton realized it was not just a wary feeling. His body seemed to slow, fear was welling up in him, and his skin tingled, hairs standing on end. The fear was palpable, and he realized it was unnatural. Thoughts in his mind were fogging, but he could still identify that this level of uncontrollable fear was not characteristic of him.

The realization cleared his mind, and he focused on locating the source of the feeling. Dread washed over him from the south and, as he turned, he saw that Jaxon, gazing in that direction, had already reached the same conclusion. Fae, too, seemed to sense the impending danger as she stood beside Jaxon.

She was looking to the south already when he saw her. She was shivering and appeared to be struck by terror. Others of the clan were now shaking their heads to clear them as well. Before Axton acted, Jaxon walked up beside Fae. Her body froze in place, staring south into the sky.

"Fae," Jaxon said.

No response.

"Fae."

He grabbed her upper arms and shook. This finally woke her out of her paralysis.

"I've... I've felt this before, but never this strong. In my old life. I don't know what it is, Jaxon."

Axton heard a blowing noise above them, drowning out what more was said. A sound like wind picking up on a near windless night. Everyone looked up to the sky searching the black for any sign of the source of the noise.

Axton saw a few eyes dart to him, and he quickly gave a silent hand signal, telling the others to ready themselves. The Bandorians all edged closer to any tree around them they could find, attempting to find any semblance of cover they could from the source of this terrifying feeling.

Suddenly, the sky was ablaze with light, blinding them all. Axton raised his hand to cover his eyes, trying to will the blindness away. When his eyes adjusted, he could see it was fire pouring down from the sky and rolling over the fields, bushes, and trees, igniting all in its path. Those hit directly by the flame instantly turned to ash, while others screamed and became charred husks that crumpled to the ground. Another group of Bandorians dove to the ground and rolled, trying to put out flames that clung to them.

In the distance, the half-elf, Fynnathias, rushed to the nearby trees, trying desperately to wake them from their slumber. Already the trees resisted the spread of the flames, igniting then dying out quickly, like a snake snapping at a victim that successfully defends itself.

"Spread out!" Axton yelled, voice echoing over the field. "Find cover! Don't make yourselves easy targets!"

The flames ended as suddenly as they had appeared, and the sky was awash with darkness again. Flames still lit patches of grass in places throughout the field. Light flickered off the healer Cairn's face as he stood above the others, up on one wagon that carried equipment, throwing shields in every direction at the waiting Bandorians. They would catch them and aim them at the sky for a small amount of protection.

"Cairn! Get off there. You are a sitting duck."

"I know," Cairn yelled back, ignoring the command, and continuing to throw shields to nearby troops.

Above, they heard the whoosh of wind once more as the enemy approached. Cairn swung an axe, severing the reins and freeing the vargr. Then he grabbed the last shield himself and jumped off the cart. But before he could get clear, the world around him lit up. Flame struck the cart, and a burst of heat-pressurized air threw wood splinters and Cairn through the air. The cart exploded. Cairn got part of the shield between him and the blast to protect his face and part of his body, but debris burned and flayed the rest. He landed somewhere beyond the cart in shadow and out of Axton's sight.

This time, the Bandorians were expecting the attack, and they saw the enemy. It was not long before the first cry went up, naming the creature.

"Dragon!" The shout could be heard by all, and others echoed it.

Axton's head snapped back and forth, trying to take in all the information as fast as possible, attempting to devise some kind of plan to get his people through this.

"Horst!" Axton said. He hoped the minotaur was close by.

"Chief?" Horst came running up from behind. Gorst and Korn were in step behind him. Axton was glad to see they already had the arm-held ballista with him.

"Can you take it down?" Axton asked.

"Not likely. We are trying to track it, but it disappears too quickly in the darkness."

"I have an idea."

Tom, who Axton had not noticed before, because of his small but burly stature, took this moment to speak. Tom was the gnomish Engineer who had become a Bandorian but maintained some of his Gnomish tinkering and had built many of the trinkets, especially siege weapons, that they now used extensively.

"Horst, if I strap five flashers to your bolt, how long would it take them to reach max height?"

Horst stroked his chin hair, thinking it over quickly. "Probably until the count of five."

Another flash of light and an explosive boom as the dragon hit the other cart, this time farther away. A line of fire burned through three more of the clan. Axton could hear the screams, see the outlines of bodies in the fire, before they fell dead and scorched.

He steeled his mind and ignored the pain, sadness, and guilt. There would be time for mourning later, and it did not help his clan in this situation. He cleared his mind of everything but stopping the creature.

Axton looked back and Tom was already busy with a knife cutting the length of fuses on five flashers. He completed his work and passed them to Horst.

"Attach all five. I have cut the fuses to different lengths, so they will go off in succession."

Horst nodded. He looked over at Korn and Gorst.

"You two, get ready. When the sky lights up and you see the dragon, you take it down. Aim for its heart!"

Horst took the flashers and attached them to his loaded ballista bolt.

Axton, understanding the plan, called out. "Torch!" He only had to wait a moment before a nearby Bandorian ran over with a flame. Axton took it from him and readied himself.

Korn and Gorst raised their ballistae for the sky near the last location they had seen the dragon. Horst aimed straight up. Axton brought the torch over and lit all five at once. Horst immediately pulled the trigger to let the bolt fly.

They all could see a small light as the fuses burned on their way up, then there was a bright flash of light as the first flasher exploded. The sky lit up and even the white of small clouds reflected the light across the field. The next flasher went off, and all could see a blinded and stunned dragon high in the sky flapping its wings as it stayed in place, trying to get its sight back.

The dragon was a rich amber-red colour as its scales reflected the flashed light. Colossal muscles moved under its thick skin, beating the great wings back and forth to keep it aloft. Above the dragon, riding on its back, was a dark figure clad in all black robes, with no skin showing except his white crooked hands holding the reins to his powerful stead. The figure held his other hand up, covering his eyes; the flash had blinded him as well.

The dragon's massive head whipped back and forth, exposing sharp jagged teeth as it roared in frustration, and it let out another burst of flames, this time aimed at the sky. The sound was deafening, but Korn and Gorst's aim did not falter. Now, even if not for the flashers, the flame produced by the dragon provided more than enough light to expose it to the minotaurs.

As the dragon hovered in the air, flapping its wings, stunned, Gorst fired his ballista at its exposed chest. The bolt was strong enough that it pierced the chest, but just barely. It was unlikely the wound was deep enough to kill the beast outright.

The dragon let out another howl and dove towards them. Korn saw the resistance of the beast's hide and decided on another tactic. He took aim and fired. The second bolt sailed past the beast's chest and instead impaled the beast's shoulder just below the wing. It tore through the muscle and sinew, wreaking havoc on the creature's ability to steer its flight.

The dragon had been aiming to just brush by the ground, but now it smashed into the ground instead. Dirt, mud, and fire soared into the air around the dragon as momentum dragged its body along the earth.

Bandorians in the area had seen the descent and gotten clear of the crash before it happened. Now, though, they converged on the downed dragon. It was hurt and grounded, but it would not stay down for long.

Like ants over the scorpion, the Bandorians descended on the dragon, jumping onto its body, and burying long swords and axes into its flesh. Blood poured from the many incisions on the dragon's body. It tried to get up on its legs, but only rose a fraction before collapsing to the ground again. Finally, it spasmed one last time before falling silent.

Axton raced to where he had seen the rider thrown from the dragon's back. But when he arrived there, a few other Bandorians had already noticed the man had snapped his neck on impact and lay dead at their feet.

Unfortunate, but ultimately, they had succeeded. The casualties could have been far worse.

Horst, Tom, and the others ran up behind Axton. He stared across the battlefield and the dead that he could see close to the still burning fires. Sadness and guilt filled him. But confidence knowing that he did the best he could pushed those feelings away. They would honour the dead.

"Gather the bodies. We will burn and celebrate them once we have cleaned up," Axton said.

Jaxon, Fae, and their pack now approached. Axton saw them and felt relief. He turned to Tom, who stood beside him now. "Thank you, Tom. That stunt saved us all."

Tom stood there, the height of a child, and simply said, "Of course."

Axton raised his voice to a yell for all to hear. "Carve up the beast. Tonight, we eat dragon! We celebrate our heroes and the glorious dead!" Dozens of hurrahs answered his call.

They would carry on.

After they had eaten, Axton visited the wounded. They had collected the dead and burned their bodies on a pyre before dinner. They were no longer as concerned about stealth. If there was an ambush, it likely would have attacked during or after the dragon when they were distracted. Besides, anyone in the area certainly would have seen that battle.

He walked among the injured. Burn victims laid out on stretchers. Men and women with blistering skin, charred limbs, wrapped in tissues and salves. Groans rose to his ears as he passed. Dozens had died, more had been injured and lie here being tended to. Many more had minor wounds, but if any could still fight, then they were patched up quickly.

The burden weighed heavily on Axton, but he knew better than to let it weaken his resolve. *Self-analysis would be useful and help him learn from the situation. But people were relying on him, and doubt destroys the mind; makes it makes it weak, slow. He would not do his people a disservice now.*

Axton heard orders being barked out as he approached a stretcher raised on the back of a burned wagon. Cairn half sat, half lay there, a broken and burned leg in a splint wrapped with salve and sealed in healing leaves. His left arm, partially wrapped, was black and blistering where it was not completely covered. Two of the fingers on the hand were missing completely and the others were bandaged.

He was yelling orders to those around but was calmer in his instructions to his ward, Thyra; he knew it was important to keep her calm while she treated the injured. She was still young, and the young were more easily rattled, so with her, he was patient and reassuring.

Axton was impressed with Thyra as he watched her work steadily and meticulously with Cairn. While all Bandorians were trained in aid and healing, it was important to have a dedicated clan member to maintain the knowledge and craft of both the physical and magical healing arts. Thyra had displayed a talent for it, so Cairn had taken her as his apprentice.

"Cairn, you are injured. What are you doing?" Axton asked.

"People won't heal themselves, Axton," Cairn said. "Well, they will, but not fast enough. Thyra is gifted, but she can also use the support."

"No rest till the job is done, eh?"

Axton smiled at his friend.

"Nope."

Axton's expression turned dark. "Cairn, your arm."

"It looks worse than it is. Or maybe it doesn't. But I still have one good arm. Others were less lucky."

His words were true. "How bad is it, Cairn?" Axton asked.

"Honestly, it could have been much worse. Most will fight again. Fili asked to be released. He would never walk or fight again. We ended him just before you got here. Others will have glorious scars to share but will fight again in time. In total, it looks like twenty-nine dead, forty-eight injured who will return to battle in time, and a lot more than that just needed a patch or two and are back at it."

"Down nearly eighty troops," Axton said, thinking about it.

"Do we have enough to hold the south still?" Cairn asked.

Axton thought over it before responding. "I believe we still do. We are going to have to. Much of our food and supplies were destroyed back there. If we want to eat, we will have to do something. Most of us only have the food left in our packs, but even that will have to be shared with the scouts to keep them quick on their feet."

Cairn nodded. "The Imperials will still be moving supplies back and forth with the capital, especially if they are worried about sieges."

"Yes…" Axton nodded. "Jaxon's pack was uninjured. They are fast and can make surprise attacks on supply lines so we can restock. We will need to get them at it soon."

Axton looked up and out over the injured once more. "This was a great blow. Some said the Empire had a dragon, some have said it may have been two dragons, but we have at least seen one. We believe this one came from Southshore. Otherwise, it would have joined the battle when we fought their garrison."

"I heard that the Empire enslaved them," Cairn said. "Treated them like beasts long enough for them to become beasts. If they have more, they will be in the capital, not here."

"Either way, now they have one less." Axton looked back to Cairn. "We have already dispatched a scout to the north to inform the other clans of what has occurred. Once the injured can be moved, we march east. We will scout ahead and set up a hidden camp from which we can launch surprise attacks."

Cairn nodded. "A sound plan. We should be mobile within a few hours, at worst, by sunrise."

"Good. Thank you, my friend. Your sacrifice was noble and appreciated throughout the clan."

"Of course."

Axton looked once more at his once strong half-orc friend, now burned and broken, half covered in bandages. Cairn would heal to fight again, and he would be stronger for it. Like the clan would be stronger once it recovered, and the survivors have passed through fire. *Pity did not have the power to heal Cairn or the others; only care and support would restore them. A wise leader knew this, but it didn't mean it wasn't hard.*

CHAPTER 26

THE CARRIAGE

The carriage creaked as it made its way over the dirt trail intended for horses, not wheels, rocking back and forth as it hit large rocks or deep ruts. From their nearby hiding place just west of the road, Fae could not help but grin at the obviously unpleasant ride for the passenger inside. Based on the regalia of the carriage, it was a member of the Magisterium. It was plain to see from the grimace on the coachman's face that he was not enjoying this part of the ride, even before she considered the fact that the carriage's occupants would probably chastise him later; it wouldn't matter if it was his fault.

But this was precisely why Fae and Jaxon had suggested this specific part of the trail to lie in wait. Though Kiva had noted that two kilometres north of this location was the best place for an ambush because of the density of trees, Fae had mentioned that it was the obvious place, and the soldiers would be at their most alert. Jaxon pointed out that while this location did not have trees that came as close to the sides of the trail, the bumpy nature of this section caused by the heavier exposure to rainfall would slow down the carriage and have everyone paying more attention to the carriage than the surrounding foliage. The ruts made any attempt at a quick escape by the carriage impossible.

Bullock was the one to bring up that the soldiers would also be the most relaxed here because they would have just made it through the place where they expected to be attacked.

"Is it just me, or has Axton been sending us on most of the assignments lately?"

Erika crouched beside Fae in the dense foliage. Fae shifted to get comfortable, her back pressed against the rough bark of a nearby tree. Kiva and Jaxon crouched alongside them, their weapons at the ready. The four of them huddled close together behind the small cover that could be found. Despite the close quarters, they maintained a tense silence, waiting for the right moment to strike.

"Well, that is what happens when all the other packs have someone out of commission, and our asses are too pretty to get singed," Jaxon said.

Fae shushed them both.

It had been several weeks since the massacre caused by the dragon attack. Immediately after the attack, Axton had sent a messenger to the north to inform the main Bandorian forces of what had happened to the southern advance. While at first it had seemed a dire event, later informants and scouts had told them that the dragon attack had been an act of desperation. There were much fewer forces between them, and Southshore after Clan Kaltor had destroyed the southwestern garrison a few weeks back, just before Fae and the others had arrived. Most of the remaining Imperial troops had pulled back to defend Southshore. They had only risked the dragon because they had nothing else to throw at the attackers.

Since the dragon's attack, Clan Kaltor had moved east through wooded areas using guerrilla tactics to conduct ambushes and small skirmishes with any forces on their way to the road joining Southshore. The clan had sent out individual packs out to harass enemies and make the area dangerous to the Imperials. Their goal was to interrupt supply lines between the major cities which would wreak havoc on the Empire.

"We were lucky to not have any of us injured in that attack," Kiva said, "That dragon fire was horrifying."

"At least if it had hit one of you two, we have a spare, so we would be fine," Jaxon said.

He let out a muted grunt as Kiva punched him in the arm.

"Guys. Quiet," Fae said.

"Sorry. My bad. Fae's right. We need to pay attention."

Jaxon raised a fist, ready to give the signal.

Scouts from the main Bandorian forces had witnessed this carriage and entourage departure from the capital days earlier and had reported to Clan Kaltor. With most of the other clans busy engaged with skirmishes west of the capital, Clan Kaltor were the only ones south enough to intercept. Because of their youth and cross land speed, Jaxon, Fae, Kiva, Erika, and Bullock were given the honour of chasing it down and ambushing it. The clan wished to know what scheme was so important to the Empire that they risked sending a lone wizard down the southern road to Southshore.

The carriage continued down the trail. Six armed soldiers escorted it, four on horseback, each with an arming sword and a shield. Luckily, no spears. The danger would be the carriage driver and the guard sitting on the watch seat on the back of the carriage; both men were armed with crossbows, though the driver kept his weapon placed beneath him and not immediately available. Drawing the ranged fire was Bullock's responsibility.

Jaxon, with hand still raised, stared across the trail, making eye contact with Bullock. He sat hidden and alone in the shrubs on the other side, invisible to all except the pack that knew exactly where he was. His job was to draw the Imperial men's attention. He was armoured much more heavily than the others for this exact purpose. With his vanguard armour of dwarven steel and a massive tower shield in his left hand, arrows would do no damage. As usual, in his right hand, he carried his massive battle axe.

This was also one of those rare moments where he wore his horned helmet. It was a large steel helm, which covered his entire face, and had two large bison horns made of metal on the top of the helmet. Bullock had worked with two dwarves and a minotaur to analyze the skull of the minotaur to understand how to best create a helmet for purposes similar to their ability to ram, so they had built it to simulate much of the structure of an actual ramming animal.

Bullock looked at Jaxon and gave a nod. He was ready.

Fae did not envy Bullock having to wear that much armour, but at least he had the strength for it. She preferred speed over strength, and it worked well for her, being the smallest of the pack.

Fae focused back on the carriage. She moved back and forth subtly to keep the blood flowing. She clenched her hand around the long handle of her deadly glaive. Her muscles tensed, and she could feel the energy from the anticipation coursing through his veins. She had that strange feeling in her stomach, like a nervousness before battle, but focused on the anticipation of the fight to come. Fae always had this feeling before a fight but had learned to channel back into herself to create feral energy.

Jaxon still had his hand up. *When was he going to give the signal?* He always predicted the best moment for these ambushes, but the carriage was directly between them and Bullock.

Finally, Jaxon took his open raised palm and clenched it quickly, then brought it down sharply. Bullock was about to have some fun.

Bullock rushed from the trees at an incredible charge, screaming and banging as he ran to make as much noise as possible. He had to make sure his distraction was effective enough for the enemies to believe that all the threats would come from his side of the trail.

Thunk. An arrow embedded itself in his shield, and Fae was thankful he had the shield this one time. Bullock belted out a chilling battle cry that had the desired effect. The men on horseback paused long enough for him to get to them. He had picked the closest man on horseback, which was now positioned between him and the carriage, and charged it with all his force and weight.

Another arrow hit his shield but did not slow him down. He smashed the horse, with shield and body, in the left flank and staggered it enough to rock against the wagon. The horse was unused to this type of motion and the wagon wheels impeded the horse's attempt to right itself. The result was a flailing horse attempting to keep itself upright and smashing against the side of the wagon repeatedly.

The wagon rocked and lifted on Bullock's side from the repeated hits. Wheels on the other side creaked and eventually snapped under the constant forces they had not been built to withstand. The driver and the rear crossbowman both fell off the carriage with their crossbows in hand, but the weapons went skittering out of reach as they each hit the ground.

The horses flailed and threw the first soldier from its back. It ran off to get clear of the confusion. Bullock and the first soldier went down together in a tumble. Bullock tried to pummel the soldier to death; he had lost his axe in the scuffle.

Two soldiers on horseback advanced on Bullock. They urged their horses slowly, wary of trampling their own man. The other three waited and looked to the forest from where Bullock had come, searching for any other enemies.

The distraction had worked. It was their turn.

"Now," Jaxon said from their hiding place in the trees.

Fae bolted forward with the other three.

Before the men on horseback reached Bullock, three daggers whistled from beside Fae. The first blade embedded itself in the armour gap on the back of an advancing soldier's neck, the other two blades clattering off the steel armour of the other. One soldier collapsed dead off his horse, but the other soldier turned to face the new threats. He saw the four other members of the pack charging them.

Kiva had another two blades in her hands. The two unarmoured men that had fallen from the carriage were back on their feet. They levelled their crossbows at the charging Bandorians. Kiva's hands whipped, and the blades whistled.

The men aimed. Kiva's first blade drove deep into the driver's chest. He collapsed. Dead. The rear guard squeezed the trigger. The second blade struck his right shoulder. His bolt triggered but shot wide, and the man dropped the crossbow. The weight of it was too much for his left hand to hold. He pulled the dagger from his shoulder and cried out in pain, blood freely flowing.

The rest of the soldiers clued into the real threat and turned. The surprise was gone, and swords were unsheathed.

The two soldiers not yet dismounted, charged towards the Bandorians, but they did not have enough room to reach a dangerous speed. One soldier and his horse reached Erika just to have her sidestep out of the way and swing her great axe into the flank of the horse. The horse stumbled and went down hard, throwing the man from its back, stunning the man.

The fourth soldier charged Fae from horseback and lined himself up, readying his sword to cleave her. As he reached her, he swung his sword down, but Fae moved with a burst of speed and switched to the other side of the horse. Before the man could adjust, she brought her heavy glaive up in a diagonal swipe. Steel ripped through the horse harness, part of the stirrup, and finally the man's left leg. The man howled and the horse's harness came apart, dropping the man to the ground as the horse ran off.

Kiva approached the fallen soldier with cold precision. She quickly put the man out of his misery with her twin swords, before continuing to the rear-guard crossbowman. He held a sword weakly in his left hand as the blood poured from the dagger wound in his right shoulder. He brought the sword up to block Kiva's attack, but she batted it out of his hand with a strike from her right hand, then ended his life with a strike from her left.

Bullock's fist collided with the first soldier's head, making a sound like the beating of a hung rug. He clasped both hands on either side of the man's breastplate and lifted him into the air, but the man was already dead. Bullock seemed to notice this and simply tossed him to the side, before engaging with the two foot-soldiers.

There was now only one horseman still left in fighting condition; the one that had been thrown from his horse by Erika's attack. Jaxon slowly approached him but did not attack. Instead, Jaxon gave the man time to stand, pick up his shield with his left hand and his sword with his right. The man came at Jaxon with an overhand swipe, but Jaxon leaned back out of the way; *the man had courage.*

Jaxon quickly shifted back, throwing himself forward, and swung his great sword sideways at the man, forcing the man to take the brunt of the attack with his shield. The man's arm buckled under the weight of the attack, and he stumbled back. He did not have time to regain his stance.

Jaxon was not one to play with someone he knew he would kill; he would make it fast. Jaxon brought his sword down on the man's right shoulder, burying it into the collarbone. When the man collapsed, Jaxon moved in and ended his suffering.

Steel clashed as Erika and Bullock collided with the final two soldiers, neither of which had been on horseback. Successful shield blocks and jabbing swords kept the two Bandorians at bay.

"Hey Fae. These guys don't look so good," Bullock said.

"Good. They are supposed to be dead."

"No. I mean, like they are not right. Something's different from the other soldiers, just look at them."

Fae finally looked up from the man she and Kiva had killed. Bullock had knocked the helmet off his opponent and Fae noticed a sickly grey face blankly staring back at them as it attacked Bullock.

"You're right. That is not normal."

"Well. Have you ever seen it before?"

His axe deflected off the shield once more.

"No. But those wizards do strange things. Maybe it's a curse."

A soldier over-extended in a swing against Erika and she lopped off his arm. It did not bleed.

"A curse?" Bullock asked, panting. "Am I going to get cursed? Fae, I don't want to be cursed!"

Bullock batted a sword swing away.

"I don't know, Bullock. Just kill him and if you turn grey, we'll know you're cursed."

"Not funny, Fae."

Bullock's swings were hesitant.

"Fae?" Bullock still wanted an answer.

Erika's axe took the head off Bullock's opponent.

"There, nothing we can do now," Erika said. "Just don't eat him and you'll probably be fine."

The head rolled and the body collapsed with no blood running.

"Gross," Bullock grimaced.

Fae looked around as she was wiping off her glaive to see the others doing the same in the grass or men's clothes and picking up equipment that they had dropped or thrown during the skirmish. The quiet after a battle was always unsettling and strange when compared to the clammer only moments before. Even the carriage stood there silent, leaning to the one side that the two wheels had snapped off from.

Fae knew that there must be someone inside, but they made no noise or movement to prove that they were alive. Just as Jaxon was cautiously stepping towards the vehicle, the door of the carriage exploded off its hinges and flew across the battlefield, crashing into the ground several yards away. Wood splintered and floated in the air.

Out of the carriage stepped a large, hooded man in the robes of a senior wizard. This man did not hold himself like a wizard, though. Even through his robes, it was clear this man was overly muscular for a wizard.

"Stand down!" came a booming voice from the hooded figure. "I will submit to be your prisoner. I choose that over death, and I have no interest in torture. Take me to your camp and I will answer what questions you have."

There was no fear at all in this man's voice, only a calm determination. The man drew back his hood, revealing a handsome face younger than expected.

"My only demand is that you take me to see Axton."

CHAPTER 27
THE DECISION

It's funny. Damitus had imagined the first time he would meet Axton face to face again many times; picturing some run in on a battlefield, or more likely one of them looking over the other's dead corpse. He had never imagined he would meet Axton again like this.

The warrior now sat across a large carved wooden table from Damitus, giving him a look that made Damitus almost glad there were others in the room: the five Bandorians that had carried out the attack on the carriage ferrying him to Southshore.

He knew a few things about them now. He had listened carefully and watched them on the walk back to their camp. They appeared to not have lived even twenty seasons, and yet the young male they called Jaxon appeared to already be something of a protégé to Axton. A role Damitus once filled for Axton and Gaer. He looked strong and fit, average height for a Bandorian, and apparently handsome enough to attract the blonde sitting at Axton's left.

Fae, they had called her. She was an odd one. She was pretty, and strong, but had the features of an Imperial more than Bandorian.

Then again, not quite. Something was off about her, but he could not put his finger on it.

The twins sitting next to one another, surprisingly, were identical, each with a shock of red hair. Last was the big male, large even for a Bandorian. He had shown he could pack a punch.

All six of them just sat there, glaring at him, waiting for someone to say the first words.

"Why the frown, Axton?" Damitus asked. "Control your emotions. Don't let them control you. Isn't that what you always preach?"

"Oh, I can control my emotions right now and still decide to frown at you."

Damitus raised an unconvinced eyebrow.

"So be it. I suppose I was the one to leave. Still, it seems like you have a new litter to replace me. And you are chieftain now." He dropped his smug look. "Then Gaer?"

"Dead. Eight years now."

"How?"

Damitus had assumed his old mentor had passed, but somehow hearing it drudged up feelings he would rather not be capable of.

"In Creet."

The blonde girl, Fae, flinched almost imperceptibly at the mention of Creet. *Peculiar.* If Damitus had not been intentionally watching them all for subtle clues, he may have missed it.

"I'm sorry." Damitus's mocking tone was gone.

"He died a good death. He did right by the clan."

It was a subtle remark, highlighting Axton's archaic idea that Damitus had dishonoured the clan. Damitus was unaffected, Axton was wise, but Damitus felt no debt to the clan. Still, a flicker from deep within him was glad that Gaer had died the way he would have wanted to.

"Moving on. As enjoyable as it might be, I did not come here to mend old relationships. I told you I would trade information for my life, and I spoke true. A danger approaches, one in which even the might of the deadly Bandorian clans cannot overcome with strength alone. A deadly threat will pour over your people like flames to a forest and leave nothing in its wake."

"You've spent too much time in the empire. It's affected your speech," Axton said. "Get on with it."

Damitus said nothing about the interruption, but gave an annoyed look. He continued, "Once the sun sets, four days from now, the Magus of Southshore will lead several other wizards in a ritual of dark sorcery, necrotic magic that will unleash a power upon your people like none you have ever seen. It will not just decimate your forces though, it will rip through you, destroying you from the inside, before it continues on to the rest of the world."

"Horseshit. No one has that kind of power," the big one said. Bullock, if Damitus remembered correctly.

"Axton, who in the Abyss even is this guy?" Jaxon asked. "How do you know him, let alone trust what he has to say?"

All eyes turned to Axton, and Damitus smirked.

Axton sighed, "His name is Damitus, and he was much like each of you."

"Damitus was a child of the Empire, orphaned at the age of eight, and brought in by Gaer and I."

Damitus scanned the others for their reactions. Most were simple, but the blonde's mouth opened just slightly before she forced it shut. *Had she heard part of the story? Perhaps adopted as well; it would explain the looks.*

"He studied magic more than others, with Fynnathias and Cairn. Before he faced the trials, he got into an argument with Gaer and I, seeing magic as a powerful tool, he wanted us to expand our knowledge in it and harness it. We did not agree."

Hearing Axton's voice and remembering his past made Damitus's hand twitch. He had not felt this exposed in decades. *No one knew his history. Except Axton.*

"We had a falling out. Damitus left before the trials, and I can only make assumptions after that." Axton looked back at Damitus. "I trust that was an unbiased account?"

Damitus nodded at Axton.

Feelings clouded his mind, like a stick raking up sediment from the ocean floor. He steeled himself to force them back down.

"Axton is correct. I will keep it simple by saying that, after I left, I used my considerable mental and physical skills to force my acceptance into The Academy of Magic, worked my way up, and have secured a place amongst the order."

"Still not hearing anything that tells us why we should trust him, let alone have taken off his bindings," one twin said.

"You and I both know that any of you could throw a dagger through my throat before I could even finish saying the words to a spell."

"He has a point," the other twin said. His comment had garnered a few grins.

"Enough," Axton said. "This ritual? What is it? How do we stop it?"

"You have pushed them too far. They were not suspecting the ferocity of your people to cripple them in battle, and proposals, once rejected due to risks, are now looking much more appealing."

Damitus's refusal to speak simply frustrated them as intended, and he could see it on their faces. *Good, they would be less likely to ask the questions he did not want to answer. He had to lead the conversation in the direction he wanted.*

"The ritual yields powerful spells for their use: ones that reanimate fallen foes and compel them to serve the archons, spells that render their soldiers resistant to death, and magics that create semi-immortals to fight in their ranks. It is a dark sorcery; immensely powerful but ultimately unstable. They need the blood of their enemy for the ritual. Your blood."

Damitus watched carefully for reactions, but the Bandorians sat stoically, waiting for him to continue.

"They have captured others of your people and they will use their blood."

Damitus did not know if this last part was true, but he had to get the clan to act, to create the urgency. And if it was true, then everything else he said was correct. It was completely possible, and even likely, that they did not have the blood they needed, and had sent him there to be killed and drained of his blood. He could think of no other reason for his forceful expulsion to Southshore and fabricated reason of being there to help with the ritual.

They feared him, and likely aimed to have him killed.

"They have been testing this sorcery for some time, carrying out many experiments without the knowledge of the people. The undead escorting me resulted from some of these tests that succeeded."

"What about the experiments that failed?" Fae asked. "Have they been carrying these out on living people?"

"Oh, I imagine so. You learn more from living humans."

Fae grimaced, but the others seemed unfazed.

"Why the blood?" Kiva asked.

"This ritual also creates a curse that slowly spreads like a plague. They will use the blood as a focus to attack people with the blood of their enemy. Bandorian blood."

"But we don't share blood. We are a culture, not a race." Axton said.

"They don't know that. They are ignorant. This spell-plague will destroy the mind but keep the body alive. It will leave the person under the control of archons, to form an army from their enemies. It will not just destroy your people when they perform this ritual, it will attack people everywhere."

"And this happens in four days?" Fae asked.

"Correct."

"Why tell us this?" Jaxon asked. "Why share this with us if you are Imperial now?" He crossed his arms as he sat back.

"I could say for revenge. I had a massive network of spies, I owned resources across the Empire, and I had access to every piece of written works that existed. I covered my tracks but, with enough time and determination, anything can be discovered. And I assure you, they had every reason to be determined. They deduced I was Bandorian, arrested me, then systematically took down all my networks. They even forced me to sign a letter and send it to my brimstone suppliers, having them send large supplies to Southshore for the ritual."

His mouth downturned into a sneer.

"But it is beyond all of that. It takes tremendous energy to create life from something that is dead, whether that be a dead mind or dead body. It takes a toll. It will slowly kill the land, the people, even the minds of those that use it. I value magic and knowledge above all else, but this is not something that grows either of those. This corrupts those that use it and everything around it. In a world ruined, there is nothing further for me to gain. I crave power, but I am not insane. This is not altruism, this is what is best for me, as you taking action is what is best for you."

"Shit," Bullock said.

"Indeed."

"What action do you suggest, then?" Jaxon asked.

"The delivery of brimstone will arrive there in three days, and the ritual will be ready on the night of the fourth day. You must rally your people and surround the city. Blockade the city and destroy anyone that tries to leave it. They will not have enough forces to break out if the spell-plague is released.

"When you have marshalled enough of your forces, you must burn the city. Lay siege to it. I will teach some of yours and help you. We can use my magic to fan the flames, and together we can burn this plague from the inside like a fever burns a disease. Magic and might, together, to end this abomination."

"No," Axton interrupted, "We will not weaken ourselves with a dependence on magic."

Damitus knew it had been a reach to suggest that, but it had been worth the attempt.

"Burn the city?" Fae asked, her lips trembling "What about the people inside?"

"There is nothing we can do for them." He tried his best to feign a look of regret. "Contain the city and destroy it. Completely."

"What about stopping the ritual in the first place?" Jaxon asked.

"How? You do not have enough people to breach the city in such a short amount of time."

No one had an answer. No one spoke for some time as they thought about the implications of what they were being told.

Finally, Axton spoke up. "I need to inform the others. You found Damitus, and you uncovered this plot. I leave it to you five for now to think on this. Come up with a plan if you can. I will not use his magics. We may have no choice but to contain the situation."

Fae's shoulders slumped, and her face was ashen.

"Keep an eye on Damitus," Axton said.

With that, he pushed his chair back, stood up, and exited the tent.

No one spoke for a time, each digesting the information and weight of the action thrust in front of them in their own way.

"Are we really going to sacrifice an entire city?" Fae asked, her voice wavering.

The blonde's eyes darted between each of her companions, and none seemed to meet hers. There was a history there that Damitus could only guess at. She pushed her chair back, stood up, and placed her palms on the table.

"Is that who you are?" The comment dripped with venom and accusation. *She had a story and the clues to it were slowly being revealed.*

"Fae, hun, there might not be any other choice." The twin with two blades said. Fae's eyes seemed to glisten, on the verge of tears.

"There might." Jaxon looked up at the others now. "We don't have the power to take the city or assault it, but we might infiltrate it. A small team. The five of us. We could sneak in and stop it."

It sounded like blind optimism motivated by the boy's affection for the blonde.

"Nonsense," Damitus said. "You can't just sneak in to stop it. Southshore knows your forces are near. They will not be letting anyone in or out without extreme investigation. The entire city is surrounded by walls of stone."

"Walls can be breached. Snuck past," Erika said.

"Even if you got into the city, you would have to infiltrate the castle as well, and the ritual will be in the castle's basement, past a full garrison of guards and troops." Damitus was letting his exasperation show. "It would be—"

"You," Kiva said, pointing at Damitus with a throwing blade in her hand. "Not another word, or I will slit your throat."

Fine. Damitus pushed his chair out and stood up, pacing along the tent wall, listening to the conversation.

"Listen," Jaxon continued. "If we could neutralize some of these barriers, we could find a way in. We have pulled off tough missions before. I have nothing yet, but we have to figure something out."

"Dammit, Jaxon. It will kill us, and you know it." Bullock slammed his fists down on the wooden table. "For fuck's sake, even Axton knows we don't have a choice." His shoulders released some of the anger and tension and his voice calmed, "Jaxon, I want to die in a good fight as much as the next Bandorian does, but I don't want to throw my life away for something we don't even know for sure is true." He placed his hands on the wooden table and stared across it at Jaxon.

Perhaps he was the smart one; at least the one thinking rationally right now.

Jaxon's head lowered as he listened. He placed his fingers above his eyes and pressed them into the bridge of his nose. *Perhaps the weight of leadership weighed on his shoulders. There was no official leader in a pack, but one usually rose to be the facilitator of discussion.*

Jaxon lifted his head to stare back at the largest of them. "Bullock, I know, trust me, I know. But we might not have a choice.

Even if we send for help now, it may take time to convince the other clans. Axton doesn't need us. He can still send riders north to rally the others while we do something."

The twins stayed sitting in their chairs around the circular table. Fae stared nervously at Jaxon, her face paling. The two boys stood, locking eye contact, neither breaking.

Damitus was curious how this argument would turn out and watched attentively and silently. He retreated further towards the wall of the tent in the darkest corner of the room, and the others seemed to lose awareness of him.

"I know what I am asking of you, all of you," Jaxon said. He looked at Bullock, then around the table to include the others as well, "but we have to find a way."

"What if he is lying?" Kiva asked.

"Unlikely," Fae said. "Axton said he was a Bandorian once. Besides, did anyone in the room get any sense that he was lying or that his story was off at all?"

The four others shook their heads gently in response. Damitus knew better than to outright lie, when simply revealing the correct nuggets of truth would do so much more.

"A sneak attack by five of us is the best option," Jaxon said. "Even if it is all a lie and a trap, a trap being sprung on five of us, is much better than it being sprung on the entire clan."

A subtle movement of Fae's hand caught Damitus's attention. She raised her hand to her bracer, seemingly without knowing it, and traced her finger over the trim. There was a small gem or amulet there, embedded in the bracer. Something about the design was familiar, like something he had once seen in an old book.

Fae stood. She placed a gentle hand on Jaxon's chest as she came to stand beside him. "I am with Jaxon. We have to do this; there is no other way." She paused for a moment. "If someone doesn't do something, it means extinction."

The importance of this moment was not lost on Damitus. The

Venesterium mixing life and death magic in the unholy necrotic union of the two could be catastrophic.

They could create this plague, create an army, but they would be unlikely to stop there. It would destroy the minds of the world and corrupt the land.

Their army would crash over the highlands of the Craeg like waves of the sea rolling over the pebbles of beaches. This threat would annihilate the Bandorians. They would be driven to extinction, and their nation of free peoples would be replaced with an Empire of slaves and servants. Eventually, it would even destroy the minds of those that ruled, and would turn the world to death and darkness, where nothing truly died, and nothing truly lived.

That was a fate he could not allow to come to pass. That was the fate that now weighed on the minds of this small pack. It would be impossible to breach the walls of Southshore with such a small army, and even if they did, they would never survive the assault. But they were not going to just give up, not while the world could turn to darkness and despair.

Fae looked over at Bullock. "Come on Bullock, no use fighting it. Are you in?"

Bullock let out a roar as he kicked a small stool across the room; it clattered into a crate of food, before coming to rest in a few pieces against the tent entrance. Bullock let out a quieter growl this time. "Of course, I'm in. It doesn't mean I have to think it's a good idea." Finally, he stomped over to stand by the other two.

A quiet, almost imperceptible disagreement started on the other end of the room. In whispered voices, Kiva and Erika were holding each other's hands and arguing, but Damitus could make it out.

"Erika, this is crazy, and you know it," Kiva said. "There is no way we are coming out of there alive." She squeezed Erika's hand tighter. "Just because Jaxon says we should do it doesn't mean it is a good idea. Even if we do manage to sneak into the city, there are guards everywhere. We'll never make it out alive. I won't let you get yourself killed and leave me without my twin." She squeezed Erika's hands to keep her from pulling away.

But Erika did pull her hands away. "Kiva, you have always been the brave one for me, but now it is my turn to be brave for you. We have to go, and you will come too, but I need to decide for us this time. If you decide not to come, I will not make you, but I know you will."

She finally stepped away from her twin and crossed the floor to where the others now stood, watching their conversation.

The four of them now looked over at Kiva, waiting for a decision to go and likely throw away their lives, possibly not even succeeding in their goal; or stay and live until a spell-plague ravages the world. *At least in one scenario, she would live a lot longer.* Kiva paced back and forth, just looking at the floor and talking to herself inaudibly. Finally, she noticed everyone was looking at her and she raised her eyes to face them. "Yeah yeah, I'm coming too, don't worry. I won't let you all get yourselves killed and leave me here to be bored by myself."

She too finally crossed the floor, and when she approached the others, she looked up at Jaxon and said, "Alright, wise leader, what is your plan to get past two stone walls?"

Jaxon's mouth turned up in a slightly sly smile. "I've been thinking about that and might have an idea, but we will need Tom." Tom had been a Gnomish Engineer even when Damitus was with the clan and if he was needed, then this was certainly not a conventional plan.

The night was dark, with no moon and only starlight to illuminate the world beyond the campfire light. Damitus's intelligent eyes watched the five brave men and women leaving. The rest of the camp clambered to ensure everything was prepared for an assault of the city if needed. They had told him of the plan, and he had provided what information he could, though he urged against it.

He sat there for a time, in the dark flowing robes of the Magisterium, watching; always watching.

Finally, he rose from the stump he rested on, to get a better view of those that would willingly sacrifice their lives to such a hopeless cause. Respect, sadness, frustration, and contempt all flowed through his mind, and he took a deep breath before speaking out loud. Not to anyone in particular, just to himself, and whatever gods existed.

He spoke slowly at first, but with certainty, "How deluded you are. Valiant, but deluded. What is honour to those that are dead and cannot use it?" His voice then lowered in pitch before continuing, "The first casualties are always the courageous."

He stood there alone in the darkness with only the flickering light of the fire to illuminate him. Then, when no one had their eyes on him, he stepped back into the darkness and, like one shadow being swallowed by a larger one, vanished.

CHAPTER 28
OVER THE WALL

Fae looked up at her lover as he gave her a nervous grin that did not help her feel any more at ease.

Jaxon sat on the wooden seat attached to a monster of a machine. A mix of wood craftsmanship, massive metallic springs, levers, and pulleys. Fae was familiar with all the principals in theory, but this machine confounded her. It was the size of a medium-sized tent and looked like the war machines one used for bringing down castle walls. The difference was that instead of a large boulder at the end of a large rotating arm, there was just Jaxon, sitting on a wooden platform at the bottom of a large track, which pointed about forty-five degrees to the sky.

Please, gods, let this work.

"Tom, are you sure this is going to work?" Jaxon asked. "I am really not feeling that optimistic about our chances at the moment." He looked down at the gnome, operating the controls of the large mechanism. The gnome's head was shaved bald except for a topknot, and he had enough muscle on him to look more like a dwarf than a gnome.

"This was your idea, Jax." Then he let out a laugh that made him sound like a madman.

Jaxon gave a wary look at their old friend, "My idea was to get us over the castle wall. It was your batshit crazy idea to launch us like giant stones."

The gnome gave a shrug and responded as if it did not matter, "Meh, you didn't say no."

"Yeah, I'm beginning to question the sanity of that decision."

Fae did as well. It had been her push to save the people of Southshore, but after going through the ideas to find the best possible plan, she wasn't so sure any longer. *A part of her wondered what she was even doing here, and who she even was?* She realized her hand was holding her bracer once more, and she thought of her nana and her gem within.

Now she stood there with a culture of people she could never quite forgive, launching a man she loved, perhaps to his death, then committing to a suicide mission with the people she thought of as family. She had never intended to end up here in life. She had once been determined to find her nana.

"Oh, buck up Jax," Tom said, turning back to the controls, "At least if this works, I'll be the first gnome to pull this off."

"You mean no one has ever done this before?" Jaxon spat the question at Tom in terrified surprise.

"Relax, we had built out the theory a few times back home, and I've done the calculations. I'm usually right about these things. Just remember to hold on to your knees so you fly like a stone."

"Oh, burn me."

Wringing her hands, Fae tried not to let her fear show. She couldn't believe she had agreed to this. *Why had she not stopped him? No, it would be fine.*

Jaxon leaned forward on the seat he sat on, grabbed his own knees, pulling them to his chest, stared at his destination, and nodded.

"Punch it, Tom!"

The spring engaged with a click, accelerating the wooden seat Jaxon was crouched in, speeding him up the track, and launching him high in the air towards the city wall. Like a boulder, he tumbled with his limbs tucked in, sailing through the air at an intense speed. He got closer to the city walls, hardly slowing down as he continued up towards the top of his arc.

Tom's voice echoed in Fae's mind at that moment. "You will know when you reach the top of the arc through the air, because you will feel weightless, and your stomach will lurch. Open your arms and legs straight; the sail will do the rest."

Fae saw Jaxon do as Tom said, stretching his limbs. The sails that Tom had secured to his arms and legs made him look like a flying squirrel as he sailed through the air.

They watched as Jaxon opened and the sails caught the air, but he was not holding the position correctly. The sails flew every which way as Jaxon moved his arms; he had to stabilize them. Tom looked over to where Fae was also watching.

"Yeah, he's dead," he said. His was so matter-of-fact that Fae kicked him in the shin for it.

"What?" he snapped back. "At least the Imperial Guards will be confused as shit when a body comes crashing down into their town. Can you use that to your advantage somehow?"

"Shut it, Tom. Just watch, he'll figure it out." *Dammit, Jaxon, figure it out.* She pressed her hand to her forehead to block out the light and continue watching.

After a moment of flailing, Jaxon got control of the sails, as Fae predicted. Then, like the flying squirrel he so resembled, Jaxon soared through the air high above the city. Finally, Fae lost sight of Jaxon over the city walls.

Tom got busy prepping the machine for another launch. Fae was still looking out over the horizon, watching for some sign that Jaxon still lived. She knew she had no control over what she would see, but she still hoped.

She saw it, the signal. A red flag was raised over one of the four castle towers. Fae let her excitement over seeing proof of Jaxon's survival grow in her for only a moment before she centred herself and remembered her duty.

"That is the signal."

She spoke so methodically that Tom did not catch what she implied right away.

"What?" Tom asked in utter confusion, "Wait, he made it? Well, I'll be a humped thistleback; that crazy son of a bitch. I expected him to become a crater in a shopkeeper's stall."

When the jubilance had worn off, he looked over at Fae, "Alright girly, your turn."

Fae looked at the launcher, then at the tall city wall in the distance.

"Burn me."

Fae's feet delicately touched down on the stone walkway of the tower. Unlike Jaxon, she had not had trouble balancing her sails during her flight, and she had enjoyed the experience of weightlessness and flight. The feeling had been exhilarating as the air brushed through her thick blonde locks.

She began detaching her sails as she looked around. Jaxon sat on an unconscious or dead guard amongst a pile of smashed wooden kindling and equipment. The tower was a mess. Broken chairs and weapons were strewn around, and a second guard was crumpled against the door. Any furniture in the watch post seemed to be in pieces.

Jaxon just sat there, grinning.

"Your handiwork?" Fae asked.

"Yeah, I put the first guy into the weapons rack, but I didn't see the second guy at first. Had to improvise with that chair."

"Smooth."

Jaxon slowly got to his feet, rubbing a visible bruise on his arm.

Kiva landed next, not as delicately as Fae, but still with enough grace. Bullock, who was after her, did not land gracefully, coming in faster than the other two. He planted feet on the ground and had to take some stutter steps, then braced himself against the far wall to stop himself. Despite this, though, he kept his footing and dignity. The only one left to still land was Erika.

"Hey, handsome. Catch me!" Came the playful call of Erika, and instead of landing like the rest, she came down towards Bullock, tucking her limbs in, twisting sideways as if to land elegantly in Bullock's arms. But she had too much speed, and she careened into Bullock, sending them both down in a heap. When they came to rest, Bullock was lying on his back.

Bullock didn't move, spreading his arms and resting his head as if he were simply happy to be laying down. Erika was sitting on his chest, looking down at his face.

"See, I knew you would catch me."

She stuck her tongue out at Bullock, then blew a kiss.

Bullock did not even bother to lift his head up. He just sighed.

"Jaxon, these two girls are going to kill me."

Jaxon gave a wry smile, and Fae and the twins giggled.

Erika climbed off Bullock and Jaxon reached a hand out to lift him up.

"Erika, please try not to break Bullock too badly before we even start the fight," Jaxon said.

Bullock smirked at the comment.

"Alright Kiva, you stay here. Remember the plan," Jaxon said. "But also remember to keep an ear to the happenings of the castle while we are gone."

Kiva mumbled something under her breath about missing all the fun, but she nodded in agreement.

It was Fae's idea. They knew they were likely heading into a trap; the best course was to expose themselves to it while keeping one person back in reserve that could rescue the rest if needed. Fae had suggested it when Jaxon talked about committing the five of them to the task. Kiva agreed she was the stealthiest and would be best for the job.

Kiva understood that while the posting would be the least exciting, if the plan went wrong, it could become interesting. *Knowing Kiva, she was probably hoping things would go just a bit wrong.*

Fae touched her friend gently on the shoulder and Kiva gave her a smile in return. "See you on the other side," Kiva said, and Fae just nodded before she turned to go.

The four of them left Kiva there and quietly descended the tower stairs. They stopped at the door that led out of the tower and onto the castle wall. The castle wall encircled most of the castle grounds, including the gardens, courtyard, and entrance. The wall eventually circled around to the back of the castle keep, which had no rear entrance, and acted as a rear castle wall.

When all were ready, they cautiously opened it.

The guard on the other side of the door looked bored, leaning on the wall, looking out on the city, and kept some of his weight on the polearm he held. When he saw the door open, he instinctively got out of the way to allow others to pass him by. It was not until Jaxon's short blade was in his gut that he seemed to realize that the newcomers were not residents of the castle. They stashed the body back inside the tower.

They continued creeping along the castle wall towards what would usually be a castle keep, however as Fae looked up at it, she thought it looked more like a tall palace than what she would call a castle. Instead of a baron's keep as she had seen before, with its sharp stone corners, this castle had sweeping rooftops and elegant windows. The decadence of it made her stumble as she was immediately taken back to her childhood, where everything around her had more to do with the impression of wealth that was projected, than the realistic usefulness of a thing or person.

She hastily regained her pace, and with a quick glance around, she was glad to notice that the others had not noticed her momentary distraction. As she crept, she appreciated the silence of the leather boots she wore.

They approached the end of the wall and faced a door that led into the castle. Uncertainty loomed over Fae. She knew this might be the final moment of calm before facing whatever lay beyond its threshold.

Pausing in anticipation, they waited for Bullock to take the lead. His towering presence would conceal their numbers should there be any guards on the other side. With bated breath, Fae stood ready to follow him into the castle.

Bullock looked back to ensure the other three were ready. He placed his hand on the door handle and squeezed as he pressed forward. The door swung open in his grip, and he strode in as if he belonged there.

The room was a guardroom, which was not surprising considering its location just off the entrance. Inside, three guards sat at a table on the left, passing the time by playing cards, and a fourth guard was sitting on a bench along the right wall, leaning over as he fiddled with a clasp on his armour.

Bullock was through the doorway and into the room with the other three directly behind him, before any of the four guards noticed who they were.

As the guard sitting at the bench noticed, his eyes bulged. That was Fae's cue. She glided out from behind Bullock and slid her blade in his side, right where his armour was open from him fiddling with the buckle. He let out a small squeal as it pierced him. The other three guards jumped up from the table as they noticed as well. They knocked the table hard; chips went flying, but the table did not completely tip, and the farthest guard stumbled as he tripped over his chair.

Bullock was the first to act, swinging his great axe into the side of the first soldier. It dug into his ribs and crushed part of his breastplate. He let go of the axe, as it was stuck in the first soldier, and he launched himself over the table at the other two, attempting to throw them into disarray before they could draw their weapons.

He succeeded with the first man he hit, but before the other man went down in the heap, he drew his blade enough to raise it and cut a line across Bullock's bare right arm. Lucky for Bullock, though, the sword had not been held with any genuine support and only drew a minor cut, clattered to the ground instead of digging a deep cut. The three crashed to the ground with Bullock throwing fists.

The farthest of the two men that had drawn his sword rose again, out from Bullock's reach, but Erika's blade slashed down through his shoulder, ending his life.

The last guard was laying on the ground, squirming under the weight of Bullock. Bullock brought both fists down in a powerful haymaker to the man's face. He stopped squirming.

Jaxon had bypassed the fight and made his way to the other side of the room, ready for any repercussions the noise from their assault may have caused. So, he was prepared when the door opened and a guard with a spear looked in with shock.

The guard was quick to respond and lunged at Jaxon. Jaxon swung his armoured left arm inside the jab and deflected the blade away from him. Mid deflection, he pivoted and brought his hand down to clutch the outstretched spear. A quick pull on the shaft of the spear brought the guard forward a step and right into range of Jaxon's sword. He sunk the blade into the abdomen of the guard, and, with a gurgle, the guard sank to the floor. Jaxon pulled him forward out of the doorway and quietly closed the door.

"Good work, people," Jaxon said.

"Nowhere good to stash the bodies," Erika said.

"Just leave them where they lay."

They all crept out of the room and into the corridor beyond, closing the door behind them. The corridor stretched to the left and right, with more doors along the wall to the left and a few to the right before it reached a staircase.

Jaxon made a hand signal, pointing to the staircase. Fae nodded.

She knew they had to get to the lower levels of the castle where any rituals would be performed. Then they had to find some way to sabotage it.

They turned right down the hall, moving towards the staircase. As they crept down that hall, a door opened ahead of them. Out walked a noblewoman and a nobleman dressed in decorative armour.

Jaxon grabbed the woman and clasped a hand to her mouth to stop the scream that was about to burst forth from her. Bullock grabbed the man by the back of the collar and smashed him into the opposite wall. He crumpled to the ground once Bullock released his grip.

Fae bound the woman's feet and hands, while Erika gagged her mouth. Only then did Jaxon release the noblewoman. They grabbed both bodies and threw them into the room that nobles had come from.

Bullock was the only one still fully in the hallways when Fae heard a noise from the nearby staircase. She turned and saw a confounded soldier standing just at the top of the stairs.

The man was clearly a guard on duty, adorned in a gambeson shirt, metal greaves, and a sturdy helmet atop his head. In their attempt to hide the bodies, they had not noticed his approach. The guard's sword was still sheathed, but as awareness dawned in his eyes, his hand reached for the sword, and he opened his mouth to yell.

CHAPTER 29

DISTRACTION

Axton approached the gathering of Bandorians with a sense of relief, seeing his friends Bao and Brakan were already there, along with two other elders of the clan, Aisling and Gregor. Fionnula of clan Eldur also stood by, accompanied by two members of her clan. They formed a circle around a clean-cut tree stump that had been turned into a makeshift strategy desk.

After they had received the details from Damitus on the plans of the magi in Southshore, Axton had sent a runner north to find other clans and inform them of the dilemma. Clan Eldur had been found first and came as quickly as they could. Axton was glad that Fionnula had been wise enough to send the runner on for more support.

"What are we looking at?" Fionnula asked as she gestured to the open field beyond the trees they stood in.

At the other end of the vast open field stood a formidable army of Imperial troops, their banners and armour glinting in the sun. They were clearly waiting for a reckless charge by a disorganized group of savages, and the Axton planned to use that against them. Axton looked at Bao to explain.

"We sent a strike team in to sabotage the ritual our messenger told you about. We gathered here and made as much trouble as we could to get their city forces to come out and engage us. Goal being to distract the forces away from our strike team. Also, if our strike team fails, we will have to blockade the city and hopefully contain the spell-plague. They had outnumbered us more than five to one, but thanks to you," Bao gestured at Fionnula and her people, "it is closer to five to two now. They also have wizards hiding in the back of their ranks. Only acolytes, we believe, scouts could not spot a full wizard or archon. But the acolytes will still be the problem. If we cannot neutralize them quickly, they will rain fire down on us."

"What about right now?" Fionnula's second asked, a burley half orc with a scar down the left of his face and an eye missing. "Are we worried the mages will drop fire on us right now and just ignite the forest? I notice they haven't yet done this. Why? I am sorry, but we have only fought troops so far."

"We had expected this as a risk," Bao said. "As we have moved west, Fynnathias has been taking care of this. He has awoken the trees and warned them of the potential of fire" She pointed her hand over to Fynnathias, the half-elf in the clan. He was the only half-elf in their clan, though he had sired several offspring that were part elf and were now young children in the rookery.

Fionnula, being part elf herself, seemed to understand, but One-Eye still had a raised eyebrow, so Bao elaborated.

"There is still some magic in the trees, but they usually slumber. Before we launched the war, some of the magically attuned Bandorians of the clans showed us that the trees could be woken, and if spoken to, they could gather their magic to resist the fire, since it is the one thing the trees fear above all else. They are not invincible, but it takes the mages too much sustained fire. They do not have the time or power to burn down a forest."

"Neat trick," he said.

"So, to combat the wizards, our thought is to send a small group comprising three packs around to flank them. They have backed themselves up against the forest behind them, and their left flank is much closer to the forest on that side than it should be. This will let a small group get close to them. But we will need to make sure their primary force is distracted."

"So, we will have to launch a frontal assault to keep the rest busy?" Fionnula asked. "That is a lot of mounted combatants."

"Two hundred mounted knights by our count," Axton said.

"How do we deal with that?" Fionnula asked.

"Oh, we have a plan," Axton said.

Bao gave a wry grin and looked over at a much larger minotaur Bandorian. She called over to him, "Horst! Do you still have the ballista ready?"

Horst called back, "You bet I do! And Korn and Gorst each brought one as well. Are we going to use them on that first clump there? They gathered so nicely for us." A wide grin spread across the minotaur's face.

"Not just yet, but soon," Bao called back, then she looked back at the group of them. "Horst will brief any of your clansmen that are on the front line, so they are ready. Horst and his troops have used similar tactics up north against the Fomorians or Giants."

"We need our forces to pull the infantry out as well," Axton said. "This will also ensure that the wizards have a more difficult time dropping an inferno on all of us at once."

"Will our flankers have to worry about the mounted units turning back on them once they engage with the acolytes?" One-Eye asked.

"Uncertain," Bao said. "Ideally, their focus will be on the primary fight. By the time they realize the enemy is behind them, they will be too disorganized to mount an assault. If they do attack, the forest is close enough for our troops to fall back into the cover of the trees if need be. Their horses are not designed for forests." Bao paused while she allowed the plan to sink in.

"So, who is going to the flank?" One-Eye asked.

"Bao, Brakan, and I," Axton said, "Along with Astra's pack and

Fenn's pack from our Clan. We will circle the perimeter and get behind them."

"You're not staying back to lead the frontal assault?" Fionnula asked.

"No," Bao said. "Horst has more experience with this than Axton or I and can lead along with yourself, if that is acceptable to you."

"Fine by me. I'll coordinate with Horst."

Axton was pleased to see Fionnula's clan at ease with their plan and able to work so seamlessly with his clan. The battle would certainly be a challenge and they could still see defeat, but this was a challenge that they would appreciate. Axton felt this was a good plan, and it was a Bandorian plan; It was direct. It was not so complicated that if one piece of the plan failed, all would be lost. *Time to go hunting.*

"Captain."

The commander signalled Captain Titus up to approach him. Titus had been waiting for the chance to speak with the commander; the man had been occupied when Titus arrived.

"I was told you and your battalion just arrived on your way to Southshore," the commander said. "Is that true?"

"Yes sir," Titus said.

"Your orders?"

"Right here, sir."

Titus reached out his arm, a hand containing the parchment orders he had been given. They showed he was to clear the roads to Southshore and then report to the commander there. Before he had arrived though, he had received word of this pitched battle and that the commander he was to report to was here and not in Southshore. So, he'd led his battalion here.

The commander pulled at his white moustache as he read over

the orders. After a few moments, he folded the parchment back up and handed it back.

"That will do, Captain. You have reported in. Please lead your battalion to the castle within Southshore and report to the magister there. He will probably be able to find something useful for you to do. If nothing else, it will be good to have extra troops there."

"With the respect of Deus, sir, would it not be better for my men and I to assist with this battle? We have been fighting these people for months. They are not as simple as they appear."

Titus's words were true. They had battled these people in the north, and he had lost many in those battles. Like ghosts, they would rush out of places hidden from view, rarely fighting in a pitched battle. They were brutal, though they had left his injured to be retrieved. And while they did not take prisoners, they also did not kill those defeated opponents. However, Titus had been taken "captive" once.

He and his men had been surrounded. There was no winning, and he knew his men would have all been killed. He ordered them to stand down, and he surrendered; the lives of his men were his responsibility. The Bandorians had laughed at first, but then had taken their weapons and armour. They had sent some of his men on their way with a small amount of food to return to the capital, then threw him and the others in fighting arenas. Him and his men were made to fight bare knuckle against other Bandorians; one on one fights, no weapons. The fights had at least been fair.

Titus remembered his fight. The man had been young, using him to gain experience. Titus had stood his ground longer than any of the others in his group of prisoners. He had landed several hits on his opponent, but he had been tired from the battle, and he was unused to the strange fighting style of the opponent, while the opponent had been fresh and used to his. Just when his opponent had pinned him and he thought the man was going to break his arm, the pressure had been released. They had picked him up, looked over for injuries, then fed and sent home with the rest of his troops.

He had returned to the war and he and his battalion had learned to adjust their tactics; they learned from their defeats. They stuck more to the woods, launched their own surprise attacks, posted guards as he had seen the Bandorians do years ago when he and the mage, Damitus had ambushed them.

"Sir, they are planning something. They will not just be attacking your men straight on as you expect them to. Use our experience."

"Captain, you may have experience fighting them, but you have no experience as a commander and do not know what it takes to lead an entire division. I am not accustomed to having my orders questioned. I gave you an order. Now carry it out."

Titus's shoulders slumped. As a captain, he knew there was no arguing with the commander's decision. He had never led a pitched battle before, and his experience counted for little here.

Resigned to his orders, Titus turned his horse and rode back. Regret tugged at his heart as he thought of the soldiers out on the battlefield and his inability to make a difference.

His experience did count, though. He had never led an army in a pitched battle, but he had seen others do it against these people, and he had seen them lose. He likely knew more than any other of the leadership involved in the upcoming battle. The commander was making a mistake, but Titus knew the man would not listen to him. He was foolish to ignore useful information about the enemy. Titus would not make the same mistake. He was a man that listened to the advice of his men.

He rode his horse away from the front line and back to his troops. He would lead them to Southshore and set up defenses for the eventual siege. At least his men would not die because of poor orders from an arrogant commander.

CHAPTER 30
ALARM BELLS

At the same instant the guard opened his mouth to yell, Bullock charged. He gave the man a good body shove and launched him off the top of the stairs. Fae formed the words to yell stop, but it was too late; the guard hit the stairs partway down. Fae grimaced at the loud crash of armour from the initial impact and the guard continued to crash down the stairs. The sound of metal clashing against stone echoed through the halls.

The others ran to Bullock's side.

"Ashes," Erika said.

And just as the curse left her lips, a guard appeared by the dead body at the bottom of the stairs. He looked up and spotted them. *So much for their plan.*

"Intruders! Intruders in the castle!" Somewhere in the distance, they could hear an alarm bell blare.

"I hated all this sneaking around anyway," Jaxon said.

Jaxon quickly disappeared into the room next to them. Moments later, he returned with an elegant metal curtain rod in each hand, without the attached curtains. Both were longer than a man. He threw one to Bullock.

"Get ready."

Bullock caught the curtain rod as Fae and Erika readied their weapons.

Soldiers appeared at the base of the stairs and charged up them two at a time. Jaxon and Bullock waited and braced themselves on the top two steps. When the guards neared, they both jabbed out with the curtain rods. They collided with heads and chests, sending the guards toppling into more guards and throwing many of them down the stone staircase. Screams and yells resounded along with the sound of broken bones and head impacts. Jaxon threw his curtain rod aside.

"Erika. Flask," Jaxon said.

Erika unclasped a small flask from her belt and threw it to Jaxon. He caught it, shook it up, and tossed it down to the base of the stairs. The guards were clumped there, tangled in fallen bodies and the flask smashed, liquid fire bursting forth, flowing through armour and bodies to burn everything in its path.

Screams carried up the stairs, and the guards writhed on the ground. The fire did not last; the unit behind them stomped out the flames and made their way up the stairs. The guards eyed the rod in Bullock's hand and refused to get close, knowing that the pole would just knock them to their deaths.

With the guards not willing to engage, the four Bandorians charged down the steps, careful not to trip. When they approached the guards, Bullock was in the lead, still holding the curtain rod like a lance. He used the rod to knock the swords out of Jaxon's path.

Jaxon launched himself, feet first, into the soldiers. They began falling and colliding with bodies behind them; Jaxon, however, used his impressive agility and speed to maintain a balanced, coordinated fall, while the soldiers tumbled uncontrollably.

Fae flinched; *one of these days that boy was going to get himself killed.*

Jaxon rolled, wielding his twin blades. As he partially tumbled down the stairs with the other soldiers, he hit marks and dropped soldiers he collided with.

Fae and Bullock charged after him, with Erika taking the rear. The first soldier that had not been downed by Jaxon reached Fae and tried for a clumsy overhand swing of his sword, which she batted away easily with her own sword. The sound of metal sliding over leather filled the air as her wrist blade emerged on her left hand; she jammed it under the man's helmet and into his neck. Bullock and Erika charged past her and helped finish the rest of the guards.

When Fae reached the bottom, Jaxon was down in a pile of bodies, stabbing and attempting to block incoming attacks. Fae lunged forward to parry a blade headed in his direction. She opened a soldier's guard and stabbed him in the thigh. He buckled over in pain, and she jabbed her wrist blade into his neck.

The Bandorians quickly dispatched the remaining guards and found themselves in the long hallway below.

Jaxon experimentally touched his bruised limbs. "Ow."

"You'll be fine," Erika said.

Jaxon shrugged.

Fae found a guard that was still alive but laid prone on the ground. She squatted down and pressed her knee to his throat, putting pressure, but not enough to hurt.

"Where are the stairs to the lower ritual chamber?" Fae asked. "We'll have more important things to do if you tell me."

"Tha-that way mam, please don't kill me. The kitchen, down the hallway. Straight through there. The stairs are just off the main hallway."

Fae looked in the direction the guard pointed. The castle was still ringing with alarm bells and more guards were on their way.

"Let's go!"

She bolted off down the hallway towards the kitchen with the others on her heels.

They passed through the kitchen with no more incident than a few shocked and terrified cooks.

The stairs were long, and dark where torch light did not reach. The pack found themselves in a very short corridor which opened into a large ritual chamber, deep underground. The stones were cool, and the air was stale.

They stepped cautiously through the open archway doors into the chamber, and their eyes scanned the room. In the ritual chamber, the roof was higher, and rounded like a giant upside-down bowl. The walls, roof, and floor were all rough stone. The room was lit by candle sconces spaced evenly along the outer walls.

The four Bandorians stepped in and spread out around a large circle in the centre of the floor that took up most of the room. Fae squatted to get a better look. Lines on a massive five-sided red star lay inside the circle; it looked like the lines were drawn with blood.

Bullock poked at a dais with the end of his axe. It had a bowl-shaped indentation in the top surface of it that appeared to be for liquid. The dais was one of five that stood at each corner of the star.

Fae stood, confused. Besides those items, the room was empty. It was exactly as Damitus had described it, but none of the indications of a ritual were there. No strange items. No books. No vials. Nothing else.

Had they arrived too late? Could they have missed it altogether? They were silent as they looked for some clue to what they were missing.

Fae could barely make out the sound of alarm bells now. The bells seemed more distant than they should be, as if a wall of eerie quietness had fallen over the place. She did not notice it at first, but she noticed it now.

The others moved into the circle, while Fae continued to examine the outer walls and an empty table with a red velvet on it.

"These symbols…" Erika said.

"Nothing I've seen," Bullock said. "Hey Fae, this writing is strange. You are from the Empire. Do you recognize these?"

Fae looked up from some markings on the wall she was examining.

"What's that?" Fae asked.

"Over here," Erika called.

Fae began walking over to them, but as her back foot crossed the edge of the large circle, there was a large flash of light that blinded them all, and everything went dark.

CHAPTER 31
A DARK PLACE

Two acolytes spoke with a superior mage Damitus did not recognize. He was not familiar with the mages of Southshore. The acolytes would know little, but the mage likely had the information that Damitus wanted.

Decadent oil lamps, spread in long intervals along the walls, dimly lit the stone corridors, but there were still alcoves with dark shadows to serve Damitus's needs.

With alarm bells ringing elsewhere in the castle, he could only hear a muffled discussion as the mage whispered instructions to the acolytes, both holding tomes with excess scrolls that peeked out from within their bindings. He remembered, with a fondness, his own pursuits of knowledge, much of which was contained in the tomes of the ancient libraries. While the acolytes wore simple robes, the mage had robes with fine embroidering, a necklace, and bangles around his wrists. *Yes, the mage would do well.*

Once the mage finished speaking, the acolytes walked away. They passed by Damitus's hiding place, but they did not notice him.

The mage then walked a short way down the corridor and entered what appeared to be his study. Damitus could see him lift a scroll and peruse it. *Good, the man was focused on it.* Damitus stepped further into the alcove and faded into the shadow.

The mage reached for his desk while holding the parchment. He held his hand out to a cup which seemed to be filled with cold tea, wiggled his fingers, and steam rose from the cup once more. He lifted it to his mouth while reading and took a small sip.

A fire pit along the wall that had been providing the light for the room flickered and dimmed. The mage turned a curious eye on it, but as he did so, Damitus stepped out of the shadow of a nearby bookcase.

Damitus waved his hands at the mage, and the man froze in place; the cup of tea fell from the man's hand and hit the floor, shattering into hundreds of jagged pieces. The mage was frozen for only a moment, however, when the amulet from around his neck sparked and fizzed before cracking and falling to the floor. He moved once again, spinning his head around. *A defensive enchantment on the amulet then; only usable once, though.*

Damitus was caught off guard and the mage turned his whole body towards Damitus, but he was too slow. As he formed the words for a spell, Damitus recovered, slid behind him, and wrapped his arms around the man's neck, cutting off the air to the man's lungs and making it impossible to speak a spell.

The mage kicked and flailed his arms, trying to injure Damitus and shake him off. But the mage was weak. He had never been in a competition of physical strength before and after a short time of it, his body went limp in Damitus's arms.

Damitus, still holding the man, dragged him three paces to the door. He closed and latched the door, then waved his hand, speaking the words to put out the fire. It would appear as if the mage had gone to bed for the night. Satisfied that he would have some time before the mage would be missed, he held the man tight, and in a flash of fire, they both vanished from the room.

The mage lay on the coarse sand in nothing but his undergarments; Damitus had already stripped him. The fire beside him cast flickering shadows on the barren landscape. There was no sun, moon, or stars in the sky—only darkness. No searching in any direction would find anything but more sand. It was always dark here; this place was likely not on Tal'am. Damitus had discovered this place long ago, and it remained a secret known only to him. It had served his purposes for some time now. The only tome that referenced this place had been owned by the horse lords, and they had been sacrificed to provide Damitus with their knowledge. *A species gone. Their knowledge was his. Great things come at a cost.*

Damitus was now wearing the mage's clothes, bangles, and all. His hand traced a continuous circle, blowing a gentle breeze into the smoke of the fire and carrying a small amount into the man's lungs. After a few minutes, the mage finally launched into a coughing fit as he returned to wakefulness. Damitus stopped his wind spell.

The mage's watering eyes widened as he saw Damitus. He threw up his hands and opened his mouth to launch a spell, but it was no use. The words came out raspy and broken from his smoke-filled lungs. His voice was too hoarse to form proper words, certainly not the precise pronunciation needed for spellcasting.

"We are going to have a conversation, you and I," Damitus said. "I have some questions and you will answer them. This is a one-way process. It does not go both ways."

"Who the hell do you think you are?" The mage croaked.

Damitus spoke the word, waved his hand, and flames burst from the sand, erupting in a pillar of fire, scorching the man's feet. He tried to let out a scream, but his voice cut out once more. The smell of cooked meat filled the air, and when the fires died down, the mage's eyes were wet, whether from the stench, the pain, or both.

"You heard me the first time, do you understand?" Damitus asked.

The mage just nodded his head. *Good.* Damitus had many other means of torture he was more than willing to use, but the man had broken quickly. *Loyalty to the cause was weak within the Empire.*

"What are the plans for the ritual? Are you and the others still planning on performing it?"

"Yes," the man said. He tried to continue, but cut himself off with another cough as he croaked out his answers. "We are performing the ritual tomorrow night."

"How? You require the blood of an enemy. Do you not?"

"Yes. We were supposed to meet a traitor mage in Southshore a few days ago; a mage that was born of these barbarians. They hired a band of mercenaries to assassinate him and bring his blood. The mage never showed up though. The mercenaries told us they set the trap, but the man did not appear. We doubled their debts to the Empire for their failure."

The mage paused, appearing to be working out something in his mind. The fools had figured out some of Damitus's past, but they incorrectly thought he was born of Bandorian blood, if there even was such a thing.

"Wait, are you the mage they were to kill?" The mage asked. "Damitus?"

With a word and a swift gesture from Damitus, a surge of electricity erupted from his hands, enveloping the mage in a torrent of raw power. The mage's agonized screams pierced the air as his body contorted in anguish. Damitus stopped and more tears poured from the mage's eyes.

"Stop. Stop," he whimpered.

"I said the questions and answers go one way," Damitus said. "Nod if you understand."

The mage weakly nodded.

"If you did not catch this mage, then what blood are you using?"

"They have alerted us that there are barbarian intruders in the castle and more gathered in a field northwest of the city. The mages and the magus left a trap in the ritual chamber for them. We only need the blood of one enemy, we—they, the magus, and the other mages will have it soon. I was supposed to be a part of the ritual as well."

"And you still will be. Now tell me everything I need to know to be you for the next day and join the ritual," Damitus said.

The mage's eyes bulged with terror.

Damitus spent the next half hour torturing and interrogating the man to gather every bit of information he would need to blend into the castle life until the ritual. When he had everything he needed, he drew his knife and killed the mage. Then he stepped back, disappeared into a flash of fire and was gone.

CHAPTER 32
EYE OF THE STORM

From his hiding place amongst the trees, Axton looked over the field. The tranquil meadow exuded an eerie serenity, belying the approaching storm that loomed in the hearts of those gathered. An eastern wind played with the long grass as it passed, blew between soldiers, and caused each unit's flag to wave through the air. All was silent except for the flapping. The Venesterium army's battle drums had stopped for the moment. The army waited tensely on the eastern edge of the wide field, less than a day's march from Southshore.

From his hiding place, Axton's eyes scanned across the field to the western side. The army of Bandorians, his clan mates and those of clan Eldur, looking like a mix of demons, monsters, and barbarians, stood along the western treeline of the battlefield. They lacked a standardized attire of the Imperials, giving them a disorganized look, but Axton knew every piece was custom made for the warrior that bore it. Their disorganization was a deception; they held close to the trees, all to further confound the enemy. There was no way for the Imperials to know how many of them lie in wait beyond the treeline.

To the north and south of the large meadow stretched dense forests, offering ample hiding places for those who wished to remain unseen. Axton and his companions had chosen the southern forest, which the Bandorians had reported as running perilously close to the Imperial army. The trees here were thick, with their dark canopies blocking out much of the sunlight. It was the perfect place to conceal themselves from their enemies.

Axton, Bao, Brakan, and Sara, along with Fenn's pack of seven and Astra's pack of six, were crouched in the underbrush just south of the Venesterium army. They had found a place where the bushes were close to the edge of the woods, but still grew tightly enough to make them invisible to their enemies out on the field. The few scouts the Imperials had positioned in the forest to alert of such an ambush now lay dead in the bush behind them.

Axton shifted his weight from foot to foot and changed crouching positions regularly to maintain good blood flow. He would need it for the charge, and he knew they hid themselves too well for the slight movements to cause a risk of them being seen.

From their vantage point, they could see the entire battlefield. Axton saw the foot soldiers in front, ready to respond to the command. The mounted units were behind them, followed by a small contingent of archers, and finally the few wizards, two of which were on horseback marking them as generals, and most likely full wizards, not archons but certainly senior. The Bandorian packs could see the flags, identifying the units, gently dancing in the wind. Every face they could see was looking straight at the primary force of Clan Kaltor. *Exactly as Bao had predicted.*

The primary Bandorian force stepped out further from the forest, still in seemingly unorganized ranks. Their back ranks were still within the forest's edge; their plan relied on the Imperials assuming that there were few others still in the forest. Axton's clan mates yelled and shouted. They beat their weapons against their shields. Their voices sounded feral as they echoed over the battlefield. Axton's arm hairs stood up as pride welled up in him at their bravery.

Venesterium foot soldiers who had not seen battle before bristled at the show of ferocity, but the trained mounted units were unaffected, and a reminder shout to hold steadied them. Clans Kaltor's and Eldur's voices died out, and the Imperial army held ground, giving no sign of being unsettled.

After only a few moments of relative silence, an enemy commander barked a loud command. With what seemed like a single motion, the Imperial army's foot soldiers all took a sidestep to make gaps in their line and let the lances through. The horses trotted steadily as they advanced to the front of the enemy lines, with a confident spring in their step and their heads held high, projecting a regal and proud demeanour that mirrored that of their riders, who carried themselves with the assurance of men who knew themselves to be above others. The sound of thudding hooves echoed through the meadow.

There were still so many of them. Anxiety rolled over Axton as he watched them move with such precision.

Once all the horsemen had made it to the front line, they stopped there and waited. The call of another command rose from someone in the line of horsemen and the horses were urged onwards. First the horses began a slow walk, then sped to a trot. Voices of the horsemen, and their footmen counterparts who waited behind them, began as a slow rumble and got louder as a roar grew from the Imperial army. The horses sped to a canter, and as they finally broke into a full gallop, the voices died down. They could no longer be heard as the sound of rolling thunder grew from the beating of the horses' hooves.

Everything hinged on the next few moments. The Bandorians had excelled at raids and skirmishes, but this was war. A full pitched battle, and the Bandorians lacked experience or training for this. A bead of sweat coalesced on Axton's brow and he blinked it away when it ran down into his eye.

The Bandorians stood opposite the advancing lancers, not moving, not making any sound at all; just waiting. They had put all of their faith in Bao and her plan. *Axton could only hope it was not ill-placed. An image grew in his mind of his clan being run down by lances, and he shook his head to clear it.*

The horsemen grew closer and closer.

Fifty yards.

Half a heartbeat passed by, and the lancers gave out a battle cry in anticipation. Axton imagined the fury in the wide eyes of the charging lancers. The audacity of the Bandorians to not simply turn and run would cause rage in the horseman's minds.

Forty yards.

The lancers continued at top speed. Axton hoped for the rage to turn to confusion. The lancers would be trained, experienced with this type of manoeuvre, and expecting their foes to turn and flee.

The clans did not move, did not even flinch. *The lancers were so close. Why had Fionnula not made the call yet? They were running out of time.*

Thirty yards.

In a flash of movement, many Bandorians jumped to one side or dropped to a low crouch, and finally Axton could see massive men behind each of them. Not men, but hulking beasts of fur and horns; Horst and his minotaurs, all carrying enormous weapons, ballistae, too big for a human to hold, while others positioned weapons that sat on the ground, aiming them at the advancing army.

Some lancers pulled back on the reins from surprise, while others charged ahead. A shout rose from somewhere in the Bandorian lines. Fionnula's voice. "Fire!"

Twenty yards.

Weapons went off in rapid succession.

Some of them, being ballistae, threw massive bolts across the battlefield, impaling horse or rider and causing both to fall or veer off immediately in the wrong direction. Other projectiles were spinning lengths of rope with weighted balls on the end: the bolas. These raced through the air but much closer to the ground, they clung to the horse's feet and immediately tripped them, smashing them into the ground and throwing the riders into the air before coming down hard on the ground.

Chaos ensued as the lead horses collapsed at the head of the charge, while other horses peeled off going their own way, or even more detrimentally, veering into the centre of the charge causing massive collisions and tripping other horses.

Ten yards.

It caused a chain reaction and destroyed the lancers' momentum as the organized charge became a disorganized stampede. The charge tripped and crashed into itself as it tried to control its motion. Horsemen not thrown from their mounts stopped and pulled their reins to the side to avoid crashing and injuring themselves.

Like a violent wave, the charge crashed and broke on deadly rocks before coming to rest at the feet of those who had put their faith in Axton. He let out a breath he did not know he had been holding.

Zero yards.

Silence. No one moved. A palpable awe fell over the battlefield.

A Bandorian boot came down hard on a lancer's head with a crunch.

A bloodcurdling war cry; the Bandorians launched into action.

Bandor warriors threw themselves into the mass of horses and bodies, slashing and stabbing through Imperial forces.

Foot men on the other side of the field could do nothing but look on in horror as every weapon imaginable was used to carve and hack their mounted comrades to pieces.

Axes cleaved, swords slashed, and hammers crushed. The sounds of battle travelled across the field for all to hear.

Axton stifled a satisfied laugh as the small number of remaining horsemen turned their horses and fled.

Uninjured men that had been unhorsed ran back for their own lines. The agile Bandorians overtook them and cut them down.

In the shrubs nearby, Axton stuck his hand out to remind the others as much as himself to hold fast and resist the urge to charge forth and begin their own onslaught.

Finally, as the noises died down, a boot stepped down on the body of a horse lying dead on the ground, and a lone Bandorian raised himself above the rest of the battlefield. He lifted his massive axe in the air and let out a yell in challenge at the Imperial army. As a chorus, the rest of the Bandorians took up their weapons and joined their voices.

Back in the bushes close to the rear of the Imperial army, Axton turned his head and gave a slightly stressed look at Sara, who crouched beside him. They both knew that this was the moment that could change the course of this battle.

They saw the archers and wizards readying themselves to bombard the Bandorian army and attempt to send them scattering, or to crush them beneath a shadow of arrows and burning mortars of rock and fire. If the Bandorians could not draw the footmen away from the others and leave them exposed to the two packs waiting in the bushes, then Clan Kaltor's army would need to fall back to the woods for shelter and try to draw the Imperial army into the woods where they could engage them one on one.

But Axton was close enough to see the Imperial general's dumbfounded look.

Then the moment passed. The general's face turned from confusion to rage and Axton tensed, waiting to see what he would order of his troops.

"Attack!" The general's voice was desperate with the sound of madness. "Destroy all of them, destroy those bastards!"

Axton was unsure what the command meant, and from the swivelling heads of the imperial troops, so were they. *Who was he ordering to attack? The infantrymen to charge? The archers to volley? The wizards?*

"Infantry advance. I want their heads."

Finally, the command Axton had been waiting for. The general had calmed enough to make a coherent command.

Axton kept his hand held out. They just had to wait for the infantry to be too committed to turn back. If the general had been a tactician, he would have bombarded the Bandorians with arrow fire, but Axton knew they were mages first, not strategists, and their plan had taken advantage of that.

The footmen crossed the field and neared the halfway mark. Axton prepared to make the call to the three packs. All eyes were on the battle on the western edge of the field.

His time had come, "Now!"

The calm of the treeline exploded with the charge of the Bandorian flankers as they burst from the foliage.

Astra levelled her modified crossbow and aimed at the magic wielders. She fired, and the bolt flew, carrying the cargo to its destination.

It struck a mage and erupted into a plume of smoke. Two other bolts, fired from similar crossbows, burst, expanding the cloud.

Nearby wizards choked on the smog, hacking and coughing spittle from their lungs. Those not choking formed the words to their evocations, preparing to attack their undiscovered attackers, but polluted air made the delicate pronunciation too challenging to vocalize.

The Bandor packs closed the distance to the wizards as quickly as their legs would allow. Axton knew their time was limited; the smoke bomb cloud would clear, and they would be visible once more.

Axton could hardly see the wizards they advanced towards, only their shadows like wraiths in haze, but he knew they were there. Even before he could penetrate the cloud, fire erupted in an unaimed hurricane over the battlefield. The Bandorians let their speed carry them through the onslaught. Blades drawn, they tore through the confused army, hacking limbs and slashing throats as they charged. Robes billowed, blood showered, and innards burst forth as mage after mage fell in the initial assault.

The inexperienced acolytes, unfamiliar with the heat of battle, were slow to react and, one by one, the Bandorians struck them down, and cast them aside, slaughtered.

Axton finally broke through the smoke. A line of confused archers took stuttering steps back, one even tripping. A line of Astra's berserkers charged them just ahead of Axton.

But as the smoke bomb had caused confusion for the wizards, so too did it lead to an inability to ensure all were dead. As the first Bandorian warriors from Astra's pack reached the grouping of archers up ahead, Axton felt the hair on his arms raise with static electricity. Lightning arced from the gnarled fingers of a still breathing wizard, racing across the battlefield at the speed of light, tearing through the lead Bandorian after hitting two others.

Two members of Astra's pack dropped, burned and charred, to the ground. One dead and one breathing in short, raspy gasps. The third was only grazed, suffering burns, and dazed, but able to shake it off in time to fire a wrist bolt back at her attacker. A stream of blood flowed down the temple and cheek of the wizard from the thick needle embedded in his skull. He collapsed to the ground.

Smoke snaked up from two archers; the arc of lightning had also claimed their lives.

Axton reached the clump of archers, and he ripped through one archer with his great axe. He hastily advanced to the next one, but stumbled on a dead body, partially losing his balance. His agility kept him from falling.

One brave archer took initiative and used the moment to swing the bow like a staff at Axton's face. It connected with a crack. The archer momentarily stunned Axton and knocked the axe from his hands.

The archer advanced on him with his short sword, attempting to take advantage of the momentary drop in his guard. Axton's hand flew forward, grabbing the archer by the scruff of his shirt, and broke his nose with a headbutt. The archer's body went limp.

Axton's eyes widened as he witnessed flames swirl in a nearby mage's hands. He still had a hand on the archer's tunic. He grabbed the archer with both hands and pulled him in between himself and the mage just as a meteor of fire and rock slammed into the limp body.

The eruption catapulted Axton like a stone through the air, and he came crashing down into a pile of dead bodies. Blood flowed down his left arm from a deep cut in his shoulder.

He noticed the sharp edges of the corpse's, too slowly drawn, daggers and realized he had come down against the blades. Axton gave the wound a brief glance and tried to wiggle out of the pile. He looked up in time to see the wizard advancing, lightning crackling in his palms, and a threatening grin on his lips.

Before the wizard could raise his hands to let loose the lighting, a blade whistled through the air and embedded itself in the wizard's neck. He produced a gurgling noise as blood bubbled from his mouth and his eyes rolled back. He then inelegantly collapsed to the ground. Axton watched to see if the wizard would move again. The body twitched once, then simply splayed on the ground, motionless.

Axton took a sigh of relief, then let his eyes trace the trajectory of the blade that had saved him. He followed it back until he saw Fenn marching towards him. Fenn neared him and reached out a hand to Axton, offering to help him up. "Thanks, friend," Axton said as he clasped the hand and Fenn pulled him to his feet.

"You looked like you could use a hand. Though I must confess, it was amusing to watch you try your hand at flight," Fenn said with a friendly laugh. He clapped Axton hard on the back.

"Burn you, Fenn," Axton grunted and gave him a teasing glare. They turned to survey the battlefield.

All around them, they could see the enemy army in disarray. The archers had been quick to break rank and were making a mad dash for the forest. At their heels were wizards that valued their own lives more than any loyalty to an army. They were desperately sprinting for the trees to the east and back towards the city of Southshore, terror apparent in their eyes. The smoke had masked their numbers and made them appear greater in strength than they were.

A few wizards remained. Blinded by the pride, and the belief that they, single handedly, had enough power to defeat their attackers. Axton could see Sara advancing on one as a blade of ice formed and raced towards her. She kicked up a nearby shield in time for the ice to shatter into pieces against it. She dipped her shoulder and let the shield glance off her side.

She reached the wizard just as he realized he should have turned and run with the others. She sunk her blade into her opponent's abdomen in one smooth motion, making a sound like a sword being sheathed in its scabbard. The wizard doubled forward as his eyes bulged in surprise and he let out a noise of shock.

Sara drew her sword to the side and let the wizard slide off it and fall to the ground of the meadow. His eyes stared hauntingly at his fallen companions.

Farther west on the battlefield, a flash of blue-white light went off catching Axton's attention. A wizard, who had summoned a magical blue blade, connected with Brakan's broad axe. The force of the blow had destroyed the sword, which had resulted in the large flash.

Brakan drew his axe back and swung down on him a second time. This time, the axe connected with the magical barrier wrapped around the wizard. The shield made an echoing splitting noise, and the axe stuck, embedded in it. Cracks spread from the place that the axe sat fixed.

The land slanted up a few feet close to the two combatants, and Bao leapt from the higher ground. She had her glaive gripped with both hands and brought it down hard. It connected with the back of Brakan's axe and drove the embedded weapon deeper in the pale blue outline of the wizard's shield.

The cracks continued to spread and multiply, their glow intensifying briefly before the shield shattered, releasing the energy into another explosion of light.

Brakan covered his eyes, but the blast blinded and stunned the wizard. Bao, blinded by the light, rolled away from the encounter. Brakan, however, recovered quickly and stepped forward.

He brought the axe above his head, then around to his side as he whirled it into a heavy cross slash. It cleaved the wizard's side and hurled him down into a heap of bodies. The wizard did not move again.

Brakan raised his axe and his head darted from side to side looking for another target to no avail.

Unit banners, flags, weapons, and the dead were all strewn on the ground, abandoned. Some would escape, but there were not enough forces left, and they could not organize with those that were left to mount a counteroffensive. They would likely retreat north.

Axton and Fenn approached Brakan and Bao, and as Axton came closer, he could see a substantial amount of blood on Brakan's left shoulder. The back of that same shoulder had a puff of smoke coming from a small flame still burning. Axton looked at Brakan with a raised eyebrow.

"Brakan, you're still on fire a bit there," Axton said. "And it looks like you've lost some blood."

Brakan turned his head to see the flame and attempted, without success, to tap it out. Bao was back up and patted it out for him. "I gotcha, big guy"

"Thanks, girl."

"Brakan? The blood? It looks like a lot," Axton repeated the question.

"No, I am fine." Brakan turned back to Axton and Fenn. "Most of the blood is not mine. And these flames they use don't seem to be as hot as an actual fire, something about them being magic and unnatural. I am uncertain, but it seems like they might be different."

Back at the main engagement, a call went up to pull back, but the call came too late for many of the soldiers, who were already too engaged in the battle to retreat.

Some of the force charged back to protect the wizards, while others remained. Those who stayed were butchered by Bandorian forces while those who rushed back, found no one left to protect—the wizards were now scattered—and they were unsure of what to do next.

"Looks like more fun heading our way," Brakan said.

Axton recognized an opportunity. "Fenn, you take your pack north into the forest and then west to regroup with our forces. We will take ours to the south and do the same. I think Astra has already headed north into the forest with her wounded." He pointed through the smoke. "Let them chase you and pick them off. It should split them up enough and add to their confusion."

Fenn nodded and called out to his pack to head north immediately.

Axton, Bao, and Brakan darted off, grabbing Sara on the way. As planned, several of the infantrymen that were on the south side of the line ran after the pack, with no better orders being given. The ones to the north ran after Fenn, and a final group intent on protecting their remaining archers and wizards ran east into the forest, looking to regroup with what remained of the army. The forest acted well to scatter the infantrymen further, and the pack ambushed and killed many of those that followed them.

When they returned to the primary force of clans, the last of the army was being swept up or retreating and the fighting, for all intents and purposes, had ended. Fenn and Astra had already returned; nothing stood between them and Southshore. They did not yet have enough to launch an assault, but they would approach the city and watch.

The clans regrouped and moved west into the forest. They would mop up any stragglers as they moved southeast.

CHAPTER 33
TITUS ARRIVES

Titus felt a gentle shake of his shoulder wake him from his slumber. He looked around; stone walls with wooden braces, a guard window, and an uncomfortable pain in his back met him. Sunlight shone through the window. It was morning. He recalled he had been sitting with some of his men in the watchtower along the wall of the city gates.

The city walls did not look exceptionally strong compared to the castle; made of wood and stone, they were shorter than he would like. He was concerned they may fall under a focused attack as he had seen the inventive solutions the Bandorians had used to overcome obstacles.

As he looked around, though, he only saw the soldier that had woken him just now. When Titus had arrived the night before, he had sent his men on foot to get the first night's rest, while he ordered those on horseback to take the first watch. Once the foot soldiers had slept, they arose to relieve the horsemen in shifts. Titus had stayed awake with his men into the early hours of the morning but had come inside to socialize with soldiers and rest on the wooden chair he was sitting on. *He must have drifted off.* He was alone with the soldier now, and looking out the doorway, he saw none of his men on the wall, only the city guard.

"Captain," the soldier said. "Are you alright? You fell asleep, and we did not want to wake you. You need your rest, too."

"I'll be fine, thank you. What time is it?"

"It is after midday, sir."

"Damn. I suppose that makes sense. What news of the attackers?"

Titus had been awake when word came of the loss in the fields northwest of the city.

"They have not advanced from what we have heard. We have sent another set of scouts out to see what they are doing."

"Good. And where are our other men? Why are none of them out on the wall?"

"Sorry Sir, but the magistrate ordered that your men pull back to guard the castle. He said the walls have enough defenders on them."

"What?" Titus asked with more anger than he meant to. His soldier stepped back a pace. "Sorry," Titus said. "You did good to wake me. Thank you for the information. You can return to your post."

The soldier left to return to his post. Titus put a hand on the back of his chair to help him stand up; his body was sore and stiff. Falling asleep in armour was a terrible idea, and he felt pain in multiple parts of his body. He moved his shoulders, getting as much range of motion as he could to work out the joints.

Once satisfied with the feel of his body, Titus made a quick pace from the wall and through the city, not bothering to provide a friendly smile to those he passed. He was unhappy with the magistrate commanding his troops away from their assignment, even if the man had the authority to do so.

Some time after leaving the guard tower, he finally arrived at the magistrates' state room and an administrator informed Titus that he would have to wait as the magistrate was occupied. Titus was, for once, glad of the magisterium bureaucracy for giving him power in this one situation.

"In a state of emergency regarding the protection of an Imperial city or town, the magistrate must grant the senior military officer the rank of captain or above an audience."

"I... yes, of course," the administrator said. He clenched his jaw. "But you must wait here for me to inform the magister."

The administrator disappeared into the office, and when he returned, he finally allowed Titus in.

"Magistrate Cicero," Titus said to the man.

"Captain," Cicero said.

The magistrate was a portly man, but his height made him appear commanding, even as he sat in his chair behind his desk. A second administrator was beside him reviewing records of numbers with the magistrate. If Titus's memory served him correctly, Magistrate Cicero of Southshore had been a member of House Dotharr. He had not been gifted with the powers of magic, but still had considerable political power, opting to become a magistrate instead. In some ways, just a puppet for the Magisterium, but the man would want for nothing.

"Sir, why have you ordered my men off the city walls?"

"Captain, the city walls are strong enough to hold a general siege, even without your men."

"These Bandorians will not launch a typical siege. They are anything but predictable. My men can help hold them at bay."

"Either way, it is irrelevant, Captain. The people pay their taxes, and the taxes pay for their protection, and we have provided that. Nothing more. The castle is the key asset, if your men are on the city walls and there is a breach, then all of your men are stuck outside of the castle behind enemy lines, instead of being in the castle making use of its fortifications and weaponry to assault the enemy."

"But Sir, if the walls are destined to fall, now is the time to act.

My men could organize an evacuation. We still have the possibility of getting the citizens out; over land, and others we can get out by boat. Why wait, Sir?"

"Titus, do not think of me as uncaring. I am a generous man and have brought this up to the magus, but his instructions were clear. We are to focus entirely on the castle. The city is expendable. I am not happy about having my city—my base of power—threatened either, but he is a magus."

"A magus is here? Where? What magus?"

"Magus Pious. They sent him here a few weeks ago from the capital."

"Pious? Pious Delphos?"

"Yes, that's right. That was his name. Why? You know him?"

"Oh, I know him."

It had been almost an hour since Titus had left the magistrate's office, and still his ears burned hot with anger as he sat at a desk. Even his face muscles were sore from the angry expression he wore. It had been years since he had reported to Magus Pious Delphos. He had been Acolyte Pious Delphos then, and he had taken command of the Western Imperial Army. Titus had argued with the man in Creet about the need to burn and massacre an entire city, and now Titus was in the same place, with Pious willing to sacrifice an entire city of innocent people just to accomplish his own goals.

Titus would have a talk with Pious, magus or not. Titus did not care anymore, but before he did anything rash, there was one important thing he had to do.

Titus signed his name and returned the quill to the inkpot at his makeshift desk. He rolled the parchment, preparing the letter to be transported. He warmed the wax on the nearby candle, then let the wax fall onto the parchment. After a second, he pressed his ring into the cooling wax and sealed the message.

Titus looked at the letter, then rolled into a small scroll. He tapped it twice gently against his palm, then let his head sink. This would start to make things right. He tucked the letter into his tunic under his armour. He would keep it safe there until he was certain he wanted to send it.

CHAPTER 34
BLOOD AND CHAINS

Fae was not sure what happened next or even how much time had passed as she returned to consciousness, but she thought she could remember the sound of a guard's metal shoes on the stone floor and a cruel, dark cackling. The bruising under her arm confirmed her foggy memory of rough hands lifting her.

Her head ached, and she tried to blink to clear her blank vision, but realized she was in total darkness. She lay on her side on something hard; it dug into her hip and shoulder. Stone. She reached out probing fingers in the darkness and noted that her hands were chained together. She thanked her luck that they were chained in front of her instead of behind her back; having her hands in front of her would put less strain on the muscles and allow them to relax. *She would need her body responsive and flexible soon.*

Fae could tell now she was lying on a floor indeed made of stone. She traced her hands along the rough cold cobblestones; her fingers feeling along the gaps. The stone had moisture on it. *Condensation.* The air was still stale. *Still underground?* She tucked her body and rolled onto her knees to allow for some mobility, the movement shifting her chains, the sound echoing against the hard walls. *It must be a dungeon. Makes sense.*

Her body shivered in the chill air and noticed they had stripped her armour, and her weapons. Now she sat in only her undergarments and chains.

As she continued to feel around, she heard chains move a little way away. They were not hers.

"Jaxon..." she called out. She hoped whatever else was down there was not dangerous. An image of a dungeon beast that ate prisoners flashed in her mind before she could rid the fear from it. The Imperials would not have kept her alive just to let something kill her in a dungeon.

She called out again, as no answer had responded to the first call, "Bullock, Erika? Who's there?"

"Quiet, quiet, I'm here." It was Jaxon's voice.

She sighed a breath of relief. Chains clinked and she could tell Jaxon was moving. He crept across the floor to meet her in what she could only assume was the middle of the cell. His chains stopped him from reaching her.

"Where are the rest?" Fae asked, hoping to hear more chains moving as she asked. No sound came, though.

"I don't know, it is just you and I here. I was searching around the place while you were still out. Three walls and prison bars on the fourth wall. There is a bit of a seating area beyond the bars, and I believe there is a staircase or a door beyond that." Her eyes were adjusting, and she could vaguely make out his hands gesturing towards the cell bars and door. "I am guessing your chain is attached to the opposite wall from mine."

"How long has it been?"

"Hard to say, but I don't seem to have soiled myself and my beard stubble has not grown in yet, so I'm willing to guess hours instead of days. Do you know what happened out there? Everything just went black for me, and I woke up here. I couldn't reach you."

Her chains still had some slack in them, so she shuffled over the stone to get closer to him. She found him with her hands and stopped, with her thighs resting against his. She could feel the touch of his legs and knew they had striped him as well.

They both sat on their knees next to each other, pressed side to side. She grabbed his hands in hers and rested her head against his shoulder.

"I don't know either," she said. "I just saw the white light, then black as well. They dragged us here, but I remember nothing else."

He turned his hands over and squeezed hers tight for reassurance.

"I am glad you are here with me," he said.

She pressed further against his side and continued to nuzzle her head against him.

"Any thoughts on how to get us out of here?" Fae asked.

He pressed his head gently against hers in return, "Nothing yet, but we should stay sharp. An opportunity will appear in time. They mean to keep us alive, or we would be dead already."

"Jaxon, I... I'm..." Fae's voice trembled.

"I know Fae. We will be ok. We knew this was a possibility and Kiva is still out there." He placed his lips on her forehead and gave her a tender kiss, "Remember our training-"

"Learn as much as we can, pay attention to everything, and wait for the opportune moment," Fae said, cutting off Jaxon with a repeated quote from their instructors. "Don't worry about me. I will be ready."

"I know," A smile crept over his face before becoming thoughtful once more.

They sat silently resting against one another for some time, occasionally adjusting. After what felt like an hour, Jaxon spoke up again.

"We should take turns resting so we have our energy. We will need it when it comes time to make our move. You can rest first; I don't feel tired yet."

Fae thought to protest, but it made no difference who slept first, and she was already leaning against him. She lowered herself into the closest thing she could find to a comfortable position and tried to relax her muscles.

The two lovers sat like that for hours, taking turns laying down and using each other to soften the stone ground. The hours wore on and all sense of time faded. They alternated between talking, meditating, and sleeping to pass the time.

There was no noise from outside their cell, and Fae could only guess the time by the pain of hunger. When she finally heard a noise from beyond her cell in the darkness, she was fairly certain a day had passed, at most. The hunger, which had been a dull pain, had transformed into a persistent, gnawing ache. If she didn't eat soon, her body would begin to gradually consume its own reserves, burning through muscle and fat. It would be a problem if they starved to the point of weakness. When the opportunity came, they would need their strength.

Her fears eased when a man entered with a torch that burned her eyes with its brightness. He approached the metal cell door and slid a metal plate and jug through a slot in the bottom. It contained two small pieces of stale bread and a small amount of water. Fae reached for the plate and passed Jaxon his piece of bread. She wet her tongue with the water so she could eat the bread, passed the jug to Jaxon, then began consuming the stale bread. *This would not be much, but it would keep their bodies from eating them from the inside.*

The second time that the man came, Fae hoped for food, but instead, four guards and the jailor flanked him. The jailor put the key in the door and opened it to allow the guards in. They approached her and Jaxon confidently, without fear of two bound prisoners.

Fae and Jaxon stood up without prodding. The guards misunderstood the motion and thought they were accepting the role of prisoners, assisting them in being taken away. They were mistaken.

The four guards stepped close to the prisoners, intending to guide them out of the room.

With a blur of motion, Fae yanked her bound hands over the first guard's head, wrapping them around his neck. She jerked his head down and delivered a hard knee to his face. His nose broke and blood gushed. He crumpled to the ground in a heap, holding his face.

Before the other guards registered Fae taking an action, Jaxon grabbed the shirt of a second guard and head-butted him. The guard brought his hands up to protect his face and Jaxon released the shirt so that he could deliver a punch with both hands. His fists connected with the guard's sternum, and he fell to the ground, gasping for air.

The third guard brought his pike down towards Fae. She sidestepped it and shoved the guard with her shoulder before the fourth guard advanced on her. The pikeman stumbled towards Jaxon, and he wrapped his chains around the man's neck, choking the guard and bringing him to his knees.

The jailor was cowering in the corner, not wanting to get involved. Something hard hit Fae's temple, and she dropped to the ground.

"Stop!"

The fourth guard had brought the butt of his crossbow into Fae's head, and before she could engage with him again, the guard had leveled his crossbow at her, aiming it directly at her chest. The jailor was stunned.

"Let him go or the girl dies," the crossbowman said, but Jaxon thought he heard the hint of fear in his voice. Fae snarled at the man, wanting to kill him for using her as a bargaining piece.

Jaxon glared at the man so hard Fae thought the man might just turn and run right there. But the guard held his ground, so Jaxon improvised. "Drop the crossbow or I will snap this man's neck."

"I... I-" the man stammered, "I have the crossbow. It is faster and will kill her first" a small amount of confidence creeped back into his voice as he finished the statement, but then it was Jaxon's turn.

"If you kill her, how long do you think it will take me to break this man's neck, then get to you? I will crush your skull with my bare hands, and you will feel every second of it," Jaxon said through barred teeth. "Take your crossbow, back away slowly and leave up those stairs with your life."

The jailor had already inched back towards the stairs, wanting no part of the entire exchange.

The threat was enough to make visible beads of sweat develop on the crossbowman's face. It seemed to have the effect that Jaxon was hoping for. The last guard's eyes froze with terror, and he slowly lifted his crossbow, intending to aim at Jaxon and backing out of the dungeon.

He did not get the chance.

As soon as he pointed the arrow away from Fae, she launched to her feet, pushing the crossbow up out of the way, and bringing her fists into the man's chin. His teeth clacked. Fae followed up by kicking the man in the kneecap and he collapsed, screaming in pain.

"What was that about?" Jaxon asked.

"The ass sucker punched me with his crossbow when I wasn't looking."

"Fair enough," Jaxon gave a nod.

They ignored the jailor as he crept along the wall to the exit.

Just as the jailor neared the stairs, though, a guard captain came down the stairs with another six guards, all with crossbows levelled at the Bandorians.

"Pathetic. These mongrels are little more than savage animals. But a savage animal still has a bite," the captain said.

He looked down at the two Bandorians in disgust, his gaze settling on Jaxon who still held the remaining guard.

"Bandorian, release that guard or it will be both of your lives."

They were defeated, and dying there would help no one. Jaxon released his grip on the guard and the guard scrambled out of the cell in terror, almost tripping a few times as he went.

Fae stood up off the ground and Jaxon pulled himself up tall. His scowl disappeared and a friendly smile replaced it. With a quick tone change, he addressed the captain.

"Captain, welcome. What can we do for you today?" Jaxon asked.

The guards' expressions morphed into confusion at the change in attitude of the two Bandorians, as they no longer seemed interested in fighting. The captain ignored them.

"You four, lead them to the ritual chamber as requested. You two, keep your bows on them. If they flinch the wrong way, shoot them. Try to not kill them, but make sure they don't forget who is in control here."

The four guards entered the cell and roughly began pushing Fae and Jaxon out of the cell and towards the stairs.

As they were led out of the dungeon, a guard shoved Fae along while the others guided them through a labyrinth of hallways. They arrived back at the ritual chamber they had blacked out in, only this time it was not empty.

Along one side of the room, an altar was illuminated with candles and adorned with the gore of one or more dead animals. Surrounding the altar were goblets filled with blood, bowls containing strange materials, and what appeared to be the brimstone Damitus had mentioned earlier. The room had an overpowering foul scent, with the stench of fermented urine mingled with the pungent odour of the brimstone. Fae wrinkled her nose, attempting to block out the noxious smell to no avail.

Along with all the expected trappings of a ritual, there were four wizards standing at each dais, in each corner of the star. All but one wizard was old and gnarled and they cloaked themselves in dark, wine-red robes with hoods that obscured their faces.

In the centre stood a man draped in black and golden robes. The gilded trim of his cowl contrasted the shadow that was cast upon his face, but it was his golden chain that clued Fae into who he was. The chain drew elegantly down his neck over his chest to end with an amulet. An eye with two serpents circling around it, the symbol of the Magi, the symbol of Deus. He was a magus; from the Order of the

Magi, they explored the very essence of magic as they served the Empire and praised Deus, Lord of Magic.

Fae had learned about the magi, first from villagers in Creet, then more from her Bandorian education. Within the Magisterium, the mages and acolytes performed spells and accomplished magical tasks while answering to the archons. They used magic for practical purposes, but the magi studied the foundations of magic. They were the quasi-religious zealots of the Magisterium, implementing Deus's supposed divine goals; the only magic users that knew more than the magi were the archons, and rumour had it that there were only eleven of them.

The magus was here to lead the ritual.

Along the centre of the circle sat Bullock and Erika, facing each other. The guards had forced them to sit on their knees with their arms chained behind their back and connected to metal ringlets secured to the floor on the outside of the circle.

"Jax!" Bullock said, as he noticed Jaxon and Fae enter.

He looked glad to see the two of them, but he quickly pinched his lips together, to avoid giving any information away. As the guards shoved Jaxon and Fae closer, Fae saw a small pool of blood behind Bullock. Lashes covered his back from a whip that a guard had used on him. Fae had heard no screams earlier, though and she felt a sense of pride for her friend.

The guards unbound Jaxon and Fae's wrists then bound them once more behind their backs, chaining them to the ground like Bullock and Erika. Forced to their knees, they faced the centre of the circle and looked right at each other. Erika gave the two newcomers a wink. "Well, this should be fun. All our favourite people are here."

Jaxon shrugged and gave her a smile. He then spoke up so the guards and wizards could hear him. "Can we get some wine for this party?"

"Shut up, savages!" a croaky voice, like sandpaper being dragged over a metal edge, echoed from the mage behind Jaxon. The mage gave Jaxon a kick in the ribs.

"Guards, leave us," the magus said. "You Barbarians are going to play nice for us." He had positioned himself at the dais in the centre of the star.

The guards that had led them into the room all gathered at the stairs up to the castle and ascended them.

"We are going to ask you some questions, and you are going to answer them, or we will torture your leader here," he said, gesturing to Jaxon and a larger mage with a masked face and a whip stepped forward. He gave a crack of the whip on Jaxon's back. Blood dripped.

Jaxon grimaced with the pain for only a fraction of a second before a smile came back to his face and he laughed.

"You hear that? These bluntaxes think that I'm the leader here. They really don't have a clue, do they?"

Jaxon then turned his head to address everyone else in the room. "I'll answer any question you have. It's not like I have any secrets."

The magus ignored Jaxon's taunts. He walked around Jaxon to look him in the eyes. He towered over the Bandorian and spoke slowly in a demanding tone.

"Where are your forces hiding? And what are they planning? I want to know about their planned troop movements."

Jaxon snickered at the questions before responding.

"Hell if I know, last time we saw our forces, they were in the woods launching a bunch of idiots over castle walls to spend time with you folks. But they'll be long gone by now. As for any other forces we have, they are likely up north still engaged with your larger forces, which I would assume you already know."

Jaxon's voice deepened and became more threatening as he glared deep into the magus's eyes.

"As for us four, we are just here to kill you."

"Fine," the magus said. "Don't cooperate with us."

The magus nodded at the mage beside Jaxon and a large crack sounded in the chamber as the whip ripped across Jaxon's back once more. Two more cracks of the whip followed, and Jaxon's face creased with pain, but he did not cry out or give any verbal sign of suffering.

Fae spoke up this time. "You don't get us, do you? We do not have any secrets. We do not scheme, we do not plot, we do not conspire. Those are the machinations of your people; it is not our way. We face our enemies, ensure they understand the might we bring down on them, and then destroy them." Her voice was icy as she described her adopted culture to those from the culture of her birth. "There is no need to torture a Bandorian; we have no secrets to keep. Everything we are is plain to see laid out in front of us, and if you decide to torture us anyway, you'll never break us."

The magus stared at Fae, then gave a nod to the wizard, out of sight behind her. She heard a crack and searing pain exploded up from her back. She screamed. Jaxon had a resolve that she did not. She felt warm blood running down her exposed lower back. She lowered her head.

An icy finger lifted her chin, forcing her head to rise and look into the cruel eyes of the magus, now crouched in front of her.

"Chatter, chatter. Perhaps you will talk, little birdy. Do you know more? Know things about your companions outside our walls, and to the north."

Fae said nothing.

"No? Perhaps if I give you some incentive."

Raising his left hand, palm facing downwards, he pointed it towards Jaxon. At first, there were only small sparks emanating from his hand, but they quickly grew in size as bolts of electricity leaped from his fingertips and coursed through Jaxon's body, burning and wrapping as they entered him.

"No!" Fae screamed.

Fae and the others looked on in horror as Jaxon's body contorted and convulsed in agony. Blue lights of electricity snaked across his flesh, moving from one part of his body to another, engulfing him in a crackling blue aura of electricity.

As suddenly as the bolts started, they stopped once again. The smell of burned flesh, where the larger arcs seared his skin, wafted through the air to fill the noses of the others. Jaxon's body stopped convulsing only for a fraction of a second before his muscles tensed again, but this time, it was his own doing. A low growl grew in volume, and it took Fae a moment to realize it was coming from Jaxon.

The magus raised his hands and again a grasping prison of electric bolts wrapped around Jaxon's body. Fae saw a crazed look of pain in Jaxon's eyes. The electric arcs stopped, and Jaxon collapsed to the ground.

"Stop." Fae said. Her voice cracked with desperation, and she leaned back on her heels, hand still tied behind her. She felt the heat of rage build in her, but her head slumped.

The magus, facing her, came closer and crouched once more so that their eyes met.

"Now, are you willing to talk?"

He was so close, their faces could almost touch, and she could feel his hot breath.

Fae took advantage.

From her knees, she launched herself forward. The magus, already balancing precariously, lost his stability and fell onto his back. Fae was on him in seconds, her fury fuelling her speed. She had a knee on his throat, ready to press down.

"No, please... don't..." The magus's voice sounded sad. Desperate. Terror sparked in his eyes.

This was it. She could crush his throat in a heartbeat. The mages would be distracted. The other three could get the jump on them, maybe kill them all before they realized what was happening. She could kill him. It would be so easy. Wouldn't it? The rage inside her faltered; it scared her, and she pulled back. She paused.

Too late.

The magus spoke a word Fae did not understand. Light exploded in her vision and her muscles spasmed, wrenching her body and slamming her arms against her shackles.

It stopped as suddenly as it started. Fae was lying on her back looking up as the Magus stood over her, a menacing smile on his face.

"For that, your man dies," the magus said. He turned to the mage behind Jaxon. "You, kill him."

As the mage next to Jaxon stood back, the least gnarled mage stepped forward. "Allow me," he said.

"No. Leave him alone," Fae said. Her voice cracked and came out weak.

"You hurt him, and I'll snap your necks," Bullock said. He snarled and gnashed his teeth at them.

The mage lifted his hands and spoke strange words. Fae screamed, pulling on her chains once more, focused on getting to Jaxon.

Jaxon looked over at Fae, gave her a smile, and then, he was gone.

A flash of fire exploded over him. The heat and light blinded them all, forcing them to turn away, and when it was done, Jaxon was gone. His shackles now rested in a pile of ash and char. His body burned to cinders.

"No!"

Fae's body would not respond. It would not let her move from her place on the ground. She cried out, but after a time, her throat hurt and became raspy, eventually giving out. Her body heaved with great sobs, and water blurred her vision as tears poured from her eyes. From her position laying on the stone ground with her arms still bound behind her back, she could not see Erika, but she saw Bullock on his knees with his head hung low and tears falling onto the stone floor.

The mages and the magus whispered amongst themselves, ignoring them as they mourned. Fae continued to cry, and she crawled towards where Jaxon had been. She tried to reach the shackles, just to touch something that had touched him moments before. Something to remember that he had existed. *There was nothing left of him.*

She crawled closer and closer, trying to reach the shackles, but her chain pulled taught and yanked her back just before she could reach them. She fell onto her side once more and lay with her head against the stone, just staring at the shackles. So close, but unable to reach them.

"I can't reach him," Fae whimpered. "I can't reach him."

"Take her blood now," the magus said.

Fae could not see him any longer, but could hear him. She heard someone approach her from behind then a knife was poked into the back of her neck, not deep, just enough to bleed. It should have hurt, but she just felt numb, like the pain was there, but it was someone telling her it was there instead of her feeling it. She also felt blood running down the back of her neck and mage hands holding her down, but she was too defeated to struggle.

She saw another mage approach her with a glass phial. He crouched over her and placed the phial against the back of her neck, and she knew he was collecting her blood, but she did not care. He stepped away and approached the central dais. His phial, she could see now, was filled with her crimson blood. He poured it into the dais but stopped as he reached half of the phial. He tucked the remaining blood into his robes and stepped back from the dais. It fizzled and then seemed to settle down to a calm bubble.

"It will take a bit for the mixture to be ready," the magus said.

The rest of the mages retreated to the staircase side of the room, behind where Jaxon's ashes lay. One mage grabbed a bundle she recognized as Jaxon's gear and carried them up the staircase.

Fae's eyes burned with further tears. She continued to stare at the ashes that used to be him.

Jaxon was dead.

He had been a rock for her, in a life that had been chaotic and confusing, always encouraging her and believing in her. He was gone. *Because of her.*

She tried to move closer to the shackles again. Her chains still held.

"I can't reach him," Fae whispered. "I can't reach him."

She had hesitated. What had she been thinking? *The rage had scared her, and she didn't know why; she should have been able to control it. She had passed the trials and become one of them, had lived with them for half of her life, but always there was a fear in her of who they were and if she wanted to truly be one of them. And in the end, that fear, that hesitation, had doomed the one she loved.*

"What is she saying?" Erika asked.

"I can't tell," Bullock replied. "Fae," he called to her in a whisper. "Fae."

His voice sounded far away. Like the pain, she was numb to it, and she did not respond.

"Fae," Erika tried her name as well. "Fae, honey, snap out of it. We need you to help us think. Better to die fighting our way out of here than bleeding out on the stone."

Still, Fae did not respond, but tears continued to fall sideways off her face and onto the stone her head lay on. Her body did not heave any longer with sobbing, her strength too far gone.

"Bullock, I think we are on our own here," Erika said.

"But Jaxon is always the one that figures out how to get us out of situations like this," Bullock said.

"Well, now, it needs to be us."

Fae heard more rustling of chains behind her as Bullock tried to test the strength of the metal.

"I can't reach him," Fae said.

It was no use. She had failed them. Her chance had come, and she had let it slip through her fingers. She could die here; everyone had to die sometime. It would be easy. Quiet, just like sleep. Fae closed her eyes and rolled over further, her will to fight gone.

"I can't reach him."

CHAPTER 35
FIRE

Damitus sighed and dumped the bundle he carried beside the two bodies that lay on the ground in front of him. Everything was dark around him, but the small fire provided enough light. It still burned from earlier; in fact, the fire never went out. A handy charm he had picked up long ago. He smiled at his handiwork and remembered that it had surprised him that magic worked at all in this place.

He put his hands on his hips, considering what he had just done.

In front of him lay the dead body of the mage he had murdered and taken the place of. The other body was that of a young man, not yet dead, but badly beaten and bloody, with several minor burns on his half naked body. He was toned and fit, and his lungs rose and fell with his breathing.

The young man pushed himself off the ground to a position on all fours. He shook his head, throwing sand from his hair, and looked up at Damitus.

"Where am I?" he asked.

"To be perfectly honest, I am not sure," Damitus said. "I can say you are in a safe place and that I have brought you here. I have only seen this place referred to once, in an ancient book gained from beyond the Empire, which also provided the arcane instructions to get here. And back. In that book, this place was called Nihinvalan, which roughly translates to something like nowhere. But as I am the sole owner of the only book to reference it, and to my knowledge, the only person in all Tal'am to know of its existence, it works as an excellent sanctuary for my purposes."

"And what would your purpose be, might I ask?"

"Most recently, it was to save you from a very painful death."

The young man furrowed his brow and moved his eyes back and forth, trying to remember.

"Right. The magus. So, you are telling me I am not dead then?"

"No. You are not," Damitus said.

The boy looked at Damitus now and moved to a kneeling position in which he could sit back on his heels.

"I remember you. You were one of the mages. I thought you killed me."

"I did not. And while I appeared as a mage of Southshore, I assure you, I was an imposter."

Damitus now drew back his cowl to expose his face to the young man. Realization spread across the man's face, and he grinned as he let out a snicker.

"Damitus. Ha."

"Jaxon," Damitus said.

"I thought you were still with Axton," Jaxon said. "I figured he would still have you bound and maybe gagged."

"I slipped away," Damitus said in a smooth tone.

Jaxon laughed and shook his head. *He seemed to find this quite humorous.* Damitus considered the man. *He could certainly be of use if he was implemented at the right time.*

"Well, I guess I owe you my thanks," Jaxon said.

"Yes, you do. But you also owe me a bit more than that."

Jaxon raised a skeptical eyebrow.

"I am going to leave you here. Get some rest and tend to your wounds as best you can. Your equipment is there." Damitus pointed to the bundle he had dropped on the ground earlier. "I have left some food and water there as well. Get suited up and wait for my signal. I am going to return to the castle and continue to skulk around. I will do what I can to sabotage the ritual and kill the magus. The knowledge that exists in Southshore must die with him."

"Makes sense so far."

"I may need you in a short while, and I will bring you back to the castle at the opportune moment to assist me in my mission."

"I can agree to that."

"Good. Rest, but be prepared. When you feel a heat grow in this place, you will know it is time. The heat will come mere heartbeats before you are transported directly to a place in space within the castle. Draw your weapons and be ready."

"I understand. I'll be ready."

"I leave you now." Damitus began to turn his head.

"Damitus," Jaxon said.

"Yes?"

"Thanks. For all of this."

"I do this for reasons beyond helping you."

"Still..." Jaxon's bravado was gone, replaced with sincerity.

"You're welcome."

A flash of flames erupted around Damitus, and he was gone.

Fae did not know how much time had passed. She felt like she had been lying on the floor for an eternity, locked in her pain and loss. Erika and Bullock continued to whisper behind her, still chained. Two mages were circling the ritual star and chanting something in an unfamiliar language, while the magus and another mage talked close to the staircase leading out of the castle basement.

Fae was no longer crying, too emotionally drained to continue, feeling as if sleep should claim her but refused to. The sounds of activity in the room had been consistent enough to almost be unregistered by her numbed perception when she finally heard something new. The sound of a person in armour coming down the staircase. She had a clear view of the entry from her place on the floor.

A man in segmented steel armour walked down the stairs, holding himself high, and addressed the magus, "Magus Pious."

So, the magus had a name. Pious. A flash of hatred reawakened her mind enough to pay some attention to the conversation.

"Captain Titus," Magus Pious said, "What do you want? My time is limited."

Pious waved off the mage he had been talking to, and the mage joined the others in their chanting.

"There is a buildup of forces less than a league away from the city walls. The Magistrate told me you ordered my men to be posted inside the castle instead of the city walls. I seek permission to reinforce the city walls with my men. The current posts on the walls are not enough to keep the enemies from taking the city if they attack."

"Request denied, Captain. Maintain your defence of the castle."

Titus firmed up his tone and leaned closer to Pious as he continued, but Fae could still make out what he said.

"Pious, if you do this, the people of the city will not stand a chance. There will be little to keep the enemy from taking the city. "

"Titus, the castle is all that matters. Maintain your defence of the castle and move any of your remaining men in the city to the castle walls instead."

Titus no longer leaned in or seemed to care if anyone else heard him.

"Dammit Pious! And leave the people we have sworn to protect to die?"

"I swore no such thing. I only owe my allegiance to the might of the Empire. It matters not if we sacrifice the citizens."

"Like we sacrificed the citizens of Creet?"

"Watch your tone, Captain Titus."

"I know you remember Creet. You were just an acolyte then, but I still had to obey your command; to fire upon the city. We burned down the town and massacred thousands of people. And now you ask me to do it again?"

Fae's body froze. *What did this man just say?*

The Empire fired on her town? All those years ago. Massacred the citizens? The memory flashed back to Fae; fire and screaming as she ran through the town. Bodies, weapons, and blood strewn on the streets. Her mind focused on a detail that had never seemed important to her before; firelight had rained down from the skies. At the time, fire had been everywhere, so there was no reason to focus on this. Nor was there reason before to focus on the arrows sticking from burning houses, seemingly of no importance beyond being further signs of battle.

"Do not try to act righteous to me, Titus. You carried out my command and lit the arrowheads of the men that fired. We both did what we had to, and now we must do it again."

"You are right, Pious, we are both to blame. But the difference between you and me is that I have regretted following that command every day since."

"Titus, you have already used up my patience. I gave you an order. Carry it out."

The two men locked eyes for a moment. Besides having been taken aback by what Fae had heard, she was also stunned by the captain's willingness to risk both his career and his life by showing disrespect to a magus.

"And Titus. We will never speak of what happened in Creet ever again."

"No. We won't."

Titus's eyes burned with hatred of the man. He stared at the magus for only a moment, then he turned and left, walking up the stairs.

What happened in Creet?

Creet. In one night, everything Fae knew of the world had shattered.

The Empire was not stability; it was tyranny. The citizens traded safety for slavery. There was no goodness in the Empire. The Bandorians were not the evil that had ruined her life, but her saviours.

The fear that had always been in her heart, the fear that had kept her from truly accepting herself as one of them, the fear had held back her killing blow; the blow that would have saved Jaxon's life. That fear was gone. And while her heart ached deeply for an avoidable loss, it also somehow felt whole.

Fae gritted her teeth and clenched her fists, scraping on the cold stone behind her. Jaxon would not have wanted her to weep or mourn, especially, not now. He would have told her to think—to use her anger as a focus. And she had no shortage of anger now. The muscles in her back tightened and rippled, tense and ready for use. She let the rage grow, and she pulled on the chains, but they did not budge.

She looked around the room, taking in her surroundings to better prepare herself. She saw her equipment hung along the wall on the bench by the entrance, saw her bracer with her nana's amulet embedded in the leather. It helped her focus her rage further. She felt power build.

But just then alarm bells rang out, much like they had the previous night, echoing through the halls from all directions at once.

A moment later, Fae heard metal footsteps tap on stone, growing closer as the steps came down the staircase. A guard, of apparently lesser rank than Captain Titus, only in a light mail armour, loudly clambered, running into the room. His chest heaved, quick deep breaths, too winded from running to speak.

The magus approached him, and the other three paused their chanting, and moved closer; the bells were loud enough to make hearing less easy. They stood waiting to hear what the man would say.

With little patience left, the magus barked at the guard, "What on earth is going on, Sergeant? Has the enemy attacked?"

"No sir, a fire. The entire eastern wall of the castle is on fire," the guard blurted out between gasps for air.

"What?" the magus screamed at the guard. "How could the eastern wall be on fire? It's made of stone!"

The guard had regained his composure and no longer breathed as heavily. Despite that, he did not seem confident about delivering his news.

"Yes, sir, but it seems it was coated with oil. Someone seems to have left a bucket of oil on the eastern turret and it has been leaking for the last day, it seems. Easily enough, it caught fire, and we cannot stop it. It has gained enough heat that some of the internal rooms have caught fire as well. We cannot put the fire out with water buckets alone. At least not in time to save that part of the castle. All guards are already on the wall attempting to douse the flames."

Oil leaking for the last day, happened to catch fire?

Kiva.

In her sorrow, Fae had forgotten about the unknown fate of Kiva, but this circumstance was exactly the reason they had left one of them hiding in the castle.

This was their chance; all the mages and the magus were distracted. Again, Fae pulled on the shackles, binding her arms behind her back still. She'd not had enough time to think through a way to escape them yet. She had spent too much time wallowing instead of focusing her rage and pain. The pain was still great inside her, but she focused her rage into strength. She pulled hard on her bindings. *She had to get out.* The shackles cut into her wrists, and she felt warm blood trickle onto her fingers.

She had to do something. Even if it was just to die fighting, anything was better than being shackled. She pulled harder and harder, ignoring the pain. Once again, she looked at her bracer hanging along the wall and the amulet within. She thought of it and everything she had become, and rage-fuelled power grew in her. Then, one moment, her hands were in the shackles and the next they were not, as if she had just slipped through the solid metal of the shackles. Her wrists burned where they had pulled against the iron, but she did not care because her hands were free. Fae did not have time to understand what had happened.

What was she to do about a magus and three mages? They had been distracted so far by questioning the guard.

"Sirs, we have no natural way to put out the fire fast enough. We need magical help. Are your wizards able to...," his sentence dropped off, and he let out a gurgling noise as his eyes glazed over as if no longer there. Then the guard dropped to his knees and fell forward onto his face.

A black throwing dagger was buried in the back of his neck and crimson blood dripped from the wound.

Two more daggers flew out of the doorway to the staircase and were followed by a dark shape running down the stairs. Kiva burst through the doorway just as the one blade found a wizard. The blade embedded itself in the mage's eye, and the man screamed in pain before falling to the ground. The other blade sailed by one mage as he moved his head to the side just in time. It nicked him though, leaving a deep gash of crimson across his face.

The magus recoiled back in terror. He waved his hands and spoke a word quickly enough to throw up a barrier just as Kiva's longer blades unleashed a flurry on him, showering sparks as they collided with his barrier. Every time his barrier fell, he would bring forth it anew and Kiva would continue her assault.

The unharmed mage stepped away from the deadly Bandorian woman, right towards Fae. She did not let the opportunity slide, swinging a leg, and tripping the mage. He crashed backwards towards Erika who had, at some point slipped the chains under her butt and feet to get them in front of her. She was ready when the mage fell. She wrapped the chains around the man's neck and squeezed, letting the air slip out of him, slowly crushing his throat. Life left the man and Erika threw him to the ground.

Kiva continued to assault the magus.

"Kiva, don't let up," Fae said, "Don't give him time to cast anything except the defence."

Fae leapt towards the last mage, the one with the gash across his cheek. She recognized him as the one that had taken the vial of her blood and poured it into the dais in the centre of the ritual star.

As she approached, she watched his hands as he sprayed fire. Fae dove to the side and rolled, narrowly avoiding being burned. The mage backed up to the rear of the room and had nowhere to go.

Erika was searching the mage she had killed for a key. When she finally found one, she began unlocking her shackles as Bullock waited close by for his turn to be freed.

Kiva continued her attacks on the magus, both moving closer to the staircase.

Fae got to her feet once more and readied for a charge, but she was too slow. A wall of flame erupted in front of her eyes, blocking her path to the back of the room where the final mage stood. She lost sight of him through the fire, and she searched for a way to put it out. She looked back to check on the others.

At the staircase, up several steps, more sparks flew and flashes of light as Kiva smashed blades, alternating between left and right, attempting to bring down the barrier or at least force the magus to continue raising additional barriers. Lacking the time for a more powerful spell, the magus said a quick word, and a gust of wind threw Kiva from the staircase and onto her back.

Instead of unleashing a destructive spell, the magus just turned and fled up the stairs and back into the castle.

Finally, with no material to continue to fuel the fire, it dwindled, and Fae rushed forward past it, but there was no mage.

"Fae to your left," Erika called.

Fae looked left just in time to see the black cloak of the mage standing in a doorway in the back of the room. *Where had the door come from? It had not been there before.* The stone doorway began to slide back into position.

"Fae, don't let it close," Erika said.

Kiva threw her last blade past everyone and to the back of the room, but the last wizard disappeared a moment before, and it clattered harmlessly against the tunnel wall as the stone entryway sealed itself behind the wizard.

"Dammit" Kiva cursed.

Erika had gotten Bullock's shackles off, and they ran towards the doorway.

"Quick, get the door open," Bullock said.

Fae was already searching along the stone when the others arrived. They tried to pry the stone apart, but it had slid into place and was not budging. Bullock added his weight to the efforts, but still, it did not budge. Bullock looked at Fae, and with regret, he shook his head. They would not be following their quarry that way through the castle.

The last wizard had escaped and while they had foiled the plans for now, they noticed the instructions for the ritual were missing, confirming Fae's suspicions that the escaping wizard had taken them. *If the magus escaped, and regrouped with the mage, they could begin work on the ritual once more. Fae and the others would need to face that, eventually, but for now, they had to find a way out of the castle.*

Titus had put it off for too long. Dread shook his hands, and he held them up to inspect them, but could not stop the trembling. *Strange how fear can permeate your being enough to wrestle control from that which you control most.* Muscle tremors had gripped him before, always when the memory of Creet surfaced in his mind.

He had long denied what he knew he must do, but clarity now filled him, and he gained control; his hands no longer shook.

The letter he had written was concealed against his breast beneath his tunic, deep under his armour. But he could hide it no longer. Sergeant Grierson and Walton stood before him. He reached under his chest plate and pulled the letter from its safety, exposing it to his sergeants; he would have to tell them.

He'd put this off for far too long. He had hoped to get back to his wife and tell her in person. Tell her everything. Tell her about Creet. Tell her what they had done. Tell her why he had become distant. He was trying to protect her. He wanted to look into her eyes to tell her, but he had not been given the chance, and now he may never be able to. So, he would do what he could.

"Walton, I need you to get this letter to my wife. Do not let anyone know what you carry. Guard her while she reads it and provide her assistance if she requires any. I give you this as an order, so if you are stopped, you can speak the truth: that you were doing as ordered."

"Sir?"

"Go now and return only when my wife has released you from service," Titus said.

"Yes, sir."

Sergeant Walton took the sealed letter and tucked it in his chest, then he walked out of the castle barracks.

Sergeant Grierson stood before Titus with a strange look in his eyes. The garb he wore was a contradiction; he wore armour of segmented steel only reserved for officers, though he only had the signate of a sergeant. Like Titus himself, limited to only ever being a captain by his social status, Grierson was fated to never be an officer because he was of even lower birth than Titus. But Titus knew that experience could make up for training, and Grierson was as valuable as any of his officers, which is why he had been put in charge of a platoon and often acted as Titus's second.

"Sir, what is it? You are speaking strangely, Captain," Grierson said.

"That letter tells my wife of things that happened in Creet and other orders I have followed. Orders that I have carried out before my time commanding this battalion as well as during. You have been with me for a long time, but you were not in Creet."

"Right, I was taking news for you to the capital."

Titus sighed deeply, "I am sorry, my friend. What we did in Creet has weighed on me for a long time, and the atrocities I regularly see eat at my heart. I have had grievances with The Empire for a long time, but tonight I have been asked to pull our men from the city walls and let the people die. I offered the plan to evacuate the people and was turned down despite the magus knowing it could be done. No longer will I carry out their commands. I am leaving tonight; I will not return to the army. If I am lucky enough for you to forget this conversation, they may report me as missing in action when an attack comes, instead of defecting. Do as they command you and keep your head down, my friend."

Grierson looked shocked, but after a short time, he seemed to understand. His wide eyes drew down into focus.

"Captain, you and I both know that I am not the smartest of men, but from you, I have gained some wisdom. You have taught me to learn the minds of our men and I feel I can speak for them. Your men and I, we do not follow the Empire, we follow you. If you leave tonight, we all go with you."

"I cannot ask this of you, my friend," Titus said.

"I didn't hear you ask Captain. And if you order us not to, then you deprive us of the freedom which you claim for yourself."

"Well said, friend. So be it."

"So, now what?" Grierson asked.

Titus pondered for a moment. "We need to gather the men. There is a small eastern entrance to the city. If we are lucky, it will be safe from attack. We will open the gate and hold it. We must get as many of the people out as we can. If we are lucky, our disobedience will not be noticed in the chaos."

"Sounds like a plan I can get behind, Captain," Grierson smiled and clapped his friend on the shoulder, "Let's go."

CHAPTER 36
ESCAPE

Pieter stood on the city gatehouse wall in his simple city guard uniform, watching the burning tower. He was dumbfounded and in awe of what he was witnessing.

The flames lit the night sky near the Southshore castle walls, turning a dark moonless night bright as day in quick flashes. Buildings nearby flicked from black to orange and back to black quickly as they reflected the light of the castle walls. Like a snake's tongue, the flames licked the side of the eastern castle wall as they tried to climb and recoil back down. Creaking and crackling sounds echoed as the wooden beams and internal structures burned and lost their strength. As guards and servants threw pales of water against the fire, the flames subsided for only a second before returning with a fury. It was out of control, and none could tame it.

He shook out of his stupor for a moment to look over at his companion, the other guard on duty with him. He did not know the man well; the other guard belonged to the day shift and was covering for some men from Pieter's squad that had been assigned to castle duty because of the events going on within.

Pieter could not remember his companion's name; when they

had been introduced, he had been too focused on making sure he introduced himself in a stately manner, to ensure he impressed his reporting officer. He realized only afterwards that he had neglected to pay attention to the man's name.

The other guard must have looked identical to him in light chainmail shirts, cinched around his waists with a buckle scabbard that held regulation arming swords. *Foolishly, the other man had wasted the time to put on his helmet; the tiny guard helmets barely offered any protection, anyway.* Pieter had taken his off some time ago and held it in his hand beside him.

The shine in the helmet, though, brought Pieter's attention back to the burning castle wall. He was supposed to be watching the road leading up to the city from the surrounding treeline, but nothing mattered compared to the horror he saw in front of him.

Something in his mind pulled at him. He thought he heard a strange sound from behind. The soft plotting of paws. Lots of them. *He would turn in a moment.* Animals were not a concern, but the fire was. *What could have started a fire like this? It was a stone wall. Nothing short of oil could burn on a stone wall like this. How had it spread so quickly?*

A half angry, half panicked shriek broke Pieter and his companion out of their stupor.

"Close the gates, you idiots!"

The two guards saw their officer running from the nearby guard house waving his hands and yelling at them. Pieter scrunched his face in a puzzled expression, but before he could figure out what had the officer in a fuss, he heard a short thunk like the sound of a butcher slamming his blade down into a wooden cutting table.

He noticed movement in his peripheral and turned to see the helmeted guard stare back at him, a blank expression on his face and the butt of an arrow sticking out of a gap in his helmet. The guard teetered, took a partial step towards the edge of the wall, and tipped slowly over the edge.

Pieter heard the moving wind of his companion's fall for only an instant before the loud thud sounded of him hitting the ground, dead.

A shot of panic surged through Pieter, and he ran to the gate wheel to drop the gate before the attackers could enter. As he took his first steps, he finally noticed the increasing sound of feet on dirt directly below him, running through the gate at a shocking speed. He kicked the lever, finally releasing the gate as he heard the clashing of swords below him inside the wall. He looked out over the edge of the wall and saw stout men and women astride massive wolves that he had never seen the likes of before. They were all halted mid charge while attempting to enter the city. They turned now and pulled back out of archery range.

He took a moment to look on in pride, knowing that he did his job; he saved the city from an invasion. The gate was down and his compatriots in the streets below would soon deal with the remains of the attacking force trapped inside the gate. He crossed his arms in satisfaction before he turned back to see if his companion guards on the ground needed any help mopping up.

As he tried to look down at the streets below, it shocked him to see an enormous, gauntleted fist block his vision. Time stopped just long enough for him to realize he was being punched, and he thought, "Oh hells."

"Really, Axton, you carry around a gigantic axe, two hand axes and three daggers, but you decide to punch the man instead?" Bao chided.

Axton grinned with satisfaction, then shrugged at Bao as she walked over to the gate wheel and drew it back. The gate lifted slowly as she pulled on the handles to the wooden wheel, starting the gear and pulley system.

"You know, it can mess up your hand a bit if you don't connect correctly, but it is oh so satisfying when it hits," Axton said.

Bao just rolled her eyes at him in response.

He picked up the limp body of the man he had just stunned, walked to the edge of the wall, and tossed him over to land hard beside his dead companion.

The gate was still only part way up as Brakan's voice came up over the inside edge of the wall. "Hurry, will you?" Then he posed the question clearly meant just for Bao. "Love! What is taking so long?"

He was below on the ground, and ensured, along with a dozen of their clanmates, that the defeated guards stayed down.

"We made enough noise, reinforcements ought to be here any moment."

"Axton decided to take his time to line up a solid punch to a guard's face, instead of just swiping him and moving on," Bao said, with only a hint of playful annoyance in her voice.

Bao finally raised the gate high enough for the rest of the forces to make it through as another call came over the edge of the wall from Brakan, "Did it connect? Did it make a nice crunch?"

By now, Axton had found a rope and tossed it to Bao for the gate wheel. He gave her a look to say, "See, I am not the only one." Bao just gave a soft laugh and tied off the wheel so that the gate would stay open even if a guard tried to release it.

Beyond the gate, the other Bandorians began charging through the city gate. A swoop of wind could be felt blowing up and out from the entrance as they charged through the porthole to the city.

Bao called to Brakan, "We're coming!" and she grabbed Axton by the shoulder and pulled him towards the edge of the wall, though he needed little encouragement. They both leapt off the wall and landed square on a different vargr for each of them.

"Vargr worked well," Axton said.

"Nice of Clan Sterkt to send support when they got word," Bao said. She leaned down and gave the vargr a scratch behind the ears.

"Let's go!"

She kicked the side of her vargr, and they made off after the other Bandorians that had already charged into the city.

Fae led the charge up the dungeon steps to the main floor. They kept to the wall at the top of the stairs before continuing.

They could hear shuffling metal footsteps as a troop of guards ran past in a scramble, attempting to make their way to the east castle wall; Fae could see the tail end of them running past well enough to notice that the last guard in the line did not even have his tunic pulled completely on and was stumbling after his companions as he attempted to button it up.

Fae held her hand out, indicating for her friends to hold up and stay low. None of the guards even came close to noticing them as they ran east down the passageway, eager to not let their home burn to the ground.

Fae drew her long sword in preparation, and Bullock did the same behind her; the twins followed their lead.

After freeing themselves, the friends had found their equipment tied in bundles along the wall of the ritual chamber. Kiva had kept watch while the others donned their equipment and made ready to fight their way to freedom.

"Kiva," Fae said quietly back to the others, motioning for Kiva to step past the others. Kiva stealthily climbed the stairs up to the front. "You had more time to familiarize yourself with the castle. Do you know the way out? You should lead us."

Kiva nodded, softly stepped past Fae, and peeked around the corner that connected to the main floor.

"This way." She gestured down the corridor leading west and then quickly north.

They swiftly crossed the hallway and pressed themselves to the stone of the north wall of the corridor so that they could peek around the turn in the hallway and look down the corridor leading north.

More guards sprinted back and forth, but none were heading in their direction. Kiva took a quick look around the corner, then ducked back. She looked back at Fae and motioned for Fae to take her place, peering around the corner. They carefully shuffled positions.

"Halfway down the hallway, on the left wall; look."

Fae peeked out for only a moment. She could see that they could make it partway down the hallway, but there was too much activity to make it all the way to the northern entrance. Part way down, though, she saw a door on the left wall leading to a room that seemed to expand north, parallel to the hallway. It did not seem to have any activity in it. She hoped that anyone in that room were just civilians and would be too distressed by their sudden appearance to act.

"I see it." She slid back to face the rest of the companions so they could all hear her clearly, even as she whispered. "Okay. The hallway is mostly clear, but we cannot make it all the way down it without likely being seen. There is a door on the left wall, halfway down the hallway. It seems like a big room, and it will cover our movements closer to the entrance. We can figure out where to go from there. Kiva will lead and we can follow. Everyone good?"

A quick, subtle nod from the others was affirmation enough.

"Good. Set up and be ready on Kiva's lead."

The group set up for a quick sprint, hoping they would not be seen. Kiva peeked around the corner again, making sure there were no other patrols to be seen from the hallway, then she burst from her crouch into a sprint down the hallway. The four others were right on her heels with only enough space between them to ensure they did not trip on each other.

As they dashed, they heard orders being shouted from the far end of the hall and the clatter of footsteps. A commander was yelling for his troops to keep up with him and was about to round the corner at the far end of the hall and run straight into the Bandorians.

"Hurry with those buckets, men. That fire will not put itself out!"

Kiva and Fae were through the door and in the room while Erika was crossing the threshold, but Bullock was still yards away from the doorway. The clinking of guards' armour grew louder as Fae heard them near the corner.

Bullock recklessly threw himself through the door just as the guards rounded the corner. He came in at full speed, and the only thing to slow him down was the wooden side of a large bookshelf that he could not avoid. He turned his body mid-stride to collide his back with the bookshelf instead of taking the impact to the face or shoulder. It made a loud crack. He let out a hefty groan as he collided with his lashed back and blood flowed from reopened wounds.

Bullock slid down the side of the shelf to come to a sitting position. *He did not look good.* Luckily, it was still too loud in the castle for his collision to have roused any suspicion of intruders. Fae bent down and grabbed one of Bullock's shoulders to pull him to his feet with some help from him.

"Thanks," he said.

He leaned on Fae, and she did her best to support his enormous bulk. She looked around the room with the rest of them, getting their bearings. They were far enough into the room to not be seen by anyone in the hallway.

They took the moment to relax as they walked to the far northern side of the room. It was a massive ballroom, which was long enough to move them further through the castle. They spent the moment looking for a door to an adjoining room, but when they reached the other end, they saw that the room only had one door on its southern side; *it was a dead end.*

"Dammit." Fae realized what the others had already noticed.

They needed to get to the entrance. The Imperials had built the castle for defence and living, so while they had built the internal areas from wood, the external walls were all hard stone, with only one entrance in or out. There were windows letting light into the large room or hall that they were in, but those windows were extremely high up and built with stone frames that allowed for light to enter but were not large enough for a person to fit through.

"Everyone, look around," Fae said. "There must be something we can use."

She helped Bullock to sit against a wall. His skin looked pale. He may have lost a decent amount of blood even before she had been brought to the ritual chamber.

The girls spread out, looking for something of use. Erika pulled back a tapestry, hoping it hid something, but found nothing but a cloud of dust. She let out a cough as she cleared her throat and blew dust out of her nose. Kiva searched through a chest, looking for a possible rope or some useful tools, but found nothing but a rich woman's garments.

Fae took a few steps back to take in the room they were in and tried to work out a new plan.

"Create a distraction, maybe?" Bullock suggested. "Throw something down to the south end of the corridor we came from?" He was fishing for ideas from where he slouched against the wall.

"Not likely to help," Fae said. "Kiva already created a pretty big distraction. There are still a lot of troops left. I don't know if-"

Her sentence was cut off by Erika calling out to them, "Here."

They all looked up and walked towards where Erika crouched, picking at, and knocking on some of the wood of the northern wall.

"This wall is not very thick. Kiva, help me with this chest. It's metal and I think we can put it through this wall right here."

Kiva was quick to respond and leapt forward to get to the chest as Erika was attempting to lift it. Kiva helped lift the other side, and the two sisters brought it to the area of the wall that Erika had pointed out.

As they lined up the swing, Fae reached down for Bullock's axe. She stepped up to stand beside Kiva, placed a hand on her shoulder so he knew she was there, and readied the massive battle axe. *It was so heavy. How did Bullock swing this more than once in a fight?*

The twins swung the metal chest back and arced the ramming object back towards the wall. It hit the wall with a loud crack as fractures appeared in the wood.

As Erika and Kiva began their back swing again, Fae stepped in with an overhead swing of Bullock's massive axe and hit the precise location of the fracture; wood splintered, but the wall still stood.

Fae quickly stepped out of the way as Erika and Kiva came back on their front swing and hit the wall again, this time the wall gave way and a third of the chest went through the splintering wooden panels in the wall and stuck there instead of coming back with the twins. The two of them then reached forward and pulled the chest back through the wall, damaging more wooden panels.

Fae stepped in and began hacking at the small hole in the wall to make it bigger, while the other two cleared the chest out of the way. After only a few more swings, it was large enough that they could each slip through without trouble, and Bullock was now back on his feet. He gave his body a shake and rotated his arms in a windmill to stretch out.

"I'm good now, just needed a breather," He gave a genuine smile at the girls, then stepped forward and took his axe from Fae.

As Fae came through the hole after Bullock, she found herself in what looked like an abandoned guard break room. There was a table against the far wall that was covered in some form of cards, but curiously, no coins. Likely, the last guard out of the room had brushed them into his coin purse before leaving, when no one was looking.

As Fae surveyed the room, she heard the familiar twang of a crossbow triggering. Then she heard a muted howl of rage from Bullock standing beside her and saw a crossbow bolt sticking from his shoulder. Finally, she noticed the lone guard that had been standing in the corner, frozen in shock when they had knocked through the wall. Bullock's eyes looked wild. His muscles strained against his skin, and veins seemed about to pop.

He rushed the guard with his right palm outstretched. His hand clamped over the man's entire face and smashed his helmeted head into the stone wall. Bullock followed up with his body, pressing his shoulder into the man, pinning him against the wall. He pulled the man's head back and smashed it repeatedly into the stone wall until the cheap helmet buckled. The man's eyes went blank, and blood ran down his face. The man went limp, and Bullock let him collapse to the ground in a heap.

The rest of the group made it through the hole, and Bullock was grunting with the pain of the bolt embedded in his shoulder, severely limiting his ability to use his left arm. He leaned against the nearby table, his hand on it, bracing himself from falling.

"Bullock," Kiva rushed to him to survey his injury, placing a tender hand on his skin near the bolt. Blood trickled, but only a small amount; the arrow kept the rest in.

"I'm ok. I've had worse."

"It's not great," Kiva said. "The bolt is deep; I can't break it and if I pull it out, it will bleed. You'll lose too much blood." Her expression conveyed her concern. "I need bandages, and something to clean it."

"Not now," Bullock said. "We don't have time. Let's get out of here, then we can patch me up. I still have one good arm."

"Love, you are having a rough day, aren't you?" Kiva said.

Bullock snickered and with that, he placed his axe down while he grabbed a nearby shield. He put it against his arm. "Help strap this on. High so I can easily move. We need to go."

"He's right. We need to keep moving," Fae said.

Kiva strapped the shield onto Bullock's arm, higher onto the upper arm instead of the forearm so that he could use it without lifting his hand.

Erika was already next to the doorway, which led back into the hallway they had previously left. This time, though, they were at the very far end of the hall and out of the view of the guards and residents gathered in the central courtyard. They could see the castle entrance from the doorway. It was just a quick sprint to the gate; they could also see two guards on the inside of the entrance and another one just outside.

From the angle they were looking from, they could only barely make out the outer guard, which meant there was likely another guard on the outside of the gate. *Four guards in total.*

"It should be easy enough; we rush the two guards on the inside then just dispose of the other two on our way out the gate," Erika pointed out.

Fae nodded her head in response, "Rush them, yes, but don't get dragged into an engagement with them. We just need to get them out of the way to make our way outside. Then make a run for the city gates. If we engage with them, we will have another dozen or more guards on us in moments."

They all agreed; they knew that their only option for escape depended on their ability to keep moving and ensuring that they did not get cut off. They were each impressive warriors, but that counted for nothing if the odds became stacked enough. Even Bullock, who could take on three or more trained soldiers at a time with his sheer brute strength, could at some point be overwhelmed.

"Bullock, are you going to make the run?" Fae asked.

"I'll be good. Just don't ask me to do it twice in a day."

Fae turned to look at Bullock, an odd sight, with a shield awkwardly strapped to his arm.

As they were each preparing to make the rush, Erika reached a hand out to the side to tell them to all stop.

"Wait," she said, alerted by something.

Fae keened her ears to tell what had made Erika paused. The sound of metal armaments and armour moving in a unison march came from just beyond the castle entrance.

Erika pulled back around the edge of the doorway she had been about to step out of. Kiva licked her fingers and put out the flame of the lamp on the table, plunging the guard room into darkness. It would be hard for anyone at the castle entrance to see them in the shadows. Fae and Erika peeked around the doorway.

The noise they had heard became clear to them as a regiment of guards, most likely from inside the town, became visible as the front of their formation entered the castle gateway. The pack was close enough to listen in on the conversation.

"Bandorians in the city, sir? How?" asked a door guard. He looked like a sergeant.

"The fire distracted our guards," the newly arrived officer said. "No other questions. Get yourselves ready. They are almost at the castle. If we call the retreat, you must be ready to drop the gate once we are in."

"Yes, sir!"

Bandorians in the city? Kiva's distraction had worked better than they could have hoped. Axton must have rallied the troops to attack in case they failed. Kiva had just made it easier for them to do so.

The officer turned back to leave and defend the gate when a voice called out, "Intruders!"

A cloaked figure, some kind of scribe or advisor, rushed past the pack's hiding place towards the castle gate.

"They are in the castle. Intruders."

"What? How?" the officer demanded. "They just breached the city gate. How are they in the castle?"

"The prisoners. They have escaped. They killed the wizards." The advisor's voice was whiny and visibly annoyed the officer.

"The fire must not have been an accident, but a diversion." The officer looked pensive. He was sorting it all out and Fae's window of opportunity was shrinking. The pack stayed hidden, listening to the exchange.

"What are you going to do?" the advisor asked. "They killed the wizards. All of them!"

"I don't give a pig's ass about those wizards and their damned plans," the officer said. "What the hell is going on around here?"

No one answered the officer. He balled his fist in frustration and grumbled some comments that Fae could not hear from their hiding place back in the guardroom.

Finally, the officer called to his men, "Men get inside. You, there, lower the gate behind them," the officer pointed at the confused entrance guard, then at the gate mechanism closet, halfway between the pack and the castle entrance. "Seal it!"

This was it. Axton and the others were close by.

"Kiva, is there any other way out of the castle?"

"Not that I have found. If that gate closes, we're trapped."

It was now or never.

"We have to stop them from closing the gate," Fae said.

They all nodded.

"Go. Now."

Erika left the room first, with Fae right behind her.

Fae pointed her wrist at the guard as he approached the gate mechanism and fired a bolt from her wrist launcher. The bolt soared past Erika and tore through the side of the sergeant's neck, spraying blood. He grasped his throat and choked as he dropped to his knees.

Erika ran past the gate mechanism, jumped over the downed guard and was on the officer. The officer was surprised, but years of training saved him as Erika attacked. She swung her sword towards his shoulder. The officer's quick reflexes brought his sword up to deflect hers.

The block brought both swords high, but the officer was at an awkward angle. Erika carried her momentum forward and punched the man in the throat. He backed away, gasping for air.

Fae was near the entry with Erika now. The other guards on the drawbridge, and the few that had originally been posted at the entry, realized the imminent threat, and drew their swords and began a charge through the gateway.

"Flask," Fae said.

Erika deflected a swing from a guard and pushed the man back towards the officer. She stood with both hands grasping her sword as she took a defensive stance, staring down the officer and the remaining gate guard.

"Grab it," Erika said.

Erika leaned her hip out towards Fae, signalling for her to take it.

Fae grabbed a fire flask off Erika's belt, shook it, and threw it at the men charging up the ramp to the entrance.

The flask smashed against the lead guard as he charged into the entry hall. It ignited, burning him, and splashing fire at the entire group behind him. They went down in a heap, trying to tear their armour off beyond the entry.

The officer was breathing regularly again and stood beside a guard, ready to advance on Erika while the scribe had run away as soon as there was any sign of danger. Erika and Fae backed away from the entrance and towards the gate mechanism, determined to keep them from it. Kiva and Bullock stood behind them now.

As they backed up, Kiva threw a large pellet at the castle entrance floor just beyond the gate mechanism. It burst in a cloud of smoke, obscuring everything beyond the gate mechanism. Fae could hear the officer and others coughing.

"Hopefully that will distract them for a moment," Kiva said.

The four Bandorians set up a defensive stance around the gate mechanism, knowing that the guards would come through the smoke any moment.

"I'll take the choke point," Bullock said. He put a hand on Fae as he stepped past her. He looked like a defensive wall, with the shield strapped to his left side.

"You do fill it better, big guy," Erika said.

Bullock stepped up to the smoke cloud with his shield and a sword; he had abandoned his axe for now. Erika stepped up beside him and the two of them took up defensive stances shoulder to shoulder, covering the width of the hallway.

Fae backed up to Kiva, who was looking down the hallway they had come from. She would guard the rear. Fae stood between them so she could turn to help where it was most needed.

They waited attentively, watching the cloud for any movement. Fae could still hear cries of pain and clattering beyond. Finally, two guards, followed by the officer, emerged from the smoke.

The two guards held shields raised, which blocked the

immediate down strokes from Erika and Bullock's swords. Both guards started a thrust at the Bandorians. Fae fired a bolt from her wrist launcher, stopping the thrust of the right guard as the dart pierced him. He collided, dead, against Bullock's shield.

"I'm out of bolts."

Erika batted a thrust out of the way, then grabbed the other guard's wrist. She yanked him towards her and sunk her blade deep into him.

She was pushing the dying man away when another guard burst from the smoke and thrust his sword forward. The guard's jab clipped Erika in the side and sliced the skin along the edge of her stomach. Erika grabbed at the wound, then batted the sword out away from her. She stepped forward and swung her leg up hard, her foot connecting with the man's groin, and he dropped. He was smart enough to roll himself quickly back into the smoke for protection.

The officer advanced and brought his sword up to block Bullock's swing. The swords connected, and the officer deflected it. Bullock was weakened by the crossbow bolt still in his left arm but managed to push the officer to the left and Erika jabbed. The officer jumped back to avoid it.

The officer parried two more sword attacks from both Bandorians. Left. Right. He must have known he was outmatched. He stepped back. Then back once again. He deflected one last swing, then jumped back and retreated into the cloud and out of sight.

One last guard came through in a foolish charge. Bullock heard the footsteps. The guard exited the cloud and was immediately skewered by Bullock's sword. Bullock pushed the man off his sword with his foot. Then all was silent in the hallway. The three dead bodies lay on the floor and would trip anyone trying to charge out of the smoke.

The friends heard more yelling from in the castle, combinations of calls of intruders, and calls for more water. From beyond the castle gate, they heard sounds of shouted orders coming from the city.

All around them, save for where the four stood, was chaos. They felt an unnatural serenity amidst the turmoil, like being in the centre of a hurricane. None of them spoke; they did not want to give away their positions through the smoke, even as it was settling.

More armour clattering from beyond the smoke cloud. Reinforcements were likely coming through the gate or from other parts of the castle.

Fae stepped up to Erika and urged her back as she held her side, trying to staunch the blood. Erika stepped back and leaned against the wall, holding her side. Blood dripped between her fingers, but she still held her sword, ready if any of the others fell and she had to defend as well. Fae held her sword in a defensive stance and prepared to launch herself to aid Bullock. She picked up one of the fallen shields and readied it.

An arrow flew through the smoke and barely missed Fae's head. It clattered off the stone. Bullock turned his arm with the shield attached to increase their cover. *Thankfully, none of the guards they had seen before had been carrying bows, so they likely did not have more than one archer.*

Thunk. An arrow came through the smoke and struck into Bullock's shield, as predicted. Then another. Fae held her shield up to defend as well, and an arrow collided with it. The shield was large and swept low to a point, protecting her head and most of her torso. But her leg was still exposed, and an arrow whizzed by, cutting at her thigh, catching some of the muscle.

Fae opened her mouth to yell, the pain searing through her, but pushed her mouth against her shield arm to keep herself silent and avoid revealing her position. She steeled herself to force down the pain. No more arrows came.

Behind them, boots clacked on the floor from somewhere in the castle, getting closer.

"We have company," Kiva said, "And they have spears."

"Shit." Fae knew they did not have a good defence against any weapons with reach while they were pinned between two groups.

Fae looked back and saw the company of soldiers rounding the corner towards them.

"Any more fire flasks?" Bullock asked.

"I'm out. Fae used the last one," Erika said.

The soldiers saw them, and determination quickly replaced a look of shock as they lowered their spears and began a slow advance on the pack.

"Bolts?" Bullock asked.

"I'm out," Fae repeated her comment from earlier.

"I have three left," Kiva said.

The soldiers were halfway down the hallway.

"Throwing blades?" Bullock asked.

"Only two left," Kiva said.

"One here," Fae said.

The soldiers stopped and held their ground, not yet advancing. Silence replaced the clanking of metal on stone. The men stood wary, eyes shifting from Bandorian to Bandorian.

Fae looked in front of them once more. The smoke cleared enough to see silhouettes. "We are going to have incoming," Fae called back to Kiva.

"These guys are not advancing back here," Kiva said.

"They do not need to," a callus and familiar voice said. "We have you surrounded."

The smoke cleared further. A sharp faced man in elegant flowing dark robes stood before them. Magus Pious. Behind him, the officer and another ten guards stood ready.

They were trapped.

"Lay down your weapons or die."

CHAPTER 37
REUNION

Titus and his men had been marching for the front gates, and now they stood face to face with a group of Bandorians. Titus looked on in confusion as he tried to survey the situation through a cloud of smoke that was slowly clearing. There were only four of them he could see, and they looked ragged, but he had learned not to underestimate their fighting abilities.

He had never seen a Bandorian that was not a challenging match for even the best trained soldier. They had often gone toe to toe with multiple opponents at once and won, and in these corridors with limited width, they could hold out for a long time.

His best hope was to push through the Bandorians and force them past the entrance to the other wing of the castle. His men's spears might help with that. *They had to reach the entrance.*

Once Sergeant Walton had left with the letter for Titus's wife, Titus had gathered his officers. He had told them of his plan, and though he had told them he was defying orders, they were eager to join him. Titus sent them to the eastern gate to hold it and create a safe route for the citizens out of the city, while he and Grierson had gone through the castle gathering up the remaining troops.

He now had almost a full platoon of twenty-four men with them. He had hoped to reach the entrance without running into the magus so they could exit quietly. But plans never go as expected.

Titus looked at Grierson to see a mirrored look of shock on the man's face. Titus pulled his focus in and called an order to his men.

"Spears out. Ready, men."

The highly trained troops did not hesitate. They aimed their spears forward, in between the line in front of each of them as they stood two men abreast in the hallway. Titus stood at the front and, unfortunately, did not have a spear, but readied his sword and shield, anyway. He was ready to call the order to advance on them, but he waited a moment, curious to see what would happen next. *What were they waiting for?*

Then he heard it. A voice he hated more than any other. Magus Pious. He saw him as the smoke from beyond the Bandorians cleared.

Now what?

Fae stared daggers at the magus, as he stood looking at her with a smug smile. No one moved on either side.

The edge of fear slid into her heart. The flame of anger wavered, threatening to be blown out. She looked to her right and saw Bullock standing there, wounded and bleeding. She snuck a peek behind herself. Erika leaned against the wall to keep from falling. Kiva stood holding a long blade in each hand, the only one not yet injured. *They could not win.*

She turned back, her back tensed with fear, her eyes lost focus with sadness, her arms lowered slightly. She felt like weights pulled her down. *It was hopeless.*

The seconds ticked by. The Magus tapped his foot, patiently

waiting for the Bandorians to comply with his command to surrender.

Fae shook her head to clear it. *Fear, sadness, hopelessness—they would not help her.* She felt the emotions like swirling black holes inside her stomach, colliding, and feeding off each other. She sped them up and turned them to anger. *But anger itself would make her reckless. She knew better. She had trained for this. The emotion had to be controlled. She forced herself to relax.* The anger boiled through her, but she turned it over, like the twisting of a sword. Wrapped it around her body. Channeled it to power her arms, her legs, and movements. Her body was tight, controlled by whipcord muscles. *She was ready.*

She knew what she had to do. They did not have to win, but they had to keep the Imperials from closing the gate.

She looked at the others and readied herself. They each did what they needed to prepare as well. They twisted their weapon handles in their hands to feel the grip, moved their heads back and forth to stretch their necks. Anything that would ensure they were prepared.

The magus's eyes furrowed in disappointment. He had an answer to his demand; they would not surrender.

Eyes locked across battle lines, each finding a target.

The magus looked to his officer, "Do it."

The officer raised his hand, preparing to signal the attack.

He did not get the chance.

A yell broke the silence, a cry, from outside of the castle gates. Accompanied by some shouting. Rushed and panicked orders.

The officer turned to look out the entrance, confusion on his face. Some of his men watched him, but others snuck a peek at the noise.

Another cry echoed off the stone, but this one was lower, more guttural. A battle-cry. Then the clanging of steel on steel, and the scream of pain.

The guard officer and those soldiers with him turned white. Their eyes went wide, and horror reflected in their faces.

One of the officer's guards took one step back, and an enormous wolf-like beast came bounding through the doorway. It sank its teeth into the guard's neck, lifted him off his feet and flung him farther down the hallway, into other guards.

The officer still stood with his hand raised, ready to call for an attack, but a massive axe wielded by a man on the back of the beast took the hand clean off. The officer screamed and clutched his bleeding nub.

On the back of the beast was Axton, mowing down one more guard in his path and howling a war cry. He grabbed a throwing axe from his belt and flung it down the hallway at the third guard.

As another guard advanced on Axton, he stepped in front of the gateway and was knocked off his feet by a second rugged beast, ridden by Bao as she charged him with her sword swinging.

The companions had let their guard down, lowered their weapons and allowed surprise to show on their faces, but only for a moment. Fae realized what was happening and looked at the others. Bullock stood beside her, shield forward, holding the line. Kiva had sheathed a sword and drawn her two throwing blades. Erika was against the wall still; she had grabbed the tunic of a fallen soldier and torn a piece to bandage herself, but she did not look good. Fae worried she did not have long.

Axton and Bao were tearing through troops towards the magus as he backed up the stairs of the grand entrance. As Bao broke through and reached the staircase, the magus swung his arms and spoke strange words. A gust of wind slammed Bao and her vargr back against the entry wall. Bao was thrown from the beast, and before Axton could advance on the magus, a whirlwind of dust and debris whipped up to form a torrent around the magus. Like a tornado, it buffeted Axton or anyone else that tried to break through it to get at the magus.

Dammit. Fae wanted her revenge. She reached a previously shot down soldier, gripped the bolt that was stuck in his neck and ripped it out. She loaded it in her wrist crossbow; *it would have to do.*

She quickly glanced back to make sure Kiva was alright. Kiva launched two blades at the soldiers behind them. One blade bounced off the shield of a soldier in the front—an officer perhaps—the other soared past a well-armoured other soldier, *a captain Fae thought,* and dropped a man behind him. The captain with a shield fell back a pace, and the officer lunged forward with a spear. Kiva deflected it with her left sword, then grabbed the shaft and pulled. The soldier was not ready for it and fell forward, letting go of the spear. In one swift motion, Kiva slammed the butt of the spear against the captain, pushing him back once more, then spun it and jabbed the spear into the side of the officer on the ground.

"Grierson," the captain cried out, "Pull him back."

The other soldiers pulled the officer away from the front line. Fae, convinced that Kiva was alright, turned her focus back to the magus. Bullock was trying to use the shield to force his way through the storm around the magus. Fae gritted her teeth. The magus was barely visible through the fast winds as they kicked up debris. She took aim, pointed left, hoping to accommodate for the winds. With her only bolt, she hoped for the best and fired.

The bolt flew true. As it travelled through the buffeting winds, a piece of something hit it and it bounced harmlessly off and out of sight. *Dammit.*

Fae felt her hairs stand on end and she saw light flashing. Lightning. The magus was building up a charge of lightning in the storm; he would fry them all.

Damitus looked at the situation playing out in front of him, and he had to laugh. *It was comical how chaotic the situation had become, even without his help so far.*

Damitus, still wore the robes of the other mage, and had snuck through the castle. He had returned, determined to start more turmoil; anything to keep the magus from completing the ritual. He was pleasantly surprised to find that once he had returned the alarms were already blaring in the castle. The Bandorians were living up to their reputation.

As he had further snuck through the halls of the castle, he had heard much noise from the front entryway. First battle cries and the clashing of steel, then the howl of an incredible wind. He had felt it too as he came closer to the entrance. Winds had swept down the corridor, annoyingly tossing the robes around him.

He came around the corner and was looking at Magus Pious upon the staircase wrapped fully in an impassable torrent of wind, and ready to smite the others down with bolts of lightning. Between Damitus and the magus, down the eastern corridor, stood a unit of castle guards, many injured or dead, unable to engage because of the storm. Beyond them, in the castle gateway, he could make out some Bandorians on vargrs, though he could not make out specific details. In the opposite corridor from him, more fighting, but he could not see who.

Damitus pondered the situation before acting. He could not pierce the magus's barrier with anything that Damitus could think of. It was strong, and it was magical, likely impenetrable. He studied it further; it was a cyclone, and it was open at the top. He could drop something on the magus perhaps, though the magus would sense it and likely counter it. *And besides, why risk exposing himself? It was once again time to have someone else do the work for him.*

Damitus steadied his legs, he squeezed his fists tight, then opened his palms and began moving his arms.

"Kratas awyr ruien li'ali."

Damitus finished the spell by pointing and focusing his arms at the top of the high-ceilinged entry hall, far above the magus. Flame erupted in a burst, and as Damitus predicted, the magus sensed it. The magus lifted his hands towards the flame at its moment of appearing and water sprayed towards the flame. But from the flame came a figure.

A Bandorian man.

Jaxon!

Fae's mind screamed, and she could hardly believe her eyes. She had just fired her bolt; her last chance, and it had missed. All hope had seemed lost, but her determination didn't let her stop thinking of ways to get at the magus when he just appeared. In a flash of fire and light, Jaxon appeared in the sky above.

He plummeted, and like an angel of death on wings of fire, he dove for the magus. His sword pointed down and arms above his head, he fell. His knees crashed into the magus and Jaxon drove his sword deep into the chest of the man, tearing as they both went down. The magus collapsed into a broken bloody mess and Jaxon tumbled down the stairs. The torrent of wind stopped, and silence replaced the horrible sound it had created.

Jaxon's body finally came to a rest at the base of the stairs, lying on his back, not moving. Tension hung in the air. No one was certain of what had just happened. No one moved.

Then a single word escaped Jaxon's lips, "Ow."

Jaxon didn't move, but that single statement let Fae know he was uninjured.

A cry went up from the soldiers in the corridor opposite to Fae, shattering the silence, and they charged into the entry hall, only to collide with Bullock as he moved to guard Jaxon with his shield. Axton and Bao and the others then charged in to take on the attackers.

Elation washed over Fae. She wanted so badly to rush to Jaxon, but the sounds of battle forced her to stay. Kiva.

She turned back to see Kiva engaged with the soldiers behind them. *She needed help. Jaxon would be ok.*

Energy bursting through her, Fae rushed back on her injured leg to join Kiva.

Kiva forced back a soldier with the point of her stolen spear, then twisted it to parry a blow from the captain. Kiva was quick, but they outnumbered her. The captain got a blow with his shield in, hitting Kiva's shoulder hard and forcing her back. The captain raised his sword for a strike.

Fae's sword came down hard on his shield, forcing him back once more. He almost lost his footing, stumbling over a fallen body.

Kiva's strong jabs and Fae's shorter-range sword made for a good offense and defence as they pushed the captain and his men back. The officer had since been pulled back, along with others Kiva had stabbed.

They continued to push the men back. After a couple of yards, some soldiers backed up into the courtyard, while the captain and the others continued to back up down the corridor. Kiva branched left to the courtyard, defending the door, but not moving farther, while Fae engaged the captain.

It seemed like half of the captain's men were now injured or killed.

Fae's sword collided with the captain's and pushed it to the right against the wall. Their faces were pulled together, Fae ready to headbutt the man. When she suddenly recognized him.

"You." Her eyes were wide. "Titus."

He looked at her but did not have a look of recognition, instead it was one of confusion. Rage bubbled up once more in Fae. This man had carried out the massacre of her old home.

"I heard you. When I was chained below."

"That was you?"

"You knew him. Knew Pious. You were there with them when they murdered my family. You killed everyone I ever knew."

Titus held his shield up, going purely on the defensive. Seemingly more interested in what she had to say than the fight.

"I was a child! I was only eleven when they took me. Creet was my home. You left nothing for me to come back to. Nothing. No one. I'm all that is left."

Fae's attacks were purely offensive now, fuelled by rage. Heavy blows coming down hard against Titus's shield. He could have taken advantage of her recklessness, taken advantage of her limp, but he didn't.

Realization dawned in his eyes, and he waved his other soldiers back so he could face her on his own. Most of them were busy tending to the wounded, anyway. "You. You were in Creet? The Bandorians saved you? They took you away?"

"Yes. The magus is dead. Creet has seen some justice, but you still live."

"I... I'm sorry. I'm so sorry for what we did," The sorrow in Titus's eyes struck Fae as genuine, and it made her pause. "I have hated what I did since that day. I've felt anger for what we did and feared that the Empire would hang my family if I deserted."

She renewed the assault, sword clashing against shield, but she did not feel the rage quite the same.

"You are right to hate me, and I have no right to ask for forgiveness. We had a duty to protect your town, but we did not follow it. It is hard now to remember why specifically, except for fear. Fear of what the Empire would do to us for failure. It is not a justification, but you deserve to know the truth."

Fae pushed his sword left and gave his shield a shove. He stepped back and continued, "I just want to get these city folk to safety. My men and I are disobeying an order to do so."

"Fae, hun," Kiva said, "Are you just going to chat with that guy?"

"How can I believe you? Or anything you say?" Fae asked. She felt the rage swell in her once more.

"I don't know, though I wish I did."

"Captain," a soldier approached from the rear of Titus's men. "Remus said he knows another way out of the castle."

"Good," Titus said. Then to his men he called out, "Men retreat. Fall back to the rear of the castle and regroup there. Follow Remus."

Fae got close and kicked out Titus's leg. When he stumbled, she gashed him across the inner thigh. Not a grievous injury, but he bled.

"Sir?" a remaining soldier asked. "What about you?"

"Dammit sergeant, just go. I'll hold them back. Get the citizens out of the city!"

Titus parried a blow and then jabbed with his shield, trying to make contact. Fae caught it with her hand. She wrenched Titus's arm sideways at an awkward angle, getting a pained grunt out of Titus, then she pulled hard on the shield, and it slid from Titus's hands. Fae threw it behind her and swung again. Her longer sword had the advantage now that he did not have a shield for deflection. Fae's sword clashed with Titus's. Then she kicked him in the left rib, not cracking anything but certainly hurting him.

Fae felt the anger, but remembered to not let it consume her, control her. *Control your emotions. Do not let them control you.* The words of her friends and mentors repeated in her mind once more. She let the anger flow out of her, only keeping that which she could safely control and use herself.

This man had hurt her, but he had not wanted to. She believed he was remorseful; he seemed to only want to protect the people and his men. Hanging on to her pain did not help her, it was only a distraction. The magus was dead, and Titus had fought valiantly.

Fae held her sword out, ready to come down on Titus after he had taken a step back, when she paused. Titus stayed, ready to deflect the blow.

Fae slowly lowered her sword to her side.

"Go," she said.

Titus' eyes revealed a look of bewilderment, then it faded and understanding replaced it.

"Protect your people, Titus."

Titus did not speak, instead giving her a look of respect. Then he slowly bowed his head to her and left.

Fae stood, with her head dipped down, and her sword hanging by her side. Bodies of the dead, along with discarded weapons and shields, filled the corridor. Blood trickled from her injured thigh.

Kiva came running back out of the courtyard. *She must have abandoned her advance on the soldiers once they had fallen too far back.* She gave Fae a quizzical look.

"You, ok? What happened?"

"I let him go." Fae's voice was barely above a whisper, "He never wanted Creet to burn. He was just a part of the system."

Kiva wrapped an arm around Fae, and Fae rested her head against it.

The entire castle fell shortly afterwards.

CHAPTER 38
REPERCUSSIONS

The rising sun cast a red glow on the town of Southshore as the rays filtered through the gently resting smoke. A grey haze was in the air, the remnants of the fire. The sounds of battle had died down as the last of the military was defeated or had surrendered.

On the northwestern castle tower, the five friends lounged, celebrating their victory and enjoying the view. Healers had wrapped and applied subtle healing magic to all their wounds. Bullock's shoulder and Erika's stomach were still heavily bandaged, and Fae still had a limp, but they would all heal in time.

When Fae had run to Jaxon after the battle, he had just complained of hurting "everywhere," but he did not seem to have anything broken, just black and yellow bruises. Fae had stared into his eyes and felt the tears welling up. He had raised his head to her and tenderly kissed her forehead, then pulled her close and let her tears wet his chest.

The friends had found a cask of mead in the cellar, carried it up, and cracked it open. Four of them were sitting and eagerly drinking from the mugs they had appropriated while Fae stood, her hands clutched to her chest, her index finger tracing the curve of her nana's pendant in its seat along her bracer. She stared out over the city, at the people now peeking out from their homes, or leaving the city.

She stood there for some time, and the others gave her space. Eventually, Jaxon decided it was time to talk, and walked up beside her, close enough so that their shoulders almost touched.

"Conflicted?" he asked.

She did not look at him as she spoke, "I guess," she sighed, "Look at them, Jax. I could have been one of them. That was the life I was supposed to live. Get married off to some merchant, have babies, clean clothes, maybe work a market stall. That life was taken from me. By our clan, by the Empire. It doesn't matter. What is past is the past. I just... I don't know. That could have been me."

Jaxon put a hand on her back, giving it a soft rub, but he did not put his arm around her. It was hard for her to express what she felt. Instead, she just let her thoughts pour out of her.

"Jax, the Empire is evil. I know that. But the people are not. Their lives are all wrong. They are not slaves, but they are not free. It is something else."

"Are we free?" Jaxon asked her. It was a strange question coming from him, he who had always been so confident in his conviction. But she recognized it as a general question and less of a statement.

"I don't know. I think so. Either way, it is better. Different." Her eyes blurred slightly as tears formed. "They need to start over. Without the systems that have created this. They are weak, but they could be strong. They are broken; slaves that pretend to be free."

"It could have been me." Once again, she returned to that same statement.

"But it's not." His voice was soft, but confident.

"No. It's not. I'm not. You're right." She finally turned to him and gave a soft smile. "Thanks."

She looked beyond the walls of the city.

"It's not over, you know. The wizard that escaped. They can still carry out the ritual."

"I know. We can face that tomorrow," he smirked. "Besides, if we didn't let him go, what would we do tomorrow?"

She smiled at him. She knew it was not true; there was still a war raging, but she appreciated the joke. It emphasized a good point; the war would go on regardless, but they could chase this wizard down. *There was always something to worry about the next day, so they might as well leave it until then.*

"We will take it one step at a time," Jaxon said. He had always been better than her at letting go of the things he could not control. She smiled and let the worry fade. *One step at a time.*

As they looked at each other, they heard boots coming up the staircase to the open tower battlement. Axton appeared over the edge of the stairs, a huge grin covering his face. "There you all are. Enjoying the fruits of your labours, I see. You five have taken the city."

"With your help," Bullock said. "Couldn't have taken it on our own."

"Aye, that is true, but you were the ones that started it," Axton said,

giving a complementary smile.

"I have dispatched scouts to the north and east to track down your escaped wizard. If they can capture or kill him, they will, but don't worry, even if he escapes, we will know where he fled to. Then we can take him."

It was something, but it still did not put Fae at ease. *So much could still go wrong if they carried out the ritual.* Axton looked at her and seemed to sense what she was thinking.

"It's ok," he said. "The Empire will be thrown into such disarray by the loss of Southshore that casting a complicated ritual will be the last thing on their minds. They will be focused purely on military strength in the region."

The rationale made sense. Fae gave a sigh, smiled, and nodded at him. Axton took the cue to continue talking, "Well, you five," Axton said, addressing them all. "Like I said, you helped take the city, the castle so, we figured you should decide. The castle is yours."

The others grinned, Erika's eyes sparkled, and Kiva muffled a squeal. But Fae, she was silent.

"What should we do with it now that we control it? It could make an excellent base of operations. We were thinking that—"

"Burn it."

Fae's voice was soft, barely audible. She turned towards them all and took a step towards Axton.

"Burn it down. All of it."

The others looked at her in surprise, but one by one, they understood her reasoning.

"It is a military asset for them," she said. "It allows men to exercise strength over the region. Much more strength than the people have earned. Whoever controls this castle will have more power than they deserve, and they will wield that power irresponsibly. Power should be in the strength of body and mind, not stone. Burn it. Leave the city. The people can stay or go as they wish, but the power must be destroyed. Lest we become the very people we have sworn to destroy."

Axton's face was sombre. He looked around the party of friends and noted each one nod along with Fae's words, before he looked back at her. "It is a wise choice, lass. It will be done." Axton stepped closer to Fae. He put a hand down on her shoulder and looked into her eyes, "You done good, my girl. You done good."

Simple words, but Fae felt the pride in that statement. Axton took his hand back, then turned on his heels and made his way down the stairs. He would give the order to have the castle burned down that night.

"They will come at us hard now. They will not let this go," Bullock said.

He placed his mug down and stood up to better address them all. "We took the second largest city in the Empire. Reports are already coming in that there is an entire eastern army that has not yet been brought west to face us. We have taken the south, and now we are going to have to defend it." He looked out across the land. "We will see how powerful the Empire truly is..." he let the words trail off.

Erika stood up and placed a hand gently on Bullock's back. "You sound a little worried there, big guy. That doesn't really sound like you."

"Maybe." Bullock rubbed his stubble. "I'm just wondering if maybe we bit off more than we can chew."

Kiva stepped up beside Bullock as well. "Honey, I think it might be a bit too late to worry about that." She stood on her tiptoes and gave him a peck on the cheek. "Whatever we face, at least we face it together. Besides, I've never known you to be one to back down from a challenge."

"Well, no, not a challenge I knew I could win."

Jaxon let his hand slip from around Fae's waist, stepping forward, and smacked his hand down on Bullock's sizable shoulder. "Come on buddy, it will be an adventure. And if we die, we will die fighting and we'll die together. That's all that we can ask for."

Bullock looked up at his friend and gave a smile. "Yeah, you are right." He quickly swung his fist low and into Jaxon's abs, but not hard enough to knock the wind out of him. Jaxon doubled over. "Besides buddy, your skinny ass will die way before me" Bullock let out a good chuckle.

"I hate you..." Jaxon teasingly groaned.

Fae helped Jaxon stand back up straight. "Come on, you guys. That cask there is almost empty. Let's head downstairs and crack another. Today we will rest and celebrate. Tomorrow, we'll figure out what we do next."

Erika kicked the empty cask off the battlement and turned, not waiting to see it hit the ground. She returned to the group and the five of them disappeared as they all descended the tower stairs together.

CHAPTER 39
TALES FROM THE DRUNKEN OWL

Bam!

Beacher's hand slammed a piece of parchment onto the bar of The Drunken Owl.

"Marcus, tell me this is some kind of joke."

Lucius turned his head, after filling a pint, to read the parchment. It was a town notice. Written on the official parchment of the Empire, it had a hole and a tear at the top where someone had pinned it to a wall before Beacher ripped it off. Besides the official seal of the Empire marking it as authentic, the parchment said only one thing.

Southshore has fallen.

"Was it those barbarians?" Beacher asked. "I thought their army was north, closer to us and the capital. How the hell did they take a place like Southshore?"

Marcus sat on the stool beside Beacher but waited for Lucius and Ox to pay attention before responding. As Beacher stared impatiently at Lucius, Ox turned the paper towards himself, as if to read the message.

"What are you doing Ox, you know you can't read," Lucius said.

"I can make out a few words that I've seen before," Ox said.

Ox traced a finger below some letters and attempted to form the words. Lucius raised an eyebrow as he leaned forward on the bar; he was not convinced. Ox looked over at Marcus for an answer.

"It is not a joke, my friend," Marcus said. "We have little information right now; only word from a few scouts and early survivors. We believe there was some form of sabotage from within. Our last official report was that they had captured a group of infiltrators. Something must have gone wrong after that. There was an entire army and full posting of guards in Southshore. It was more than enough to defend against any army that the Bandorians could have had in the south."

"If they can take Southshore, what is there to stop them from coming here or taking the capital?" Beacher asked.

With all the news of war lately, Lucius had been happy to see that Beacher was in town once more. If nothing, Ox always cheered up having him around. But this news of Southshore falling changed what good tidings they had previously felt.

"Well, for starters, the entire Imperial army lies between us and the Bandorians," Marcus said. "Though, with the constant raids on our camps and sabotaging of our supply lines, our forces have been forced to pull back in the last week."

"Great," Beacher said, slumping his shoulders and taking a drink of his beer.

"But my friends, even in the worst-case scenario, it is not all doom and gloom," Marcus said. He leaned forward, suggesting once more that he had something not intended for the public to know. "Though the official statements have been that the Bandorians destroy everything they touch, the unofficial word is that, when they take a town, they have left the people to go about their normal lives once they have destroyed the military installations."

"Really?" Ox asked. His eyes lit up with a sliver of hope.

"Well, that is just a rumour I heard," Marcus said. "No telling if it is true."

Ox sighed. Beacher sat back and took another swig. Lucius knew that "rumour" meant the things that Marcus knew but was not allowed to share with others outside of the administration.

"Besides my friends, I've heard that the Empire has a little surprise for the Bandorians. A magic they have been working on for some time. They are almost ready to unleash its full fury on the enemies of the Empire. And as for Southshore, the capital has already dispatched an army south to take it back. The Bandorians may have taken the city, but now they must do something they have never done before. They must keep it. This time, we haven't just sent the army, though."

Ox leaned forward, hanging on every word.

"This time they have sent an archon."

From the Author
THANK YOU!

I sincerely want to thank you for reading my book. You took a chance on it, and I hope you enjoyed reading it as much as I enjoyed writing it. Getting this book into your hands or onto your device took over two years of writing, editing, rewriting, (rinse and repeat) with editors enough times to create nearly five drafts of the book, but finally it is done and the second book is in development.

If you interested in reading more about the war, or meeting other Bandorians, visit the link below for bonus chapters and a companion short story written exclusively for fans of the series.

www.MikeMcKinnonAuthor.com

To be notified of when the next book is coming out,
https://www.mikemckinnonauthor.com/Newsletter-Sign-Up

Acknowledgments

Thank you to my wife and family for their continual encouragement to pursue my passions and to my parents for always compelling me to take on new challenges.

Thank you to Jo Thompson for teaching me so much about writing and storytelling, to Hana Kennedy for making sense of my mess, and to Cam Skitsko for helping me on this journey.

About the Author

Fantasy and science fiction have always held Mike in their enchanting embrace, providing a canvas to explore profound philosophical questions that often elude other mediums. A devoted admirer of the works of storytelling giants like Tolkien, David Eddings, R. A. Salvatore, Robert Jordan, and the visionary George Lucas, Mike's narrative prowess gravitates towards epic fantasy and thrilling adventures.

Mike has been an avid reader and consumer of stories from a young age. He had a habit of spinning tales for anyone willing to lend an ear and writing them when they would not. He spent many years involved in different forms of music and experimenting with drawing, but his passion for arts is most pronounced in his twenty-five years of semi-professional dance.

Surprisingly, Mike spent his career in IT and business

management, but the pull of storytelling remained constant, and he eventually returned to his genuine passion of storytelling. After working on many short stories in his free time, he finally took the time off to complete his debut novel and begin his series.

His first novel, "The Bandor Child," stands as the inaugural instalment of an expansive series chronicling the Bandor-Mage war and the pivotal events that unfold during the third era.

Mike lives with his wife in the captivating city of Edmonton, Alberta, Canada, nestled alongside a majestic river valley and just a short drive away from the awe-inspiring Canadian Rocky Mountains. As a proud father of two children, he often finds himself reading to them or telling them stories he makes up on the spot in ever expanding fantastical universes. His deep connection with nature and the great outdoors, as well as his innate fascination with human history, fuels his creativity and provides the perfect backdrop for his boundless storytelling spirit.

Manufactured by Amazon.ca
Acheson, AB